THE HAYLOFT GANG

The Story of the National Barn Dance

Edited by Chad Berry

UNIVERSITY OF ILLINOIS PRESS
Urbana and Chicago

Manufactured in the United States of America
1 2 3 4 5 C P 5 4 3 2 1

∞ This book is printed on acid-free paper.

Library of Congress Cataloging-in-Publication Data
The hayloft gang : the story of the National Barn Dance /
edited by Chad Berry.
p. cm. — (Music in American life)
Includes bibliographical references and index.
ISBN-13 978-0-252-03353-7 (cloth : alk. paper)
ISBN-10 0-252-03353-1 (cloth : alk. paper)
ISBN-13 978-0-252-07557-5 (pbk. : alk. paper)
ISBN-10 0-252-07557-9 (pbk. : alk. paper)
1. National Barn Dance (Radio program)
2. Country music—Middle West—History and criticism.
3. Radio broadcasting—Illinois—Chicago—History.
I. Berry, Chad
ML3524.H39 2008
781.64209773'11—dc22 2007052621

THE HAYLOFT GANG

MUSIC IN AMERICAN LIFE

A list of books in the series appears at the end of this book.

CONTENTS

Foreword
Loyal Jones vii

Acknowledgments xi

Introduction: Assessing the National Barn Dance
Chad Berry 1

1. The Rise of Rural Rhythm
Paul L. Tyler 19

2. Music of the Postwar Era
Wayne W. Daniel 72

3. Chicago as Forgotten Country Music Mecca
Lisa Krissoff Boehm 101

4. Early Broadcasting and Radio Audiences
Susan Smulyan 119

5. Race and Rural Identity
Michael T. Bertrand 130

6. Patriarchy and the Great Depression
Kristine M. McCusker 153

7. Cowboys in Chicago
Don Cusic 168

8. The National Folk Festival
Michael Ann Williams 187

Afterword
Stephen Parry 199

Contributors 205

Index 207

FOREWORD

Loyal Jones

Radio opened up rural America by beaming in programs from far-off places, and it was a miraculous happening to us landlocked folks. In addition to novel and educational matters, it brought us elements of our own culture and values and taste. The programs at WLS and other stations that reached to our ridges and hollows transmitted the voices and music of people who were like us. We all knew a fiddler or two, or a banjo picker, someone who sang the old songs, and we had all sung hymns at church and as we worked, but we didn't know that there were so many talented people out there until we had a radio.

The National Barn Dance arrived four years before I was born, and it was a long time after I showed up that we had enough money to buy a Sears Silvertone, one that required those costly fifteen-pound batteries, long before the Tennessee Valley Authority brought us electricity, locally called "lights." Before that, I remember walking across the mountain to listen to the radio of the only person we knew who had one. It was an amazement to me, hearing those happenings from far off. The stations that I remember were closer than WLS, such as WWNC (Asheville), WBT (Charlotte), WSM (Nashville), WNOX (Knoxville), and WLW (Cincinnati), although we ran the dial at night when reception was the best and found all sorts of other stations farther off. I don't remember many radio personalities from these early years, but later, studying 78 rpm recordings and other transcriptions, I recognized those who had sung the songs that I liked best back then—Mainer's Mountaineers; the Briarhoppers with Whitey and Hogan (I learned later that my brother knew Hogan, who was from the next county); the Carlisle Brothers; the Blue Sky Boys; and Bradley Kincaid, long after he had left WLS for WLW, WBZ (Boston), and stations in between and was now at WSM's Grand Ole Opry. I was entranced by Bradley's clear tenor voice and his old ballads, lyric folksongs, and sentimental numbers. We did know Bradley by name, and of course Roy Acuff. My fascination with radio was dampened only by my father's advice, "Save that battery so we can listen to the news and the Grand Ole Opry."

Now with years of thinking about Appalachia and the South, I've come to the conclusion that rural people all over the country and beyond have much in common. Our values are tied to religion, family, neighbors, and community. We tend to be levelers, deferring to others—as good as anybody but no better—personalistic, rich in the folks we know, and devoted to our home place, although many of us left that place to improve our lot in life. The kind of music and the sentiment of those who performed reflected these values, and thus appealed to us. John Lair's homey voice, reading his countrified scripts, was totally understandable, and in introducing his performers, he made them sound like people we already knew.

It is said that when President Franklin D. Roosevelt was contemplating what was to become his "Fireside Chats" to reassure people in the Great Depression, he decided to try to speak in such a way that the ordinary working people of the country would understand what he had to say. Will Rogers, who had known hard work, said that Roosevelt did such a good job that even the bankers understood his explanation of the bank failure and his reformation of the system. In his Fireside Chats, even with his patrician accent, this wealthy elite Easterner became a welcome, genial, reassuring, plain-speaking guest in the homes of millions of working-class Americans.

WLS executives somehow chose to pitch its programming to the same kinds of people. After all, Chicago was Sandburg's "city of the big shoulders," a metropolis to be sure, but it was the city of stockyards and railroads coming in from all directions, bringing in the products of thousands of farms and ranches and taking away the machinery, implements, household goods, clothing, and supplies to be purchased by country people. WLS was then owned by Sears, Roebuck and Company, and although Sears was slow in seeing the value of radio as a means of fueling consumption, it was in business to sell things. Maybe the story about that first Barn Dance broadcast was accurate, and maybe Tommy Dandurand's fiddle band, augmented with cowbells, did horrify the listening Sears executives, but when the mail started rolling in from all those rural people, even they saw the potential of providing information and entertainment to such folks.

The National Barn Dance was an event to be looked forward to in the homes of rural people, as well as those who had left the Appalachians and Ozarks, the whole South, and the Great Plains to seek their fortunes in towns and cities. WLS introduced them to talented performers from places like where they lived or had recently left, but it also introduced them to people of a different accent and music that were acceptable, even if they listened to them mostly because radio was a novel and interesting new happening. Thus the people were reified in their own worth, and they were also opened to new and enlightening experiences.

Radio also brought them humor to lighten their load, and humor was especially welcome after the Great Depression set in. On the National Barn Dance, John Lair wrote humor into almost all his scripts and encouraged humorous repartee between Lulu Belle and Scotty, or between Red Foley and Lily May Ledford. Slim Miller, with his mournful face and manner, did mime-like humor for the live audiences and made radio listeners curious about what was going on. Arkie the Arkansas Woodchopper did humorous stories about farming, fishing, and hunting. Smiley Burnett and Pat Buttram, who both later became movie sidekick comedians, did comedy on the show. "Lonesome" George Gobel was popular as a comedian, and so were the Hoosier Hot Shots, Captain Stubby and the Buccaneers, and others.

As country music shows developed, so did comedy. Long shows, such as the National Barn Dance, needed something to provide variety and to invigorate it when it sagged from too many tragic or sentimental or not-so-good songs. Comedy served the purpose. Likewise, when performers began to do personal appearances, they were expected to entertain for the whole evening, and humor enlivened these shows as well. Entertainers knew that people craved humor and loved to laugh. Country humor also served other purposes. Even though a good many country performers had found a way to earn a living and some fame in the entertainment business, they were aware that they were mostly viewed as rubes by the larger society. Country music humor thus continued a long history of the theme of the city slicker versus the country bumpkin and gave it a vigorous new life. It was a topsy-turvy humor that elevated the country person over those who thought they were better than he was. Here are some examples, the first from Captain Stubby:

> This politician dropped in on me in the [cow] pasture field, just getting about dark. He crawled over the fence and came out there where I was, to talk to me about getting my vote. He had a toupee, and it blew off in that pasture field. He thought he found it three times. He tried on two!

> City fellow: "Hey, Grandpa, how far is it to Indianapolis?"
> Farmer: "How did you know that I'm a grandpa?"
> City fellow: "I just guessed it."
> Farmer: "Well, guess the way to Indianapolis."

In the early days of the country music industry, the decidedly rural humor was usually delivered by a country person to other country people. Thus, the jokes were in-jokes and had the effect of making country people feel better about themselves, at the expense of urban folks. But since humor approaches things in an oblique manner, and if it is truly funny, town and city people could enjoy it too. You can't be very mad while you're laughing. It served the further purpose of defining rural people as marginal people in relation to others. Most of the older musicians, humorists, and comedians whom I've interviewed saw their work as not only adding to good entertainment but being therapeutic as well. Captain Stubby said, "A lot of comedians came out of the Depression—hard times. We used humor to bolster ourselves up, and we laughed at our problems. Humor is very important in entertainment. It is the best thing in the world to have a good laugh." Bill Carlisle, a Grand Ole Opry performer, said, "Well, it's a good thing we have such a thing as humor. It's important, and I think you live longer if you can see the humorous side of nearly everything. Almost everybody had a comedian in the band, but they don't do that nowadays. But I just keep shucking corn, just like always." Wade Mainer felt strongly about comedy: "I think the people really wanted something to entertain them—maybe get their minds off of some of the hardships that they went through. They'd walk miles to see us." Charlie Louvin, of the Louvin Brothers and still a member of the Grand Ole Opry, stated, "When you do a two-hour show, you can't just sing the whole two hours. A joke here and a joke there lightens it. Music [and humor] is a great release. If you have a job you can't stand but that you have to keep, music can give you a night away from that job, or thinking of your dim future, or whatever your problem might be." He went on to talk about balanced entertainment. "If you were putting together a balanced show, you would have a comedy act, a country music act, and a girl singer." Finally, Tim O'Brien, a superb instrumentalist and singer, who did comedy with the band Hot Rize, as Red Knuckles and the Trail Blazers, reflected on another use of humor that he learned from Jethro Burns, who played the NBD for many years: "When you're putting on a show, people really want to get to know you, and you want to reveal something of yourself. The easiest way is to poke fun at yourself. It almost always works. You take your music seriously, and you respect the audience and yourself, but you can break the ice by making fun of yourself. Jethro Burns was a big hero of mine as a musician, but he was always poking fun. He was very sharp." All these musicians who had played comedy, especially early in their careers, spoke fondly of humor and its value in entertainment, and also how it made the people in the audience feel better. They talked of how exhilarating it was to possess the ability to have a whole audience laughing. They also regretted the decline of such humor, especially in modern country music.

The NBD was a successful variety show aimed at people of the vast rural and small-town regions of its listening area. It was an important and influential cultural event that lasted for thirty-six years. It was heavily influenced by the folk and commercial life of its era, and it affected the country broadcast entertainment shows that followed it, such as the Grand Ole Opry, the Mountaineer Jamboree, the Boone County Jamboree, the Louisiana Hayride, and the Ozark Jubilee. Yet it had its own cultural flavor and reflected traditions broader than those on other shows. The excellent essays in this book show the importance of WLS and the NBD under the ownership of Sears, Roebuck and the *Prairie Farmer.* These essays collectively present a convincing argument that the National Barn Dance was more important than most scholars realize. In fact, nowadays few living people even know of the show or the talented people in its cast. Stephen Parry's documentary and this book should go a long way in informing new generations about the importance of the National Barn Dance.

ACKNOWLEDGMENTS

The Hayloft Gang offers readers original essays that document the history and significance of one of radio's most important and enduring entertainment programs. Between 1924 and 1960, the National Barn Dance was a pioneering and influential Saturday evening event that eventually reached millions of listeners nationally and sparked many imitations. Along the way, it helped create an entirely new form of popular music, rooted in rural white and African American styles and forms. *The Hayloft Gang* documents the multifaceted cultural contributions of such a popular yet now largely forgotten program.

All of the contributors in this volume agreed to set aside momentarily their own work to be a part of this collective effort, and for doing so, I would like to offer each of them sincere thanks; it has been a joy putting this collection of essays together. In addition, the illustrations that accompany the articles come from a number of places across the country. I thank each person and institution who provided permission to include them here, particularly Debby Gray, a collector. I also thank Harry Rice at Berea College and Wayne Daniel, one of our contributors, for their help with identifications. Genevieve Reynolds in the Berea College Appalachian Center deserves high praise for her organizational skills, her commitment to the Appalachian region, and her all-around willingness to help. Gratitude also goes to Rodney Wolfenbarger for his many talents. My own family has rather sacrificially endured my professional commitments, and I am pleased Lisa, Madelaine, and Nat can see a tangible result. Laurie Matheson at the University of Illinois Press was always a supportive editor, and I am grateful to our copyeditor, Carol Betts, and to Diane Pecknold and the other, anonymous reader for their helpful suggestions.

There is one person, however, who deserves public acknowledgment: Steve Parry. If it were not for his dream of a documentary film—and a companion volume of essays—Chicago's National Barn Dance would continue to be, well, second fiddle to another city's radio program. This, I am happy to report, will not as easily be the case, as readers of this volume and viewers of his documentary will be reminded that Chicago was the center of what came to be known as country music two decades before Nashville and the Grand Ole Opry achieved such a distinction. I thank him for his help with this volume, particularly for so generously sharing his visual sources. For Steve Parry's vision and determination, we can all be grateful.

INTRODUCTION: ASSESSING THE NATIONAL BARN DANCE

Chad Berry

> They've invaded all the cities
> With their pretty corn-fed ditties
> And they've got the population all in tears . . .
> Them hillbillies are mountain Williams now.
>
> —The Hoosier Hot Shots

My grandparents listened. As a rural woman trying to put food on the table and take care of children in Tennessee during the 1930s, who yet also lived very much in the world, my grandmother traded some hens in exchange for a battery-powered radio. To this day, my ninety-three-year-old grandfather fondly recalls the National Barn Dance (NBD) team, including Homer and Jethro and especially Lulu Belle and Scotty, though my grandfather would say "*Looler Bale.*" Eventually, in order to find work and elusive economic prosperity, my grandparents moved closer to Chicago—to northern Indiana—and continued to listen to the Barn Dance, for it helped bring the South a little closer to them in the North.

Because of this move, I was born and raised in northern Indiana, and since learning more about the NBD I've been astonished to discover some striking connections I have with the Hayloft Gang. I grew up listening to AM 89-WLS—just eighty miles away from my hometown—though the daily fare that Larry Lujack, Tommy Edwards, Yvonne Daniels, and others served up in the 1970s and 1980s was quite different from the programming that reigned at WLS until 1960. Linda Parker, I've learned—the Sunbonnet Girl—died suddenly in 1935 in my hometown of Mishawaka, Indiana. Alka-Seltzer, one of the Barn Dance sponsors (figure 1), was made by Miles Laboratories, located in the adjacent county of Elkhart. And where I lived for more than a decade in East Tennessee was the home of Homer and Jethro; where I now live and work is where Bradley Kincaid—the "Kentucky Mountain Boy"—once lived and worked and where Red Foley was born; my daughter attended the Foley Middle School.

The National Barn Dance is closely connected to the rapid rise of radio in the United States. Between 1920, when KDKA was formed in Pittsburgh, and 1923, radio had grown to 556 stations. WLS began broadcasting on April 12, 1924, and the first National Barn Dance—probably copied from WBAP in Fort Worth—took place on April 19, in just the

Figure 1. Sponsorship by Miles Laboratories, maker of Alka-Seltzer, poured money into the National Barn Dance coffers. Collection of Debby Gray.

second week of the station's operations. It was not the first barn dance, but it became extraordinarily influential and enduring; only the one-two punch of television and rock 'n' roll would eventually do it in, thirty-six years later. Although it was local and regional, it was also national—one part of the show aired on the NBC network—and international, once it followed members of the armed forces overseas. All told, some 2.6 million people would pay to see the show live from Chicago's Eighth Street Theatre. During the Great Depression, when movie theaters charged a dime, the NBD charged seventy-five cents and still had people lining up down the block. And if one couldn't get to Chicago, then one scrambled to get a radio (figure 2)—just as my grandparents did—so that by the late 1930s, 82 percent of homes in the United States had one. But the distribution of radios was uneven in the early years. By 1930, almost half of all midwestern farm families had radios, compared to only 10 percent of southern families; hence early radio programming was much more rural than southern, even though programs such as the National Barn Dance would be remembered by many as the harbinger of country music.[1]

One of the persistent questions encountered by present and past scholars, especially those who study country music, is, Why was the National Barn Dance so popular in a place such as Chicago? Admittedly, this is an essentialist question, and if one searches for a neat and tidy essentialist answer, one will never be satisfied. The reason that some country music scholars seem perplexed by such a question is that possible answers do not always mesh with the Nashville-focused paradigm that has long dominated country music's creation myth, one that overlooked, in the words of one contributor to this volume, the preeminent radio home for country music before World War II: Chicago, Illinois. Even though a *Billboard* banner headline and article from 1943 proclaimed Chicago the "haven of the hillbilly en-

Figure 2. It was no coincidence that Sears sought a place on the airwaves through WLS, as revealed by this page of radio ads from 1927. From the Sears Archives; used with permission.

tertainer,"[2] the Chicago historian Lisa Krissoff Boehm argues that the popular image of Chicago—gangsters and gunfights—never made room for "country" music coming from the radio. Moreover, as the twentieth century progressed, Chicago could not hold on to its rural image and rural outreach. One of the benefits of an interdisciplinary approach to one subject such as the NBD is, however, that each scholar from a particular discipline sees a particular reason to highlight the importance of a radio program that pervaded the airwaves for three-plus decades. A music scholar is naturally going to discuss the program's importance to the development of a new commercial music form. A radio scholar, however, might caution that the NBD may be more important to radio history than to country music, even as a cultural historian finds connections with vaudeville and old medicine shows.

Scholars in this volume all emphasize diverse reasons for the NBD's enduring popularity as well as a number of reasons why the Barn Dance is an important component of twentieth-century cultural history. Contributors discuss the development of rural white music that eventually became known as country music; the role of urban and rural tensions in American culture during the mid-twentieth century; the ways gender and race played out in the Barn Dance and the lines that each drew; the country's search for meaningful identity through the Barn Dance; how the program was rooted solidly in industrial capitalism; the tensions associated with the rise of radio; and even urbanization and migration.

Perhaps music is the best place to start. In his piece, Paul L. Tyler notes explicitly that the music of the National Barn Dance was not purely southern music transplanted northward. Southerners may have tuned in eagerly to the program, but, Tyler argues, the music was always *rural* music. George C. Biggar himself speculated that "it is doubtful if southern folk songs or cowboy ballads were sung [on the very early shows], as very few Midwesterners of that day were familiar with them."[3] Moreover, in the early years, WLS programmers were pragmatic; they would try just about anything a couple of times to see if it worked. Indeed, the first Saturday night the Barn Dance aired was something of an experiment, but after just three weeks, more than a thousand letters had come in to WLS—from twenty states—praising the Saturday night lineup. Even though WLS was experimental, it is not to imply that the program that resulted was accidental; it was, Tyler argues, intentional. Once the show was a hit, programmers continued to include all kinds of music—from old-time fiddling to polka, from Hawaiian guitar music to ballroom dance orchestration—to satisfy as many listeners as possible. Richard A. Peterson has noted that programmers realized early on that the solo fiddler sound "proved to be extremely monotonous when listened to over early radio receivers"; consequently, by the 1930s, diversity (musical styles, performers, and instrumentation) mattered.[4] Only later, Tyler explains in his essay, did the likes of Bradley Kincaid and John Lair join the gang and, in the process, bring more southern music and musicians with them. Those who believe they know about the origins of what came to be called country music will want to read what Tyler says about the "southern thesis" of country music's origins. After World War II, Wayne W. Daniel explains in this volume, this diversity in programming increased, attempting to offer something that would appeal to almost every listener. But after the war, as the recording industry began to replace radio in terms of an artist's earning power, the Barn Dance embarked on a slow but perhaps steady slide. The death knell was rock 'n' roll.

Susan Smulyan, a radio historian, highlights the way radio both nationalized and homogenized as well as how it provided listeners with power and autonomy. But she too emphasizes the rural nature of the programming: "Farmers and radio," she writes, "seemed made for each other." Why Chicago, one might ask again? Because it was the urban nexus for hundreds of thousands of midwestern farmers, and as the reach of WLS extended considerably with the additional power of 50,000 watts in 1931, the station became a center that rural people throughout the central portion of North America—south as well as north—identified. In 1945, for example, WLS reported that it reached 3.5 million homes in Illinois, Wisconsin, and Indiana alone. And attesting to this reach, the station received more than a million pieces of mail each year.[5] What, Smulyan asks, could be more exotic and progressive than listening to a voice conveying weather information or old-time music from Chicago, hundreds of miles away? The answer of course is nothing, and it's the reason my grandmother in the 1930s was willing to part with some of her prized hens in order to take part in this national entertainment medium. And during the 1920s and early 30s, WLS was just one of many stations offering listeners a cornucopia of programming.[6] Smulyan explains that Chicago, compared to New York, for example, was unusual in its broadcasting importance; nevertheless, the NBD often achieved top-ten status in network radio ratings. Therefore, the NBD was both national and local/regional at the same time, mirroring, Smulyan says, the same "tightrope" walk demanded of radio in its formative years.

Another sure reason for success is that WLS was always pretty good at identifying a market. First when the Sears-Roebuck Agricultural Foundation owned it and then later under the ownership of Burridge D. Butler's *Prairie Farmer* magazine, the station catered to rural people. Recall that the 1920s was an era of threatening changes (racial- and gender-boundary testing) and disturbing reactions (lynchings, the Ku Klux Klan, and nativism). The new voices and the new music coming from the new technology were exciting for some and frightening to others. "High culture" came over the airwaves, to be sure, but there was a great deal of "low culture," too. Radio's democratic content—ethnic, racial, and regional—raised eyebrows among some guardians of culture, and the music of the NBD became a palliative, profitable, and alternative salve countering all those other urban choices. WLS consciously became the voice of rural America. During the Great Depression and World War II (see figure 24), WLS was out in the community, operating a soup kitchen on West Madison and later selling war bonds and entertaining soldiers and their families.[7] Its work during the 1930s and 40s was never purely local or, for that matter, regional; it was grounded firmly in issues and trends in national culture. Even in the late 1950s, when the station was sold to ABC, the new owners were savvy enough to transform the station into one that catered to urban folk (as well as urban-wannabe types outside of Chicago) with a rock 'n' roll format.

The National Barn Dance, however, refused simple categorization. If rural culture beaming out on a newfangled technology was a prime reason for its success, that alone cannot explain everything. Ironically, such a program so cleverly and deliberately cast as a folksy, wholesome, straitlaced, domestic, and rustic affair was firmly rooted in industrial capitalism,

Figure 3. In the early years of radio, new technology had to be reconciled with tradition. Here, the family gathers around the radio instead of the hearth; otherwise, things are as traditional (and comfortable) as ever. Collection of Debby Gray.

another reason, perhaps, why Chicago became its home, say, over a smaller midwestern town. Remember, WLS began as part of the World's Largest Store—Sears—and would later be sold to *Prairie Farmer* because the station had not yet generated a profit sufficient to satisfy the accountants at Sears. WLS put big bucks in an unparalleled public relations enterprise that connected with Barn Dance listeners through its *Stand By!* and *Family Album* publications as well as its numerous appearances with fans on the road. Alka-Seltzer's sponsorship of the network program brought hundreds of thousands of dollars into the coffers—roughly three-quarters of a million dollars in 1936 alone. And then there were the record contracts, which gave some NBD performers comfortable lives amid economic calamity and led to an entirely new commercialized musical form for the masses, particularly after World War II.

Certainly another important factor was nostalgia. In the 1920s the United States was engaged in culture skirmishes between rural and urban combatants. Historians now interpret the time as the Jazz Age, but the other side of the debate might prefer to call the era the Rural Music Age.[8] Whatever one calls it, by the 1930s the country was engaged in a quest for the authentic (WLS even included accented songs of Olaf the Swede on the Barn Dance), and scholars have observed how first the South and then the West would be the places those seeking the authentic would go to find it (figure 3).[9] Richard Peterson has claimed that one of the most important traits shared by both the "hillbilly" and the cowboy "siblings" was that they were "unfettered by the constraints of urban society," in spite of their deliberate constructions.[10] Naturally, the NBD, reflecting the rural–urban divide, would provide plenty of both types of these sibling images and hence would address the needs of folks uprooted by social change and economic catastrophe. The songs, the historian Anthony Harkins has argued, realistically portrayed the specters of Depression-era life: hardship, loss, death, always cast in a romantic and idealized rural past just out of reach for urban and rural folk alike.[11] Moreover, as Loyal Jones reminds us, much of the material on the NBD was also quite funny. Tragedy and comedy together make for powerful identification, after all. Some of the most successful comedy, however, such as that of Homer and Jethro (figure 4), parodied urban ways to the delight of fans nationwide.[12]

Before long, stars from the Hayloft Gang would even more explicitly address the hunger for the authentic, including those—brought especially by John Lair—from the "mountain South," broadly defined. No performers epitomized this vision of edenic Appalachia longer or more successfully than Lulu Belle and Scotty (see figures 5, 38, and 50).[13] Michael Ann Williams shows how the connection between the National Barn Dance and the National Folk Festival complemented one another. Although some of the music brought up north was known as hillbilly, the term itself was much more ambivalent, connoting, Harkins argues, rootedness, identity, and distinctiveness from the metropolis's masses. Say what one might about a hillbilly, everyone knew that such a person had clear connections to a rural and perhaps even authentic past in the upland South that also was beyond the reach of most listeners.[14] Alleged Anglo-Saxon purity aside, however, the baggage from years of

Figure 4. Homer (Henry Haynes) and Jethro (Kenneth Burns) were musical parodists who hailed from East Tennessee. John Lair Collection, Southern Appalachian Archives, Berea College.

pathologic media coverage of Appalachia (the usual stuff: feuding and violence, backwardness, odd religious practices—all the things one might categorize under "social depravity") meant that another piece of "authentic" culture had to be found; besides, in spite of all the ways southern performers were made and remade by the Barn Dance, many of the images were still latently negative.

The cowboy (and cowgirl) was seen as the perfect replacement, replete with positive images, as Don Cusic discusses in his contribution. To prove the appeal, Douglas Green once

Figure 5. Few musical partnerships were as popular or as long lived as that of Lulu Belle and Scotty. Collection of Debby Gray.

asked the cut-to-the-chase question: What little boy didn't want to grow up to be a cowboy, but who wanted to grow up to be a hillbilly?[15] Richard Peterson, however, has argued that the cowboy never quite replaced the mountaineer; instead media took the best elements of both—the music from the latter, and the dress of the former—and made a musical sensation "by dressing the singer of heartfelt hillbilly songs in the heroic cowboy outfit."[16] The problem was cowboy songs just did not sell well (can anyone identify one Roy Rogers hit?); among Gene Autry's biggest sellers was "That Silver-Haired Daddy of Mine," which was nonwestern in theme (see figure 43). But Autry's real importance to commercial success was what he wore when he sang his hit in the 1935 film *Tumbling Tumbleweeds.* If Peterson is right, it proves the country preferred the music of reputed hillbillies who simply donned a cowboy outfit. Some, like Roy Acuff, an East Tennessean, proudly resisted such a transformation, sneering, "I am very annoyed when someone calls me a cowboy." Nevertheless, music changed after such elements were replaced or blended, for old-time fiddlers and string bands faded as soloists appeared donning guitars and were followed by comedic acts and even more harmony acts taking advantage of the nuances of microphoned sound (see figure 12).[17]

Observers of American culture have also long argued that Americans have embraced technology even though it makes them somewhat ambivalent about the changes it sets in motion. Henry Ford, for example, unleashed the automobile age, but he also created Greenfield Village and, Bill Malone has reminded us, sponsored fiddle contests and old-time dances.[18] As the scholar who knows country music better than most, Malone asked us to think about the uses of the barn dance: "a term redolent with the presumed naturalness and innocence of rural entertainment—to describe continued hillbilly radio shows emanating from cities suggests an effort to capitalize on a national mood of nostalgia for a way of life that was rapidly slipping away."[19] If life seemed in flux (and when does it not?), tuning in to the National Barn Dance—the technology of radio notwithstanding—was a palliative for the malaise associated with change.

And add another bit of irony into the mix: WLS accomplished great success by a marketing program that sought to ease the alienation felt by many listeners. Paul Tyler explains in his contribution that WLS offered listeners an airwave community and sociability at a time when many feared the loss of connectedness (see figure 35). Early promoters of the NBD, he says, really believed that listeners would hold a barn dance in their homes, with music supplied by WLS. Performers, both Tyler and Kristine McCusker point out, became like friends and family, in no small part because of WLS's marketing efforts through publications and invitations to keep in touch with the Hayloft family. And write listeners did (see figures 7 and 33). Tyler explains how although the NBD originated from a public space inside Chicago's Loop, marketers and program directors succeeded in creating the illusion that it in fact was an extension of the home, especially the parlor. WLS seemed to care little whether music featured was folk or pop or even hillbilly; what mattered was whether its acts brought what Tyler calls "easy familiarity" into one's home. The cover of the 1930 *Family Album* epitomizes this idea (see figure 3).

Even as our understanding of country music has expanded over the past several decades, gender has remained, until recently, unexplored—sometimes overlooked—terrain. During the Great Depression, the NBD, while offering performers meager pay, reaffirmed the traditional and the nostalgic during the uncertainty of the 1930s. Kristine McCusker has written elsewhere about the ways the NBD directors combined working- and middle-class images and metaphors into an appealing ideal for listeners, especially in the creation of Linda Parker (née Jeanne Muenich; see figure 41);[20] in this volume McCusker explores the way the Barn Dance responded to the Great Depression's challenges on male breadwinning status. In the Barn Dance, the gendered images of performers reinforced the ethic at a time when the whole economic system seemed most in peril. It did this, McCusker argues, through both a gendered stage (where men were patriarchs and women were sacrificing mothers) and fan ephemera, which only reinforced the radio stage in listeners' homes. Also crucial to the message during the early 1930s was that the strong women and men who carved "civilization" out of chaos lived on in the values represented by the National Barn Dance. If McCusker sees the continuity of the gender status quo on the NBD in her contribution, Smulyan reminds readers that female listeners might have been inspired by the new model of opportunity afforded by the female stars of the NBD, such as Linda Parker, Patsy Montana (see figure 42), and Lulu Belle.

If Americans were unsettled about gender roles after the 1920s, historians know white Americans to have been challenged also by new racial freedoms. Again, the NBD may have been a salve for festering malaise. Anthony Harkins, for example, explains in his book *Hillbilly* that what came to be known as country music, which originated as rural white music and was billed to rural and even urban white folks, contained in fact a great deal of various and diverse sounds and traditions; it was, he writes, an "amalgam" of African American and European American traditions, blended with industrial capitalism and technology. Still, those African American forms (beat, banjo and guitar, sacred music styles and traditions, and ragtime, jazz, and blues) became very important components of what came to be cast (*whitewashed?*), ironically, as an "authentic" white music form labeled "country."[21] Michael T. Bertrand's contribution here convincingly explores this often overlooked racialization of early country music by delineating the ways white listeners identified and articulated "who they were and who they were not." Both Bertrand and McCusker explain how such "white" music was a preventive against the more dangerous sounds and freedoms of the Jazz Age. Frequently troubled by these threats, Bradley Kincaid's mountain South (even though Kincaid's birthplace was closer to the bluegrass than to any Appalachian mountain) offered listeners a white, Anglo-Saxon cultural form in which to glory amid all the unsettling change around them. He spent a great deal of time and energy on this mission, proselytizing that southern mountaineers were "a people in whose veins run the pure strain of Anglo-Saxon blood."[22] And even though "Anglo-Saxon" screams of whiteness, Susan Smulyan argues that the jazzy numbers performed by whites on the Barn Dance "may have been the closest to the black vernacular available on the radio." Nevertheless, when one looks at a picture of an eager crowd outside the Eighth Street Theatre, there are no black faces among them. Would any African Americans have been comfortable going into the theater? What do we make of Malcolm Claire, also known as "Spareribs" (see figure 36), who performed in blackface as he offered children's stories on the Barn Dance? In a photo from the thirtieth-anniversary WLS commemorative album, only one black audience member is visible (figure 6).

Scholars probing the reasons for the extraordinary success of the National Barn Dance do not always emphasize migration, but I want to do so here. James Gregory, in *The Southern Diaspora*, called for new thinking about internal migration, "one of the seriously underanalyzed issues," he wrote convincingly, "of twentieth-century American historiography."[23] There

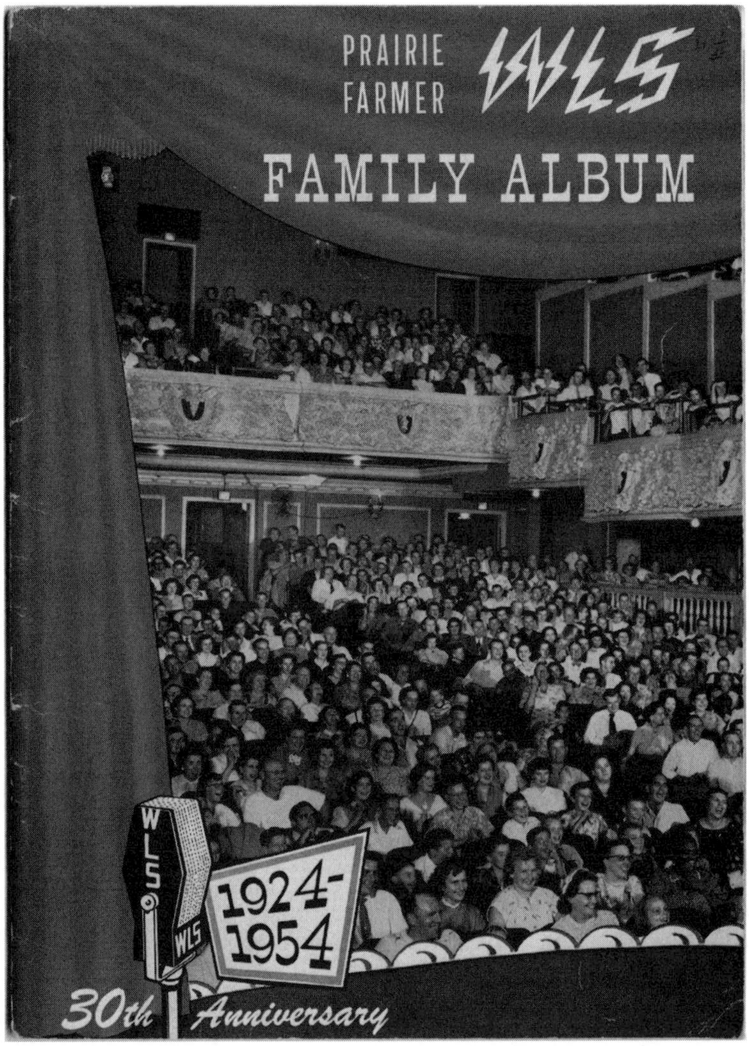

Figure 6. The music of the Barn Dance, while enriched by African American styles and influence, became codified as a white musical form. A lone black woman appears in this otherwise white audience. Collection of Debby Gray.

are two components of this massive migration that contributed to Chicago's and WLS's success with the National Barn Dance: one was the urbanization of Chicago as a destination among midwestern rural folk, but historians know little about this migration stream. The other, whose details are increasingly understood, was the out-migration of southern whites and blacks, especially to the North. Those going westward would affect radio in places such as Los Angeles, too, for KMPC created the Beverly Hill Billies (again, the emphasis is on creation, since the performers were not hill folk but from San Francisco, upstate New York, and other parts of a country whose people were on the move) and made that group a sensation in the 1930s, indicative of the national popularity of such music and suddenly making the question, "Why Chicago?" less befuddling.[24] Throughout the twentieth century, the migration up and out of the South saw departures of nearly 8 million blacks, almost 20 million whites, and more than a million southern-born Latinos.[25] Almost 30 million people, listeners as well as composers and performers, cannot relocate and fail to leave a lasting legacy; the music that was *made* by such a diasporic movement in new destinations—not necessarily *brought* from the South—is surely one of the most important cultural changes in the last century. Even George C. Biggar cast his recollections firmly in migration: "It was only natural that the Barn Dance should become popular. Here were thousands of farm families in the audience who knew first-hand the fun and informality of this type of entertainment. In the cities were thousands who had come from rural communities or had heard the old folks tell of the 'good old times.' To all of these, the Barn Dance was as refreshing as a breath of spring air."[26] And when John Lair was creating Linda Parker's life story for the airwaves, naturally he would have her born in Kentucky and migrating to the urban-industrial area of Hammond, Indiana, the same place to which plenty of other Kentuckians were moving.[27] It is futile to argue that one migration stream alone resulted in—and accounts for—the NBD's popularity, just as D. K. Wilgus explained decades ago;[28] I am suggesting, however, that the movement of people, broadly considered, resulted in losses and gains that made the NBD's themes quite appealing (figure 7).

A few examples from Mary A. Bufwack and Robert K. Oermann's *Finding Her Voice: Women in Country Music, 1800–2000*, prove that without this demographic phenomenon, such rich and diverse programmatic offerings would have been much more difficult. Lily May Ledford came from Powell County, Kentucky, while Louise Massey, reared in New Mexico, was bilingual. Princess Tsianina was a Cherokee. The DeZuricks hailed from Royalton, Minnesota, but Sophia Germanick came from the Ukraine. Or take the peripatetic John Cooper, who was working on an Ohio River lock when his daughter, Myrtle Eleanor Cooper, was born back in Boone, North Carolina, in 1913 on Christmas Eve. Eventually, he would move his family to Indiana, then to Tennessee, to Florida, South Carolina, and Kentucky before making it to Chicago as an escapee from Tennessee on moonshining charges in 1929. Myrtle, by now in her teens, got a job at a department store candy counter but, so the story goes, was fired for giving out treats to a hungry old woman. Repeatedly pestered by her father for an audition at WLS, the station's managers finally relented and listened to Myrtle, whose volume shocked them; evidently, she was unaware of the power of a microphone and all its changes on tone.[29] Having been turned down, the daughter turned down her own volume and came back with her father, and this time WLS took a chance with her in the 5:30 A.M. time slot. John Lair advised Myrtle to consult with some more experienced vaudeville stars, and her mother sewed up a calico dress with lots of ruffles, paired with some old-timey lace-up

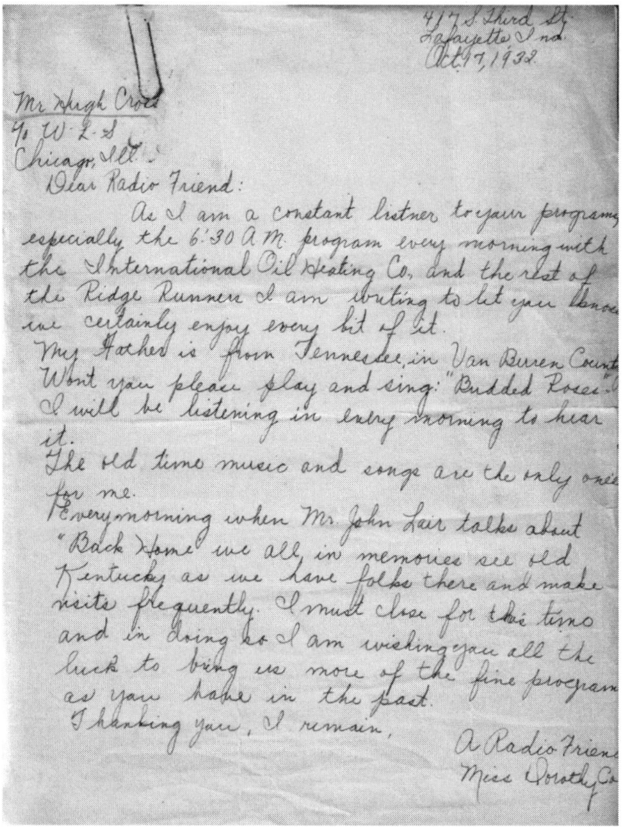
417 S. Third St.
Lafayette Ind.
Oct. 17, 1932.

Mr Hugh Cross
% W-L-S
Chicago, Ill.
Dear Radio Friend:
As I am a constant listner to your programs especially the 6:30 A.M. program every morning with the International Oil Heating Co. and the rest of the Ridge Runners I am writing to let you know we certainly enjoy every bit of it.
My Father is from Tennessee, in Van Buren County. Wont you please play and sing: "Budded Roses." I will be listening in every morning to hear it.
The old time music and songs are the only ones for me.
Every morning when Mr. John Lair talks about "Back Home" we all in memories see old Kentucky as we have folks there and make visits frequently. I must close for this time and in doing so I am wishing you all the luck to bring us more of the fine program as you have in the past.
Thanking you, I remain,
A Radio Friend
Miss Dorothy C

Figure 7. This fan letter is a reminder that women and southern migrants in the North were important parts of the Barn Dance audience. Southern Music and Radio Photographic Collection, Southern Appalachian Archives, Berea College.

boots and a pinned-on plait of hair. After her first appearance on the National Barn Dance, Lulu Belle was born; by 1936, she was deemed "Queen of All Radio." She and her eventual real-life husband, Scotty Wiseman, retired in 1958 and returned to North Carolina, where she eventually was elected to the state legislature.[30]

Ruby Blevins was born in 1912 in Arkansas and raised with ten brothers. Always dreaming of stardom—perhaps to escape her hardscrabble young life—she learned guitar and fiddle and at age seventeen added an "e" to make *Rubye* seem more distinctive. She followed her brother and his wife to California when she turned eighteen. There, she landed a couple of radio gigs yodeling and eventually became Patsy Montana of the Montana Cowgirls. After the group broke up, she returned to Hope, Arkansas, but wound up in Shreveport, Louisiana, where she received an invitation to go to Camden, New Jersey, to play fiddle and sing backup; by 1932, she had a record of her own. The following year, back in Arkansas, she and two of her brothers decided to take what they hoped would be the world's largest watermelon to the Chicago World's Fair. At twenty-one, she got the job as the female voice of the Kentucky Ramblers. Rechristened the Prairie Ramblers, the group landed a record deal, and Montana's song, "I Want to Be a Cowboy's Sweetheart," recorded in New York City, became the first million-seller by a woman.[31]

But migrating fans also had an impact on the music, and these stories are not often told. Roy Garret, for example, was born in 1934 to a coal-mining family in Lee County, Virginia. "I knew all along that I wouldn't be a coal miner," he said, "but I didn't know what I would be doing." One thing he did know was that he wanted to get out and see a little bit of the country. In 1950, at just sixteen, he went to Dayton, Ohio, and got a job at a supermarket. The air force beckoned next, taking him to Texas, and after he got out he went to Indianapolis for a couple of months and then to Harlan, Kentucky, for a short time. "Me and my cousin," he explained, "we just liked to get out and see things. We would literally hitchhike clear across the country—just barely enough money in our pocket for our next meal—and not worry a bit about it." Eventually, he went to Chicago and got a job at an A&P on the west side but eventually found a factory job in Norridge.[32]

Garret knew about the National Barn Dance before he got to Chicago. "I just knew it was there," he said, "and anywhere there was country music, I was there." Once, when his wife, Alma, from Blount County, Tennessee, was working in a coffee shop in Chicago, she met Homer and Jethro, who noticed her southern accent and asked where she was from. They too were from East Tennessee. "I decided to go down to the Eighth Street Theatre, and I liked it," Garret remembered. "It was slightly popular music then. Captain Stubby and Homer and Jethro and Bob Atcher (see figure 48) was there then." He remembered the performance he saw as a "very colorful show. I guess I was used to dingy bars—but it seemed so colorful and bright. And they always had such a big bunch on stage." He continued:

> One thing that I noticed, Homer and Jethro, when they hit the stage—one of them [was] in a bright red suit all the way down, the other one in a bright green suit all the way down. And this comedian—Cousin Tilford [Holly Swanson]—was real tall and ugly. He looked like a bulldog. And he'd drop his face down, and the audience would start laughing at him. He would look up and down the front row who laughed real loud, and he'd zero in on that person. And that person's laugh would just get louder. That would go over on the radio real good. And then they'd introduce Homer and Jethro, and the audience was just going crazy but it wasn't because of them, it was because of Cousin Tilford.

Garret remembered that as the 1950s wore on, the country was suffering mightily from rock 'n' roll, but that country music kept going in Chicago even after the NBD left WLS. He recalled, "When the Eighth Street Theatre shut down, Bob [Atcher] opened an FM radio station west of Chicago, and FM was just beginning to come in, and his station was the only one doing country music back then."

By July 1965, he and his wife moved to East Tennessee because their son was about ready to start school. After talking to Alma's sister, a music buff who complained about how hard it was to get records, Garret opened a record shop in Maryville, which would become an East Tennessee institution for four decades. "If I hadn't went in to business right away," he said of leaving Chicago, "I'd probably went back. I really missed it up there. But by the time I went back up there and realized it was nothing like it used to be, there was no way I'd live up there now."

All of the articles in this collection prove that a radio show is worthy of cultural study and understanding, that it was influenced by the time and place in which it was born, just as it in turn influenced culture around it. Early on, WLS, with its 50,000 watts of power, had an enormous reach, but so too did the National Barn Dance. As a testimony to that reach, we are pleased to present a wide array of scholars who attempt to understand this piece of twentieth-century culture from as many sides as possible. In doing so, they tell us not just about a radio program, but also about history, culture, economics, gender, and race. John Lair reminded listeners that the songs they heard over the airwaves on the Barn Dance were those listened to by their "daddies an' mammies"; in learning about these songs, we learn about a generation of folks struggling to reconcile the traditional to the changing, which is, after all, a timeless human endeavor.

NOTES

I thank Steve Parry, Paul Tyler, Diane Pecknold, an anonymous reviewer, Rodney Wolfenbarger, and Wayne Daniel for their helpful suggestions.

1. Mary A. Bufwack and Robert K. Oermann, *Finding Her Voice: Women in Country Music* (Nashville: Vanderbilt University Press, 2003), 80; Richard A. Peterson, *Creating Country Music: Fabricating Authenticity* (Chicago: University of Chicago Press, 1999), 100.

2. "Chi King Korn Heaven," *Billboard*, August 21, 1943, 1.

3. George C. Biggar, "The WLS National Barn Dance Story: The Early Years," reprinted in *Exploring Roots Music: Twenty Years of the* JEMF Quarterly, ed. Nolan Porterfield (Lanham, Md.: Scarecrow Press, 2004), 35.

4. Peterson, *Creating Country Music*, 98–99.

5. *Variety*, January 12, 1944, 38.

6. See, for example, Derek Vaillant, "Sounds of Whiteness: Local Radio, Racial Formation, and Public Culture in Chicago, 1921–1935," *American Quarterly* 54 (March 2002): 25–65.

7. See Wayne W. Daniel, "Hayloft Patriotism: The National Barn Dance during World War II," in *Country Music Goes to War*, ed. Charles K. Wolfe and James E. Akenson (Lexington: University Press of Kentucky, 2005), 83; Biggar, "WLS National Barn Dance Story," 41.

8. Bill C. Malone notes that jazz was far from being the preferred music for many during the era. See Bill C. Malone, *Don't Get above Your Raisin': Country Music and the Southern Working Class* (Urbana: University of Illinois Press, 2002), 27.

9. See, for example, Jane S. Becker, *Selling Tradition: Appalachia and the Construction of an American Folk, 1930–1940* (Chapel Hill: University of North Carolina Press, 1998).

10. Peterson, *Creating Country Music*, 67.

11. Anthony Harkins, *Hillbilly: A Cultural History of an American Icon* (New York: Oxford University Press, 2004), 89.

12. Malone, *Don't Get above Your Raisin'*, 181.

13. Ibid., 70.

14. See Peterson, *Creating Country Music*, 68–80; and Harkins, *Hillbilly*, 94.

15. Harkins writes masterfully about this transformation; see *Hillbilly*, 95–97.

16. Peterson, *Creating Country Music*, 81–82.

17. Ibid., 93, 91, 93, 106.

18. Malone, *Don't Get above Your Raisin'*, 61.

19. Ibid., 62.

20. See Kristine M. McCusker, "'Bury Me beneath the Willow': Linda Parker and Definitions of Tradition on the *National Barn Dance*, 1932–1935," in *A Boy Named Sue: Gender and Country Music*, ed. Kristine M. McCusker and Diane Pecknold (Jackson: University Press of Mississippi, 2004), 3–23.

21. Harkins, *Hillbilly*, 71–72; Malone, *Don't Get above Your Raisin'*, 14–17. Scholars of country music need to do much more research on whiteness and racialization.

22. Bradley Kincaid, *Favorite Mountain Ballads and Old Time Songs* (Chicago, 1928), foreword (Berea College Archives). Thanks to Kristine McCusker for her help with this citation.

23. James N. Gregory, *The Southern Diaspora: How the Great Migrations of Black and White Southerners Transformed America* (Chapel Hill: University of North Carolina Press, 2006), 9.

24. For more information, see Peterson, *Creating Country Music*, 77–80.

25. Gregory, *Southern Diaspora*, 14.

26. George C. Biggar, "The Early Days of WLS and the National Barn Dance," *Old-Time Music* 1 (Summer 1971): 12.

27. McCusker, "'Bury Me beneath the Willow,'" 18.

28. D. K. Wilgus, "An Introduction to the Study of Hillbilly Music," *Journal of American Folklore* 78 (1965): 196.

29. Peterson, *Creating Country Music*, 107.

30. Bufwack and Oermann, *Finding Her Voice*, 96, 78, 80.

31. Ibid., 86–88.

32. The quotations from Roy Garrett in this and the following paragraphs are from a personal conversation with Garrett, June 6, 2006.

1 THE RISE OF RURAL RHYTHM

Paul L. Tyler

> I've heard the barn dance fiddlers
> I've heard the square dance call.
>
> —from "Cow Boy Rhythm,"
> by Patsy Montana

On a Saturday in spring 1924—April 19, to be exact—a reader of the *Chicago Herald and Examiner* might have spotted a short article titled "National Barn Dance Tonight." The announced barn dance was not a soiree scheduled for a farmer's outbuilding in a rural district somewhere outside Chicago's city limits. It was, in fact, intended to attract a nationwide audience that could listen in as an unnamed old-time fiddle band sawed out square dance tunes in a studio recently constructed in the Hotel Sherman in the heart of Chicago. Attendance at this first National Barn Dance would be through a headset or a primitive speaker connected to a radio tuned in to WLS, the newest station vying for attention in America's second largest city. Any dancing would have to take place in the listener's parlor or kitchen, in close proximity to that newfangled radio set.

WLS's National Barn Dance was not the first radio program to feature old-time fiddlers. Local masters had already fiddled on stations in Iowa and Atlanta. Other significant early radio appearances by fiddlers occurred in Texas. In December 1922, WFAA in Dallas offered a concert by "Colonel William Hopkins, fiddler of Kansas City." Col. Hopkins, a forty-five-year veteran of the fiddle and bow, was accompanied by pianist Charles Krause on such numbers as "Old Southern Melodies," "Arkansas Traveler," and "Bows of Oak Hill" (the latter tune was recorded five years later by the National Barn Dance's Tommy Dandurand under the more usual spelling, "The Beau of Oak Hill"). A month later, in nearby Fort Worth, WBAP aired a show of square dance music that featured the fiddling of Capt. Moses J. Bonner, a Confederate veteran, and Fred Wagner's Hawaiian Five Hilo Orchestra. Spurred on by the enthusiastic response from a widely scattered audience, WBAP broadcast old-time fiddlers several times a month on an irregular schedule over the next few years.[1]

When the WLS National Barn Dance went on the air in April 1924, in the station's second week of operations, it was perhaps intentionally following trails blazed by the Texas stations or, closer to home, by KFNF in Shenandoah, Iowa. Most country music historians regard WBAP as the originator of the radio barn dance format, yet it is not clear that WLS borrowed either the format or the barn dance name from the Fort Worth station. But someone in Chicago must have been listening, for by the second week of the National Barn Dance, the local papers listed an appearance on the program by Cowbell Pete. According to WBAP's official history, the Fort Worth station was the first to use an audible logo, a cowbell, introduced in 1922. At WLS, cowbells became a signature sound accompanying applause through at least the first two decades of the National Barn Dance.[2]

Though it may not lay claim to having been the first radio barn dance, the WLS show soon became a dominant feature of the Saturday radio lineup in Chicago, the Midwest, and across the country. As it evolved, the National Barn Dance proved to be incredibly durable, missing only one or two Saturday nights over the next thirty-six years. It also became immensely popular and extremely influential. But in those early years of radio, when programming everywhere was intermittently scheduled—some cities following Chicago's lead in having "silent nights"—the National Barn Dance was still something of an experiment. WLS's first station manager, Edgar Bill, described how it came about:

> The truth is that it just grew up and here is how it happened. We started WLS with a large variety of entertainment programs. We would try anything once to see what our listeners thought about it. We had religious programs and services on Sunday. We featured high-brow music on one night; dance bands on another; then programs featuring large choruses. Other nights, we'd have variety or we might have a radio play. When it came to Saturday night, it was quite natural to book in old-time music, including old-time fiddling, banjo and guitar music and cowboy songs. We leaned toward the homey, old-time familiar tunes because *we were a farm station primarily* [emphasis added].

The Saturday night mix struck a chord with the target audience. According to the *Chicago Evening Post*, within the show's first few weeks "more than a thousand letters have come in from twenty states expressing appreciation of the old-fashioned barn-dance music." Letters came from a variety of listeners young and old, and several quoted in the article were written by folks living within the city limits of Chicago. Because much of Chicago's population was newly arrived from rural districts, WLS's farm-oriented programming became the favorite of many city residents as well.[3]

This distinctive pairing of a strong, rurally targeted radio station with a potent institutional base in a major metropolis explains much about how WLS and the National Barn Dance, in the years before World War II, came to be the preeminent radio home for what would later be called country music. In the crowded field of radio broadcasting in Chicago, WLS offered programming no other local station in the mid-1920s had, hoping to attract an audience that was mostly ignored by its competitors. The other half of this powerful combination was the organizational entity behind the radio station. WLS was owned successively by two large and successful corporations that provided resources sufficient to make the National Barn Dance easily the largest show of its kind before 1942.

Yet, though the National Barn Dance was a towering presence in the emerging commercial field of country music in the second quarter of the twentieth century, the last echoes of those early Barn Dance fiddlers have long since died away. A substantial paper trail tells us who the stars were and demonstrates that an extensive audience eagerly tuned in weekly to the broadcasts, traveled to Chicago and other midwestern towns to attend live shows, and snatched up souvenir songbooks and photo-filled yearbooks. The actual sounds of the National Barn Dance, however, have long been missing from our public consciousness. The artists broadcast live, and recording technology was not regularly employed to capture for posterity the sounds they sent out over the airwaves. A few incomplete air-check disks have turned up from the show's second decade, but the playing and singing, the comedy and banter that came into listeners' homes through those early radio sets can only be imagined. Before turning our focus to the main topic of this essay, reconstructing the music of the National Barn Dance, it would be worthwhile to recap the institutional history of WLS's landmark program.

GROWTH OF THE NATIONAL BARN DANCE

Through its first four years, WLS was operated by Sears, Roebuck and Company, a Chicago-based retailer that relied heavily on mail-order catalog sales. More accurately, WLS was the responsibility of the Sears-Roebuck Agricultural Foundation, chartered in 1923 to help farmers "farm better, sell better, and live better."[4] Of course, if farmers were successful at the first two of these activities, they would have more disposable income to spend on the last; and if Sears demonstrated acceptable ideals about what living better meant, and offered desirable products, a portion of that disposable income would lead to increased sales of Sears merchandise.

By 1928, because WLS had not yet turned a profit, Sears sold its station to the *Prairie Farmer* magazine. At the time, the cast of the National Barn Dance (hereafter also referred to as NBD or by the show's nickname, the Old Hayloft) included nearly thirty performers. By the middle of the next decade, even so large a cast was dwarfed by the number of performers who appeared on Saturday nights: between seventy and one hundred instrumentalists, vocalists, comedians, and other variety artists.[5] From the early days, at least some NBD stars also appeared on other WLS programs throughout the week. Other WLS artists, whose primary responsibilities were on weekday programs, joined the Hayloft Gang on Saturday nights as well.

The *Prairie Farmer*, founded in 1841, was a biweekly publication with a mission that meshed well with that of Sears's Agricultural Foundation, especially after Burridge D. Butler, a conservative crusader for agriculture, became the magazine's publisher in 1909. Under Butler's direction, the magazine provided farmers with a steady stream of information about issues facing agriculture and sought to serve by bringing them the best advantages of modernization without endangering the traditional values and meaningful symbols of agrarian culture. The *Prairie Farmer* rose from the pack of nearly fifty farm-oriented journals published in Chicago and elsewhere in Illinois to be the leading agricultural publication in the region, if not the nation. Reflecting Butler's idealistic stance, on the occasion of WLS's ninth birthday, the magazine declared that "America's oldest farm paper considers it almost a sacred privilege to serve as custodian of this powerful 50,000-watt station, acknowledged everywhere as the broadcaster with the greatest audience of the common, everyday folks on farms and in towns and cities."[6]

What Sears had started yielded an amazing harvest under Butler's *Prairie Farmer*. Always a careful businessman, before purchasing WLS, Butler sent sixty "field men" out for six weeks to discover the radio preferences of more than sixteen thousand midwestern farm families. They found that WLS clearly stood alone at the top of the list, sealing the deal. After eight years as the *Prairie Farmer* station, WLS set a record for the largest mail count received by a station in the country: "more than one million letters in the first six months" of 1936. Combined with increased advertising potential and growing profitability, WLS proved one of Butler's guiding principles, that "service had its rewards."[7]

Stuffed mailbags and many listener surveys all attested to the fact that the National Barn Dance was the jewel in the crown of Butler's media empire. Several important steps were taken in the next few years that assured the continuing prominence of the Barn Dance. In 1931, WLS became a 50,000-watt powerhouse, covering most of central North America. In 1932, due to popular demand for passes to see the show live in the broadcast studio, the station moved the NBD to the Eighth Street Theatre, where it sold out two two-hour shows every Saturday night—starting at 7:30 and 10:00—from March 19, 1932, to August 31, 1957. Starting in August 1933, a one-hour segment was broadcast coast-to-coast on the NBC Blue network. Miles Laboratories, of Elkhart, Indiana, sponsored the network segment in order to promote a new product, Alka-Seltzer.[8]

Other National Barn Dance segments continued broadcasting on the WLS airwaves through the support of a variety of sponsors. A typical Saturday night program lineup in the 1930s looked like this listing from 1933:

7:30	National Barn Dance
8:00	"Big Yank" Variety Program
8:15	Aladdin Program—Hugh Aspinwall 10/28
8:30	Keystone Barn Dance Party
9:00	Kitchen Klenzer—Three Kings—WLS Trio
9:15	Mac and Bob
9:30	Cumberland Ridge Runners
9:45	Song Story by the Emersons (Geppert Studios)
10:00	National Barn Dance (NBC Network for Alka-Seltzer)
11:00 to 12:00	Prairie Farmer Barn Dance[9]

The mix of sponsors reveals the surprising breadth of the audience for the Barn Dance. A producer of work shirts sponsored the Big Yank program, while Keystone Steel and Wire Company of Peoria, Illinois, sponsored the long-running Keystone segment. The products of the two companies were presumably useful to both farmers and those engaged in industry. The Aladdin Mantle Lamp Company, on the other hand, manufactured kerosene and oil-burning lamps that would have been particularly relevant to farmers and other residents of areas not yet reached by rural electrification projects.

Time and again, especially during the Butler years, WLS proved to be remarkably effective at building connections with its audience. By at least 1930, the National Barn Dance was being broadcast in front of large live audiences at the Illinois and Indiana state fairs in what became annual appearances. Early in the *Prairie Farmer* era, WLS Artists, Inc., was formed to book live performances of road shows. One purpose of this venture was to help staff musicians—not all of whom were full time—supplement their incomes, but another reason was undoubtedly to help meet the demand voiced by the station's listeners. In 1933, the station also began to promote "Home Talent Shows," in which listeners—usually kids—could imitate their favorite WLS performers on stage and also be entertained by real stars from the Old Hayloft.

For three years, starting in February 1935, WLS published a weekly fan magazine that started out as *Prairie Farmer's WLS Weekly* and was soon changed, after a naming contest, to *Stand By!* The sixteen-page, large-format magazine contained photographs and features on NBD artists and other WLS personalities, a full broadcast and live appearance schedule, letters from listeners, and several news and queries columns. The longest-lasting artifacts of these relationship-building activities are issues of the *WLS Family Album*, published annually beginning in November 1929 for the following year, with the last one appearing in 1957.[10] These slickly produced, forty- to forty-eight-page books crammed with photographs and homey introductions to all of the station's on-air staff can still be found at midwestern flea markets and antiques stores (see figures 3 and 24).

Several landmark occasions demonstrate the incredible popularity of the National Barn Dance throughout the 1930s. In fall 1930 two performances were scheduled for the large

International Amphitheatre at Chicago's famous stockyards. Ten thousand people were able to attend each show. According to reports, an equal number were turned away from the first show. The crowds were even bigger—20,000 per night—for the NBD's one-night-per-week appearance during September 1933 at the Century of Progress International Exposition, better known as the Chicago World's Fair. Perhaps the most stunning was the occasion in July 1939 when 60,000 people from fifteen different states somehow crowded into a public park in the small town of Noblesville, Indiana, for a Sunday picnic featuring WLS's Little Brown Church of the Air. Though some churches had canceled services so their parishioners could attend, the real draw was the Barn Dance stars Patsy Montana, the Maple City Four, the Hoosier Sod Busters, and comedian Little Genevieve. Patsy Montana remembered singing in front of those 60,000 fans as a "staggering experience. . . . These were farmers, working hard to make their chores work out so they could drive a great distance and still get home in time for evening chores."[11]

UNDERSTANDING THE MUSIC OF THE OLD HAYLOFT

What was it about the music of the National Barn Dance that so endeared it to huge numbers of rural and urban midwesterners? My attempt to reconstruct the nearly forgotten sound of the NBD's early years will start with how a WLS publicist framed the very first program of barn dance fiddlers. A glimpse of the show's future appeal shines through in the "National Barn Dance Tonight" article mentioned at the beginning of this essay. Here is the text in full:

> "All hands 'round—swing your partner—sasahay [*sic*] 'round—do, si, do—balance partners!" The old familiar calls of the barn dance fiddler will reverberate from many a concrete barn tonight, when Sears Roebuck Station WLS conducts its first weekly national barn dance over the radio.
>
> Farmers the country over, heeding the announcement of the Sears-Roebuck Agricultural Foundation, have planned barn dance parties for this evening. Young and old will have their fling from 8 P.M. till midnight, because Isham Jones' College Inn Orchestra will alternate with the fiddlers and other musicians of yesteryear. This will be the only WLS program on the air today.[12]

This short text signifies a great deal about the substance and style of WLS's attempts to serve the rural community. Living better, in the view of Sears and, later, the *Prairie Farmer*, involves such decidedly nonmaterial values as community and sociability, reaching out across generational divides, and respect for the old blended with an openness to the new. WLS could benefit farmers' lives by providing them not only timely information and educational features, but also the kinds of entertainment preferred by farm folk. The Sears catalog, of course, offered for sale many material accessories related to this vision for living better, including radio sets, phonograph records, and musical instruments. And Sears continued to use WLS and the *Prairie Farmer* to advertise its catalog and merchandise.

Unfortunately, although the full introductory announcement printed in the *Chicago Herald and Examiner* suggests so much, it did not appear in any other of Chicago's half-dozen daily newspapers. The first post–World War II generation of country music historians all missed the story, which has led to several misunderstandings about the nature of the National Barn Dance. For instance, from a local radio host and from an NBD memorabilia collector, I have heard recent retellings of the myth of the program's accidental beginnings. The contemporary spread of this narrative dates to 1966 when Robert Shelton, a critic of popular music for the *New York Times*, published *The Country Music Story*. Shelton's source was probably John Lair, an important WLS programmer during the 1930s. The myth went as follows: Saturday night arrived and "'there was just nobody to put on the air.' The station manager was in Evanston, and Tommy Dandurand, a janitor at the station, brought out a scratchy fiddle and somebody got a cowbell, and off it went."[13] From the *Chicago Herald and Examiner* notice, it is patently clear that WLS executives were more careful in their planning, and the show was no accident. And although Tommy Dandurand (figure 8) is often named as the first fiddler on the Barn Dance, it is doubtful he was a janitor for the station or the Hotel Sherman. Dandurand had been a streetcar motorman in Kankakee, Illinois, and had moved to Chicago to live with his son after losing a leg in an automobile accident two years earlier.[14]

Figure 8. Old-time fiddler Tommy Dandurand. Courtesy of Ann Lair Henderson.

Confusion also surrounds the name of the

program, which was dubbed the National Barn Dance at its very beginning. As estimable a scholar as Wayne Daniel has mistakenly claimed that the NBD was known initially as the "WLS Barn Dance," and that "National" was added to the name when the NBC Blue network picked up a segment of the program in 1933. Daniel is justified in the first half of his assertion by the casual way in which the program was named in radio program listings published daily in the papers. Often the show *was* simply called the "Barn Dance" or the "WLS Barn Dance." Through summer 1924, WLS's Saturday night program listings included a variety of names, such as "Old time fiddlers program," "National farm barn dance," and "Old time fiddlers." For a time in the fall of that year, it appears that WLS might have been trying to shift the program's focus away from the image of the barn dance, and titles like "Saturday night Mardi Gras" and "WLS review night" became more prominent. But by the dawn of 1925, Saturday night at WLS was given back over to a "national barn dance" or to simply a "barn dance."[15]

Finally, the *Chicago Herald and Examiner* announcement of the first National Barn Dance reveals clearly an essential characteristic of the early programs, a trait that would carry over for the next thirty-six years (the first half of which are covered by this essay). The music of the Barn Dance, and of WLS weekday programs, comprised a very broad range of styles and genres. On that first program, the old-time fiddlers (or fiddle band) alternated with a modern ballroom orchestra, and every Barn Dance program that followed included both pop and country artists—or to use a music industry term from before 1950, "hillbilly" musicians. This basic fact has proved problematic to most postwar country music scholars, and has led, at minimum, to the NBD's importance being understated and, at worst, to its being misrepresented in scholarly writings on country music.

Wayne Daniel summed up the contemporary heuristic problem succinctly in his opening salvo for the *Journal of Country Music* in 1983: "Drawing from standard country music reference works and WLS publications, several writers have agreed that the National Barn Dance delivered to its audiences 'a mixed musical array' that was 'decidedly more "popular" than "hillbilly."' New evidence to support this conclusion is put forth in this article."[16]

Sadly, the consensus that the WLS Barn Dance lacked a certain degree of country or hillbilly authenticity has consigned the NBD to virtual footnote status in the standard country music reference works. Cursory treatments of the show highlight the fact that Country Music Hall of Fame members Gene Autry and Red Foley started out on WLS, but they do little more than list the names of other key performers. And most histories of country music go little beyond the cursory when discussing the National Barn Dance. Though some recently published and online reference works contain solid entries on key Barn Dance performers, not much has been done to integrate their contributions into larger historical narratives. Ivan Tribe's entry in the online *Century of Country* reveals an irony that explains why the NBD has been regularly overlooked in so many quarters: "Overall, it is quite difficult to overestimate the importance that the National Barn Dance played in the growth of Country music on radio in the second quarter of the 20th century. Sadly, no anthologies of the music of performers from that era have ever been released." The music of the Old Hayloft has been roundly ignored, so it is no surprise that a recently published encyclopedia of Chicago history, besides getting the show's name wrong, characterizes the NBD as "nearly forgotten today."[17]

The National Barn Dance is not well remembered primarily because of the incompleteness of the sonic record. By the time I wrote this essay, I had identified only eight or nine preserved air-check recordings of the Barn Dance from before 1945. Most were recorded during the war years, with only a single program from 1939 surviving from the time period covered by this essay. Apparently all the surviving air-checks from the early years are of the sixty-minute-long NBC network segments. Thus only a selective portion of the entire program has been preserved. The National Barn Dance encompassed at least five hours each week and presented numerous artists who were seldom or never featured on the network segment sponsored by Alka-Seltzer. Fortunately, many NBD artists did leave behind a large body of work on commercial phonograph records. However, very few of these recordings are currently available through record company catalogs. While many rare pre–World War II recordings of rural musicians have been reissued in LP and CD formats over the last four decades, NBD artists have not been fairly represented.

This dearth of National Barn Dance artists on contemporary reissue recordings is both a symptom and a cause of our contemporary amnesia about one of radio's most storied programs. Consider the case of the biggest NBD stars: Lulu Belle and Scotty, Arkie the Arkansas Woodchopper, and the Prairie Ramblers. In an audience poll conducted in 1937, WLS listeners voted these three the most popular acts on the station. All three are noteworthy for their longevity with WLS. Lulu Belle and Scotty joined the Barn Dance cast separately in the mid-1930s and, except for a two-year hiatus, performed as a favorite NBD duo until their retirement in 1958. The Arkansas Woodchopper had an even longer run, coming to WLS in 1929 and staying with the Barn Dance even after it left WLS in 1960 and moved to WGN. The Prairie Ramblers (figure 9) were also associated with the NBD through the better part of three decades, from 1933 through about 1956, with several short periods off to work at other stations. But only two albums on American record labels were ever devoted to reissues of earlier 78 rpm recordings by these artists: that is, Lulu Belle and Scotty, *Early and Great, Vol. 1*, on Old Homestead Records, and Patsy Montana and the Prairie Ramblers on a *Columbia Historic Edition* LP. The first-ever reissue of the Arkansas Woodchopper's early recordings appeared in 2002 on the small independent label British Archives of Country Music.

This lack of representation on post–World War II commercial recordings is even more puzzling when one discovers how prolifically Old Hayloft musicians recorded during the period covered by this chapter. The Prairie Ramblers, for instance, recorded 257 pieces between 1933 and 1942, while also accompanying vocalist Patsy Montana on an additional

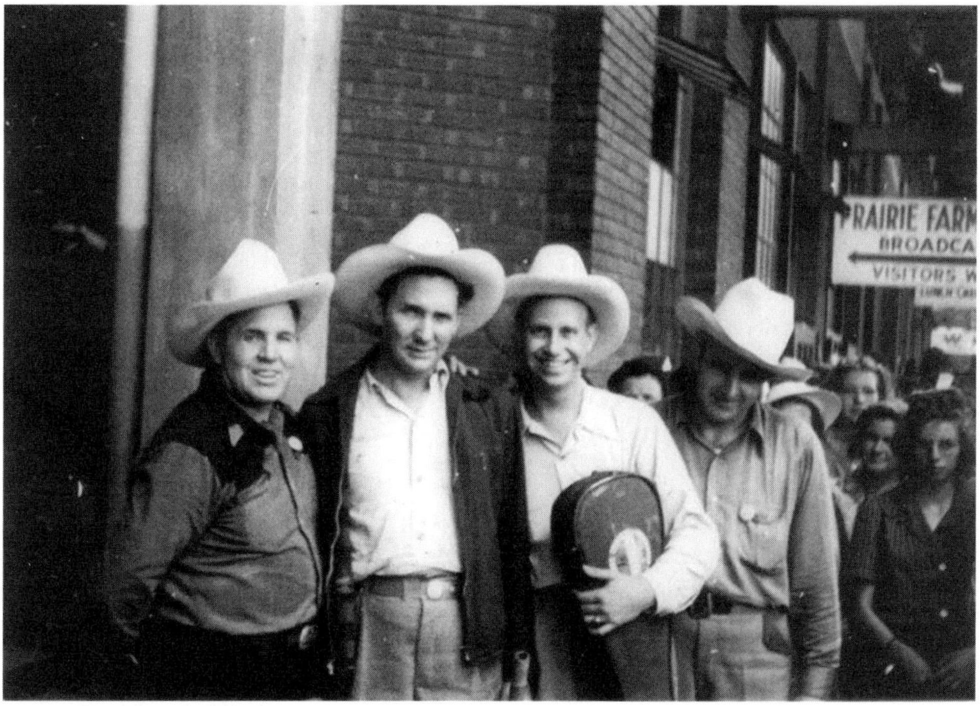

Figure 9. The Prairie Ramblers (left to right): Chick Hurt, Salty Holmes, Alan Crockett, and Jack Taylor. Courtesy of Don Gill.

87 sides. Another measure of their recording activity comes from their sixth-place standing on a list of country artists with the greatest number of recording sessions—the Ramblers and Patsy made seventy-five visits to the studio. This list, which I compiled from an analysis of the data compiled in Tony Russell's valuable *Country Music Records: A Discography, 1921–42*, contains several other Old Hayloft artists. With 115 recording sessions, Gene Autry has a clear hold on third place, while fiddler Clayton McMichen, who recorded with his own Georgia Wildcats (figure 10) as well as with Gid Tanner and the Skillet Lickers, is in tenth but would move higher if the Skillet Lickers sessions were factored in. Mac and Bob, with fifty-three sessions, are ranked eleventh, while the Hoosier Hot Shots, with thirty-nine, finish off the top twenty. It should be noted that some critics regard as suspect the "hillbilly" credentials of four of the artists at the very top of this list—Vernon Dalhart, Carson Robison, Frankie Marvin, and Bob Miller. If this is the case (and I am not comfortable with the argument), then the two most frequently recorded authentic rural or country musicians up through 1942 are National Barn Dance stars Gene Autry and the Prairie Ramblers.[18]

An analysis of Russell's discography reveals further hints of the importance of the National Barn Dance. Of the 1,588 artists that Russell includes—if their record label marketed them in any way to white, southern, rural, or small-town consumers, they are included—I

Figure 10. Clayton McMichen's Georgia Wildcats played the Barn Dance in 1933 and included (left to right) Jack Dunigan, Thomas Hoyt "Slim" Bryant, and Bert Layne. Courtesy of Juanita McMichen Lynch.

identified fifty-five as having some tenure on the WLS Barn Dance. According to Russell's own estimate, there were over 28,000 masters recorded by these nearly 1,600 acts.[19] By my count, at least 55 NBD artists recorded 2,333 of these sides, and that total could be increased by several hundred to make up for later Gene Autry and Clayton McMichen recordings. In either case, over 8 percent of all country music records made between 1921 and 1942 were made by musicians who at one time or another were members of the Hayloft Gang. Included in these ranks is an impressive array of musicians—starting with Chubby Parker and Pie Plant Pete and stretching through the Cumberland Ridge Runners and the Westerners. All were undeniably rural in origin and played and sang in styles that are today clearly recognized as "country."

Nevertheless, not all of the musicians who performed on the Barn Dance were included in Russell's discography, some because they apparently never recorded, others because their recordings were evidently not marketed for a rural audience. How do we account for the mix of popular and "hillbilly" styles that constituted the NBD? One place to start is by acknowledging that this mix never appeared to be a problem for either WLS or for much of its audience. When the NBD went on the air in 1924, a rubric for defining the difference between country music and pop music did not exist. Through the 1930s, WLS exhibited no desire to limit its audience to narrowly defined segments of taste or musical preference. And though the station's identifiably rural artists appeared right alongside such urbane veterans of the music industry as Henry Burr, who had "made more phonograph records than any other person," and Grace Wilson, "the famous 'Bringing Home the Bacon' girl," no apparent attempt was made to educate the audience about which genre each artist represented. There are two noteworthy exceptions to this rule. Bradley Kincaid and John Lair, a WLS producer and organizer of the Cumberland Ridge Runners, went to great lengths to present what they viewed as authentic folk music from the southern Appalachians. For both men, it was important to distance their representations of traditional folksong from other commercial manifestations of hillbilly music.[20]

In the annual *Family Album* that WLS began to publish in 1930, a little more than a year after *Prairie Farmer* magazine purchased the station from Sears, musical acts are not labeled or segregated by type, beyond small hints or suggestive images. For instance, Arkie the Arkansas Woodchopper had actually chopped wood and Gene Autry had been "really and truly a cowboy" before he became a singer of western songs. William Vickland, on the other hand, was conservatory trained, and the Novelodeons, who specialized in comic arrangements, were all "highly skilled musicians."[21] One might infer that WLS and the *Prairie Farmer* regarded the difference as one between musicians who learned through aural tradition, such as Arkie and Autry, and those who were formally trained. George Biggar, who had a long association with the Barn Dance as an executive for both the Sears-Roebuck Agricultural Foundation and WLS–*Prairie Farmer*, applied the descriptive "folk" in a nonacademic way in talking about the music of the Barn Dance: "We used the terms 'folk music' for traditional music, and 'modern folk music' for more recently written songs."[22] But the WLS programmers were never explicit, and we are left to wonder whether or not they intended the term "folk music" to expand to cover all the music heard on the National Barn Dance.

Place of origin was also deemed important by those who wrote copy for the *WLS Family Album* and other publications, presumably because it would reinforce connections between the performers and their mostly rural target audience. Thus, the *Family Album* pointed out that the Three Neighbor Boys "came directly from the farm in Marshall county, Illinois," while the Rock Creek Rangers, a band made up of Sunshine Sue Workman and her brothers, was from a farm in Iowa. Still, farm origins are not enough to characterize or categorize the music styles of these performers. Rural districts in America, especially east of the Mississippi River and even in the southern Appalachians, were never totally isolated from the movements of people in and out, from visits by itinerant troupes of performers or music teachers, or from the cultural influences of town-based institutions and commerce. Brass bands, church hymnals, and musical instrument salesmen were not limited to the cities. Thus there was no essential or impenetrable divide between the music styles of the metropolis and the countryside. And while traditional fiddling or older ballads and folksongs may have been more commonly found in a rural musician's repertoire, some from the country dabbled in newer sounds, such as band music, ragtime, the latest song compositions from Tin Pan Alley, sophisticated part-singing, or even jazz. In short, some rural musicians, from all parts of the United States, have been known to play music that is, according to current definitions, unmistakably *not* country music.

But the question of origin raises another problematic issue introduced by postwar country music scholars: that is, the notion that country music is primarily and, in some way, intrinsically, *southern*. The clearest statement of what I call the southern thesis is in Bill C. Malone's masterful history, *Country Music, U.S.A.* He began the first edition with the assertion that commercial country music "developed out of the folk culture of the rural South." For the second edition, Malone's definition offered more nuance while reasserting even more strongly the southernness of country music, which

> evolved primarily out of the reservoir of folksongs, ballads, dances, and instrumental pieces brought to North America by the Anglo-Celtic immigrants. Gradually absorbing influences from other musical sources, particularly from the culture of Afro-Americans, it eventually emerged as a force strong enough to survive, and even thrive, in an urban-industrial society. . . . It was only in the southern United States, though, that dynamic folk cultural expressions, black and white, evolved into viable commercial forms in our own time.[23]

There can be no argument that hillbilly or country music is comfortably at home in the South, and that a large percentage of both country musicians and enthusiasts hail from below the Mason-Dixon line. Similarly, a substantial portion of NBD artists had southern roots, and the program was well received by southerners who had migrated to Chicago and elsewhere in the Midwest. Yet there is no evidence that regional style was ever *the* determining factor in selecting or rejecting artists to appear on the Barn Dance, at least before World War II, or in the general preferences of the show's audience.

A few years before Malone's history was published, D. K. Wilgus offered an eloquent description of the multiple roots of what became country music: "Early hillbilly performers came not only from the lowland and upland South, but from the Great Plains and the Midwest. . . . That the first important hillbilly radio show originated in Chicago cannot be explained solely by the presence of Southern migrants. Its manifestation was of the South; its essence was of rural America. Southern hillbilly music seems but a specialized and dominant form of a widespread music."[24] Unfortunately, Wilgus's wisdom has been ignored, and the southern thesis has become gospel truth in the scholarly discourse on country music. Occasionally, scholars have had to make some unwarranted assumptions in order to account for the presence or absence of what they view as real country music, the southern variety, on the National Barn Dance. A few examples will suffice. Jeffrey Lange argued that a group like the Prairie Ramblers, Kentucky natives with a smooth sound and a preference for swing, were necessary on the NBD in the mid-thirties to offset the Cumberland Ridge Runners (also from Kentucky), a more characteristically southern—and presumably rougher-sounding—string band. Following this line of thinking, the Ridge Runners' appeal was limited to the southern migrants in the audiences and, by implication, the Ramblers would not be an appropriate hire for a barn dance show on a southern radio station. And in an oft-made retrospective comparison with the Grand Ole Opry on WSM in Nashville, Charles Wolfe described the WLS Barn Dance as "'soft' country—with a lot of vaudeville, barbershop quartets, polka bands, and ersatz cowboy songs."[25] Wolfe is correct in asserting that such styles were present on the NBD; but the implication that this limited range of styles adequately describes the music of the early National Barn Dance is completely misleading.

Another example of the contortions required to prop up a regional bias stems from a memorable, though regularly misunderstood, statement from a WLS executive. At some point in the early 1950s, WLS's longtime station manager Glenn Snyder—he started at the station in 1932—proposed the term "hungry hillbilly" as the antithesis of what the National Barn Dance was all about. Beginning with Bernard Asbel's 1954 story on the Barn Dance for *Chicago Magazine*, most critics have asserted that Snyder equated "hungry hillbilly" with southern styles of country music, and "he'll have none of it on WLS." A more careful reading of Asbel's treatment reveals this equation to be rash and unfortunate. According to Snyder's colleague George Biggar, the "hungry" label referred to the southern-style country bands that played taverns and honky-tonks while costumed in "fancy get-ups," like those fashionable in postwar Nashville. Though this discourse on hungry hillbillies originated in a later period, there is relevance for this essay. Biggar tied the critique of hungry hillbillies to Burridge Butler's commanding preference for a certain style of presentation, for overalls and calico shirts and a mandate that his WLS artists be natural and "ring true."[26] According to practices established in the 1930s, there would be no Nudie suits on the Barn Dance. But Snyder and company never hung out a virtual sign that read "No southerners need apply."

One further tangential observation about hungry hillbillies practically cries out to be made. Perhaps only a resident of the Chicago area would catch the possible double meaning of Snyder's positive term for the music of the Barn Dance: "uptown hillbilly." The tavern district where Snyder's hungry hillbillies plied their trade, as described in Asbel's article, was located on the west side, along Madison Avenue. Uptown, on the other hand, is a north-side neighborhood that has long served as a point of entry for immigrants and, especially in the mid-twentieth century, for white migrants coming to Chicago from the southern Appalachians and elsewhere in the rural South. Could Snyder's vision of an "uptown hillbilly" have meant a southern mountaineer newly arrived in Chicago, someone whose musical heritage was closer to the mountain folksongs promoted by Bradley Kincaid and John Lair than to artificial hillbilly songs of the music industry? It is worth pondering.

A critique is long overdue of the southern thesis, and of other essentialist explanations of the emergence of commercial country music from the abundance of rural music styles and traditions found throughout America in the first half of the twentieth century. That, however, is beyond the scope of this essay. Let it suffice that when distinctive, commercial, southern forms of country music developed in the 1940s, especially with the ascendancy of Nashville, some of these styles were alien to the goals of WLS and the *Prairie Farmer.* Still, the dominant southernness of postwar country music should not grant the southern apologists an exclusive claim to the music's historical roots. The dynamic folk traditions of string bands and songsters from the 1920s and into the early 1930s and the more professionalized soloists, vocal duos, and swing bands of the late thirties were equally developed by rural musicians from the Midwest, the West, and the North.

But if none of the definitions or genre labels offered thus far by scholars (popular versus hillbilly) or by the NBD's marketing department (folk and modern folk, songs of the mountains and plains) are adequately descriptive, how do we understand the distinctive character of the music of the Old Hayloft? I believe an answer can be found in the merging of the existential dynamics of the radio medium and WLS's reliance on the old and the familiar to win a place for itself in the homes of rural Americans. Once again, the *Chicago Herald and Examiner*'s announcement of the first show provides a clue: WLS's strategy highlighted "the old familiar calls of the barn dance fiddler" and relied on the appeal of pleasurable experiences and nostalgic memories associated with a real barn dance, a widespread institution of communal sociability that many commentators of the time feared was passing from the scene. While the station's executives initially envisioned that rural folks would actually hold a dance on Saturday nights to music supplied from the WLS studios—and some apparently did—it did not take long to realize that this was not the best use of the new medium.[27]

Old-time fiddling and square dance calls, nevertheless, continued to be potent symbols for WLS and the National Barn Dance. For four months beginning in summer 1924, the station conducted a fiddle contest during Saturday-night broadcasts with the listening audience serving as judges. First prize was awarded to George Adamson of Kenosha, Wisconsin, at one of the NBD's first remote broadcasts from the Illinois State Fair in September. In 1926 and 1927, the NBD conducted similar on-air contests for square dance callers. There were thirty-one contestants in the 1927 contest, but no announcement of who the winners were either year has yet surfaced.[28] Through the 1930s, the Hayloft Gang always included several old-time fiddlers, but by 1939 (the date of the earliest recorded broadcast I have been able to hear), square dance calling had been relegated to a symbolic and transitional role (figures 11 and 12). On the NBC network segment, the Arkansas Woodchopper delivered rapid-fire patter calls that faded out as the program went to a commercial break. A union-mandated staff orchestra supplied the fiddle breakdown for this network broadcast.[29]

Through its experiments in programming, WLS discovered that the old familiar music that worked best on radio was music better suited for the more intimate domestic spaces of the parlor or kitchen, not the public hall. Old-time fiddling and its associated dance forms belonged primarily to what folklorists have called "public" or "assembly" traditions. "Domestic" traditions, on the other hand, included the customary contexts for the singing of traditional folksongs and for family music-making.[30] In the latter part of the nineteenth and the beginning of the twentieth centuries, domestic music traditions increasingly featured

Figure 11. Dance tunes were performed by the Cumberland Ridge Runners (left to right, rear): Slim Miller, Hugh Cross, Harty Taylor, Karl Davis, Linda Parker, and John Lair. John Lair Collection, Southern Appalachian Archives, Berea College.

parlor performances made possible with purchases of merchandise from a music dealer, including sheet music, song folios, and relatively affordable mass-produced instruments like guitars, mandolins, and especially the piano. WLS and the Barn Dance found a comfort zone by concentrating on such domestic traditions, which led to a shift to smaller and more intimate acts: solo performers, vocal duos and trios, and jocular conversational skits involving the announcer, as straight man, and one or two comedians.

Soloists, like Bradley Kincaid and Grace Wilson, and small ensembles, from the Girls of the Golden West to the Maple City Four, all became as familiar as friends to the listeners at home, because they fit well with the dynamics of the new medium. Radio receivers came to be housed in large cabinets, usually crafted as attractive pieces of furniture for a family residence. Audiences listened in the comfort of their living rooms, parlors, or kitchens. In addition, the audio fidelity of radio sets after the mid-1920s far surpassed that

Figure 12. Old-time musicians Jesse Doolittle, Tommy Dandurand, Rube Tronson, and Ed Goodreau. Library of American Broadcasting, University of Maryland.

of the phonographs of the day. The radio singer's voice was more immediately present in the listener's home than the voice of the phonograph-recording artist. The NBD played up this familiar, homey quality and asked its performers to be natural, unassuming, and friendly. In constructing its virtual and musical "Old Hayloft," WLS began by modeling it as a public assembly, an old-time social dance in a rustic outbuilding. But the station reached its greatest levels of success when it reconfigured the presentation to suggest surroundings as comfortable and as homey as the parlor or living room. The Old Hayloft—the barn that housed the Barn Dance—thus became not a public venue, but an extension of the home, of the hearth.[31]

Furthermore, the seemingly natural merger between the intimacy of radio and the familiarity of old-time songs provided a way for urban popular-song artists to fit in seamlessly with the rural musicians of the Barn Dance. Based on the photographic evidence of the *WLS Family Albums*, at least some of the pop music acts reconfigured their presentation for the domestic setting of the Old Hayloft. A key element for making the transition: the use of one of the countless guitar-strumming members of the station's cast. Thomas Hoyt "Slim" Bryant, a guitarist with Clayton McMichen's Georgia Wildcats, was asked to be the accompanist for one of the station's popular-song artists in 1932. On the Barn Dance, the staff pianist—Ralph Whitlock in the 1920s and John Brown during the 30s—may be all the accompaniment a singer used, suggesting a setting like a family parlor.[32]

To better understand the import of this reconfiguration, consider that since at least Stephen Foster's era (the decades leading up to the Civil War), the American popular-song tradition was centered on public, staged performances. Star singers, who helped the music industry by promoting the latest hits from Tin Pan Alley composers, performed to orchestra accompaniment in concert settings in the popular theater and vaudeville. When the recording industry broke upon the scene, people went to public arcades where they could drop a coin in a cylinder machine and hear a singer backed by a studio orchestra. When the phonograph itself was domesticated, the music on the discs played at home continued to represent the performance practices of the assembly tradition. With the development of radio broadcasting—direct competition for the record industry—popular singers were presented a new venue with its own set of new challenges and demands. WLS and the Barn Dance met those challenges with astounding success by erasing the social distance between the performer and audience, a separation that characterized the assembly tradition. They turned pop singers into friends who had come into your home to visit.[33] Other radio stations, of course, worked similarly successful strategies. The National Barn Dance led the way by using the symbols of rural sociability and old-time music to draw into its embrace music and musicians from more formal and urbane performance contexts. Popular songs could be remade as folksongs or at least be imbued with the rural values of the Old Hayloft.

The first identifiable pop singers on the National Barn Dance were the duo of Ford and Glenn (Ford Rush and Glenn Rowell), whom Edgar Bill, the station manager, discovered in a theater on Chicago's North Side during WLS's first few weeks of operation. For the next few years they appeared weekly on the Barn Dance and also hosted a *Lullaby Time* for a half hour prior to the start of the NBD proper. Ford and Glenn were the first in a long line of small vocal ensembles in the Old Hayloft who specialized in close harmony. The list includes such groups as Ingram and Carpenter, the Harmony Girls (1924); Three Hired Men, "Swedish boys with plenty of 'mean' harmony" (1930); the Milk Maids, including Juanita (Mrs. John) Brown, a native of Adrian, Michigan (1931); Three Neighbor Boys, whose "singing has never lost its sweetness and simplicity" (1935); and the Girls' Trio, "three little girls from Des Plaines . . . perfect harmony" (1939).[34] Was the repertoire of these vocal groups country or pop? Such labels apparently did not matter to WLS and its audience. What was important is the easy familiarity with which the performers brought music into one's parlor. These singers, starring on a nationally prominent radio show, were like neighbor kids, or hired hands, or other familiar members of your community.

Homey and domestic presentations were not the entirety of the National Barn Dance. Many acts still clearly represented the assembly traditions of public performance. These acts ranged from string and swing bands like the Georgia Wildcats and the Westerners to raucous novelty groups like the Four Hired Men and the Hoosier Hot Shots. Also, the

Barn Dance always had some sort of staff band. Starting in 1924, it was the generically titled "old time fiddlers." In the early thirties, Rube Tronson's Texas Cowboys—featuring two real country fiddlers along with accordion, clarinet, and brass players—filled that role. In 1932 and 33, there was no staff orchestra, and with several organized string bands in the cast, the bands took turns playing for the square dance troupe for its turn on stage.[35] By the end of the 1930s, a staff orchestra—with union-card-carrying violinists, not country fiddlers—was on stage for at least the NBC network segment of the broadcast. Network shows from that era started and ended with big production numbers featuring the orchestra and the many-voiced Hayloft Chorus. But the heart of the Barn Dance was in the intimate and familiar presentations of small groups like Mac and Bob, Jo and Alma, Karl and Harty, the Flannery Sisters, Lulu Belle and Scotty, the Girls of the Golden West, Linda Parker with the Cumberland Ridge Runners, the Three Little Maids (the Overstake Sisters), and Winnie Lou and Sally (named for WLS). Notice how many of these artists were women. What could be more homey and domestic than that for 1930s audiences?

THE RURAL RHYTHM OF THE HAYLOFT GANG

The actual sounds of the National Barn Dance before World War II are quite elusive, for the words and pictures of the *WLS Family Albums* carry no audible signal. For readers able to render music notation into a musical performance, there are several dozen song folios published by NBD artists before 1942 that contain lyrics, piano arrangements, guitar chord symbols, and, in one case, numbers and symbols indicating where and when to draw or blow on a ten-hole harmonica. Songbooks like these would have been helpful for playing along at home with an artist heard regularly over the airwaves. But today, separated by many decades, such published arrangements are by themselves insufficiently descriptive to enable an accurate reenactment of the music of the Old Hayloft.[36]

A few examples will disclose some of the challenges encountered. When compared to their phonograph records, the song folios published for Bradley Kincaid, Mac and Bob, and others contain quite accurate transcriptions of the lyrics of the songs. Other artists' songbooks show more lyrical variation, but the differences are still relatively minor. More crucial are the differences in form that can be found by comparing printed scores and recorded versions of the songs. For instance, the songbook version of the Arkansas Woodchopper's "The Bronc That Wouldn't Bust" gives no indication that the fourth and final stanza was used by Arkie as a refrain after each of the other three stanzas on the recorded performance. In addition, for this song and another cowboy song, "Texas Cowboy," the songbook supplies yodels that are less elaborate and only half the length of what is heard on Arkie's phonograph records.[37]

The most glaring inaccuracies in the song folios are found in the musical notations themselves. Vocal harmonies are entirely missing in the folios published for Karl and Harty (figure 13) and Mac and Bob (figure 14), duets whose characteristic styles were built on close harmony. Examples of melodic imprecision can be found time and again in the songbooks. It is admittedly difficult to transcribe clearly and cleanly the vocal nuances of a traditional folk singer who employs slides, scoops, and other vocal ornaments in moving from note to note. (Such features epitomized the emerging distinctiveness of country music, including the styles heard on WLS, and were often contrary to the strictures and conventions of formal

Figure 13. Karl (Davis) and Harty (Hartford Taylor) were born and raised near Mount Vernon, Kentucky. John Lair Collection, Southern Appalachian Archives, Berea College.

Figure 14. Mac (Lester McFarland, of Gray, Kentucky) and Bob (Robert Gardner, of Oliver Springs, Tennessee) were said to have met while studying at the Kentucky School for the Blind. Southern Music and Radio Photographic Collection, Southern Appalachian Archives, Berea College.

music training in the first half of the twentieth century.) Still, the published song folios often miss basic melodic steps and turns of the performance practices heard on records made by NBD artists.[38]

A telling instance is found in the notation for the fiddle tune "The Irish Washerwoman," credited to Tommy Dandurand. The version printed in a landmark 1935 anthology (figure 15) is nearly identical to other published settings of this standard piece. My transcription of an actual Dandurand performance—recorded in the Gennett studios in Chicago in August 1927—shows some notable differences that reflect Dandurand's personal shaping of the tune

Figure 15. "The Irish Washerwoman," from *100 WLS Barn Dance Favorites;* notation by Paul Tyler.

(figure 16). In the first strain he preferred a gently curving melodic contour over the repeated jumps of the conventional setting. His second strain comprised a melodic idiosyncracy in the first half, and a distinctive rhythmic shift in the descending figure leading to the final notes. And finally, Dandurand's record featured square dance calls sung by Ed Goodreau, in what is likely the earliest recorded example of a "singing call," a style of calling that would come to rival the older style of chanted and rhymed calls known as "patter."[39]

Discs made for the record industry provide the best opportunity available today to hear something resembling the sounds of the early National Barn Dance. Still, it must be remembered that such recordings represent performances not in front of a radio microphone, but rather in the studio of a rival business concern. During the 1920s and 30s, record companies' profits dipped sharply, due in large part to the formidable competition afforded by radio. Bill Malone, for one, has argued that commercial country music developed out of the kinds of rural folk music the record companies turned to in order to develop new markets and reverse their slumping sales. Sears, on the other hand, saw an opportunity to work both sides of the aisle and entered into a complicated agreement with the Gennett label—affiliated with the Starr Piano Company of Richmond, Indiana—to produce budget records featuring Barn Dance artists on the Challenge and Silvertone labels. In later stages of the five-year deal, the WLS material recorded by Gennett was issued on Supertone and Conqueror.[40]

By the start of 1928, four Barn Dance acts—Walter Petersen, the Kentucky Wonder Bean; Tom Owen's Barn Dance Trio; Tommy Dandurand and His Gang of WLS; and

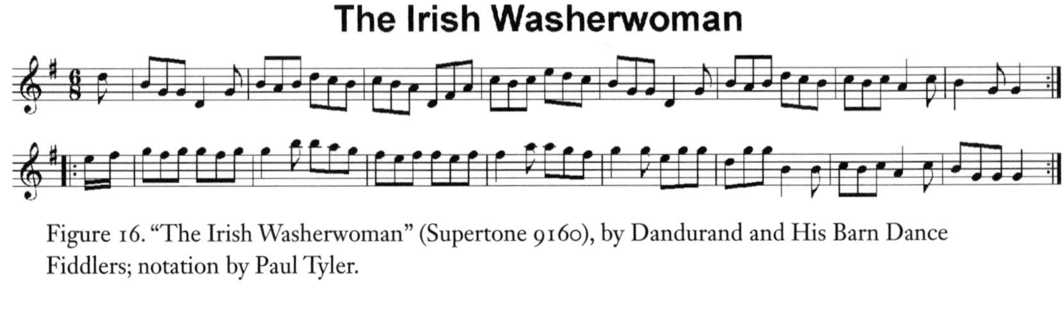

Figure 16. "The Irish Washerwoman" (Supertone 9160), by Dandurand and His Barn Dance Fiddlers; notation by Paul Tyler.

Chubby Parker—had recorded at Gennett's studios in Richmond and Chicago. Sears sold these records through its ubiquitous catalog. Weekly appearances on one of the most popular shows on radio undoubtedly provided the kind of publicity that other rural recording artists envied. Even after Sears sold WLS to the *Prairie Farmer*, Barn Dance artists Bradley Kincaid, the Arkansas Woodchopper, and Pie Plant Pete continued to record at Gennett for labels featured in the Sears catalog.[41]

The commercial alliance between Sears, WLS, and a record company reached a most interesting, and perhaps most profitable, convergence in 1931, when Sears hired Gene Autry to broadcast regularly on *Conqueror Record Time*, a show sponsored by the retailer on WLS. Because of his growing popularity, Autry had just been signed to a contract by the ARC group of record labels, which then included Sears's own Conqueror label. For its part, Sears loaded its catalog with Gene Autry merchandise, including a signature-model guitar (see figure 44), songbooks (see figure 43), and a section of Autry records on Conqueror. Topping it off was the fact that Autry became a regular guest on the National Barn Dance. The irony is that Autry, who became perhaps the most famous and successful performer associated with the Barn Dance, was an employee not of WLS, but of Sears.[42]

Here, at the beginning of the twenty-first century, it is difficult to fathom the earlier rivalry between the phonograph and broadcasting industries. Nevertheless, at some stations—most notably, WLW in Cincinnati—broadcast performers were prohibited from making records. Other professional country musicians who worked in radio never bothered to record, because the financial returns were minimal. Conversely, many of the rural string bands and songsters, who were the first wave of country music on record, never really became professional entertainers. To have a career in country music in the 1930s, it was virtually a necessity to get a good foothold in the broadcast industry, and most radio jobs for country musicians were nonpaying. Regular radio air time allowed a barnstorming act to publicize its public appearances in the station's listening area. It was through admissions and the sales of souvenir photographs and songbooks that a band of young country musicians could make a living.[43]

For several reasons, the National Barn Dance proved to be the pinnacle of the country music field before World War II. Perhaps most important, broadcasting on WLS was a paying gig. George Biggar claimed the average WLS staff musician's weekly salary was $60; those who appeared only on the Barn Dance got union scale, or about $20. As Patsy Montana (see figure 42) would disclose, however, WLS was not willing to pay female artists the same scale. Only when she relied on the bargaining power of a recent hit record and threatened to quit did WLS executives agree to a $60 salary, half again the size of the station's original offer.[44] Furthermore, because Chicago was an important center of recording for major labels (Columbia and Victor), the independents (Paramount, Gennett, and ARC), and the new budget labels (Bluebird and Decca), NBD artists had enhanced opportunities to make records.

And record they did. Through a concerted effort over the last few years, I have been able to listen to nearly 700 sides—out of the 2,333 referred to earlier—recorded by Old Hayloft artists.[45] I have heard at least one recording by nearly two-thirds of the fifty-five NBD country artists who also made records between 1924 and 1942. The musical examples assembled comprise one to three CDs worth of material (from twenty to seventy pieces) for each of the following major NBD artists: Arkansas Woodchopper, Gene Autry, Girls of the Golden West, Hoosier Hot Shots, Karl and Harty and the Cumberland Ridge Runners, Bradley Kincaid, Lulu Belle and Scotty, Mac and Bob, Louise Massey and the Westerners (see figure 47), Clayton McMichen and the Georgia Wildcats, Patsy Montana, Chubby Parker, and the Prairie Ramblers. At the other end of the scale, I have sampled only a few songs by artists like the Happy Valley Family, Lonnie Glosson, Jo and Alma (the Kentucky Girls), Fred Kirby, Pie Plant Pete, Blaine and Cal Smith (the Boys from Virginia), and the Smoky Mountain Sacred Singers (a quartet that included Mac and Bob). Some NBD artists who made records are still aural mysteries to me: Dixie Mason, the Flannery Sisters, the Dean Brothers, Sally Foster, the Hill Toppers, the Maple City Four, Tom and Don, and Romaine Lowdermilk.

Two discographical reference works have been published recently that provide complementary tools for assessing the repertories of early country music artists, including these performers from the Old Hayloft. Russell's *Country Music Records*, already introduced, provides chronological lists of each artist's recorded masters, grouped by session. Guthrie Meade's posthumously published *Country Music Sources: A Biblio-Discography of Commercially Recorded Traditional Music*, contrarily, is organized by song, which Meade painstakingly sorted into a taxonomy of song families and types. Meade's magnum opus does not include every country song recorded before 1942—as does, at least in theory, Russell's—only those that he deemed traditional according to the following criteria: "those recorded songs that have appeared in published folk song collections, as well as those songs copyrighted or appearing in print prior to 1920." Meade estimated that the entirety of recorded country music was twenty thousand masters. Further, he claimed that his definition of a traditional song covered "around 90% of the recorded repertoires of the early country entertainers, but less that 50% of later performers." The majority of the Barn Dance artists listed in the previous paragraph belong to the latter category.[46]

In what follows, I will briefly summarize the biographies and recorded repertories of the early Barn Dance's most important rural musicians and will further attempt to draw stylistic connections to other members of the Hayloft Gang by grouping the artists in rough chronological order in these categories: fiddlers, folksong artists, modern folksong artists, western song artists, and novelty musicians. These categories are for convenience and are by no means to be regarded as mutually exclusive. The repertories of many NBD performers contained material that belongs in more than one category. Nevertheless, my hope is that this scheme will help reveal both the breadth and depth of rural rhythm heard in the Old Hayloft.

Fiddlers

In 1935, both George Biggar and John Lair published nostalgic remembrances of the beginning of the National Barn Dance, and both identified Tommy Dandurand as the show's first old-time fiddler, or as leader of the first fiddle band. However, there is no evidence to verify this claim. The second week the Barn Dance was on the air, one Chicago newspaper listed the scheduled performers as follows: "Evening barn dance; special music by old-time fiddlers; features by Timothy Cornrow, violinist; Kentucky Wonder Bean, harp; Cowbell Pete, bells." It is possible that Dandurand may have been the leader of that anonymous band of fiddlers, or the real person behind the pseudonym Timothy Cornrow (another paper reported that Cornrow was "from Ioway"). Yet, through the first half year of the NBD, twenty other fiddlers' names are listed in the Chicago papers as making an appearance. The name "Fiddling Tommy Danduran" [*sic*] does not appear until January 3, 1925. Ironically, that was an evening when Dandurand was back home in Kankakee competing in a fiddle contest.[47]

Throughout that first summer, in 1924, the National Barn Dance was devoted to an on-air fiddle contest. Contestants were nominated by their local communities and were named each week in the *Chicago Evening Post and Literary Review:* for example, C. A. Pemwright of Mt. Ayr, Indiana; N. G. Aldrett of Morrison, Illinois; Chester Crandill of Hebron, Wisconsin; W. Goatschel of Oak Park, Illinois; Thomas Frill of Mason, Illinois; and unnamed fiddlers from the Iowa Farmers Union. The contest was for teams that were to include a lead fiddler, a second fiddler, and a "caller who knows what real calling means." Not all entrants met these criteria, and even the winning team included only George Adamson on fiddle and George Murdick on piano.[48]

In February 1926, the NBD's resident square dance caller, Tom Owen, a Missouri native, recorded eight fiddle tunes with calls at the Gennett studios in Richmond, Indiana. In the absence of any concrete data, most historians have attributed the fiddling on those discs, once again, to Tommy Dandurand. But a comparison of a transcription of the "Irish Washerwoman" recorded at that session (figure 17) with Dandurand's recording of a year later (figure 16) suggests that these are performances by two different fiddlers. (Further comparisons of other

Figure 17. "The Irish Washerwoman" (Silvertone 3106), by Tom Owen's Barn Dance Trio; notation by Paul Tyler.

tunes common to both sessions provide additional support for this conclusion.) The identity of the fiddler in Owen's Barn Dance Trio will probably never be known. A small likelihood exists that it is one of two fiddlers in a photograph printed several times in early promotions of the Barn Dance: Illinois fiddlers Frank Hart of Aurora and William McCormack of Marseilles are pictured along with guitarist James B. Priest (figure 18).[49]

Tommy Dandurand—born in 1865 in Kankakee County, Illinois, third generation of a pioneer French family that settled in "Le Petit Canada" in Bourbonnais Township—did appear regularly on the Barn Dance from fall 1924 through at least 1930.[50] In 1927, he made two trips to the Gennett studios in Chicago and recorded fourteen sides, thirteen of which had square dance calls. The remaining side was a medley of waltzes. These performances by Tommy Dandurand and his Barn Dance Gang were in accord with the stated rules of the 1924 fiddle contest on WLS: Dandurand and Rube Tronson, a native of Wisconsin, fiddled in a rarely recorded, archaic, regional style in which the lead fiddler plays the melody along with chordal accompaniment from a second fiddler. The caller on these sides was Ed Goodreau, also from Kankakee. On a few pieces in 6/8, or jig, time, a banjo can be faintly heard.

Since Guthrie Meade included all of the tunes recorded by the Owen and Dandurand bands in his *Country Music Sources*, they are traditional according to his definition. The same can be said for eleven of the twelve fiddle tunes, with calls, recorded in 1933 in Chicago for Bluebird by the National Barn Dance Orchestra. None of the musicians—two fiddles, two guitars, and a mandola—have been identified, and in truth, only the band name connects these recordings to the WLS show. The mandola was not all that common an instrument, however, and a mandola player, Chick Hurt of the Prairie Ramblers, had just joined the Barn Dance that year. A picture of Rube Tronson's Texas Cowboys printed in the 1933 *WLS Family Album* provides another tantalizing hint. It shows two fiddlers, both natives of Wisconsin: Tronson, the orchestra leader, and Leizime Brusoe, from Rhinelander.[51] Another puzzling fiddle band, with possible ties to WLS, recorded in Chicago in 1934, when the Rustic Revelers cut eight sides for Decca (five of which were classified as traditional by Meade). The only possible connection, the name of the band, is in this case quite a bit more tenuous. Still, the Hoosier Hot Shots, an immensely popular novelty band that joined WLS in 1933, were the direct offspring of a barnstorming comic group known as Ezra Buzzington's Rustic Revelers. Fiddler Buddy McDowell, a native of Van Wert, Ohio, who later joined the NBD in a reconfigured lineup

Thousands dance to the
unes of W-L-S Old-Time
iddlers each Saturday

Figure 18. James B. Priest, Frank Hart, and William McCormack. Courtesy of Chicago History Museum.

of the Cumberland Ridge Runners, was another Buzzington alumnus. Was McDowell the fiddler in the Rustic Revelers 1934 session? Could Tronson and Brusoe have led an actual National Barn Dance Orchestra through its paces in that 1933 Bluebird session? I doubt we will ever know for sure.

From the mysterious Timothy Cornrow to the unnamed fiddlers of the National Barn Dance Orchestra, most of the Old Hayloft's fiddlers toiled in anonymity. Though they were the sparks that originally ignited the National Barn Dance, they were clearly never the stars. There were a few exceptions, such as Lily May Ledford, a nineteen-year-old fiddler, banjo-picker, and traditional folksong artist from Lombard, Kentucky, who appeared on the Barn Dance in 1936 before heading off to Cincinnati with John Lair the next year to form the celebrated Coon Creek Girls. Homer "Slim" Miller was a baggy pants comedian and versatile fiddler for the Cumberland Ridge Runners. Upon hearing preserved transcriptions of the Pinex Merrymakers, it is evident that Miller was equally adept with old-time square dance tunes and more modern styles of fiddling, influenced by jazz and swing. Slim recorded only two fiddle tunes on commercial discs: "Roundin' Up the Yearlings," which Meade classified as traditional, and his signature piece, "Goofus," which was too recent a composition for inclusion in Meade.

Another fiddler in the same mode came to the Barn Dance in 1933. Clayton McMichen had recently quit one of the most commercially successful rural string bands in the United States, Gid Tanner and the Skillet Lickers, who recorded over a hundred sides for Columbia between 1926 and 31. McMichen, however, had grown weary of straight-ahead, old-time fiddling and was "determined to forge a new string band music that borrowed heavily from Big-Band Swing." Over the next few years, he would make strides toward that goal with his new band, the Georgia Wildcats, which featured a young, jazz-adept guitarist and fellow Georgian, Slim Bryant.[52] But based on the thirty-four pieces the Wildcats recorded in the two years before they came to Chicago, they were still firmly grounded in traditional old-time music. The path McMichen would follow toward the hot sounds of jazz and swing are prefigured in a couple of these recordings, for example, "Wild Cat Rag"; "Yum Yum Blues" (a Slim Bryant composition); and a western song composed by two Chicagoans, "When the Bloom Is on the Sage." McMichen's progressive vision was partly shared by several other National Barn Dance fiddlers: Tex Atchison and Alan Crockett, early and later fiddlers with the Prairie Ramblers, and Curt Massey of the Westerners. (All three will be introduced more fully in the treatments of their bands in following sections.) The blending of old-time fiddling with the hot licks of jazz and swing was achieved earliest, perhaps, by the Prairie Ramblers, with Atchison leading the way. Nevertheless, Massey, Atchison, and Crockett could fiddle an old-time breakdown with the best. Massey's 1934 "Brown Skin Gal Down the Road" and Atchison's 1937 "Raise the Roof in Georgia" and "Kansas City Rag"—with dance calls—would be driving enough for any floor filled with square dance sets.

In 1941, as a nationwide square dance revival was gathering steam, Alan Crockett went into the studio with the Arkansas Woodchopper's Square Dance Band to record tunes and calls for seven square figures and an old-time "circle two-step." Crockett played "Walking Up Town" for the latter, a variant of a widespread tune commonly known as "Twinkle Little Star" (not the same as the children's song). Meade identified all eight of the tunes fiddled by Crockett as traditional.

Folksong Artists

Chubby Parker (figure 19)—his given name was Frederick—was perhaps the National Barn Dance's first true folksinger. Nearly a decade after he left the program, John Lair described him as "the first to bring to radio the home songs of America."[53] His name first appeared in program listings for the Barn Dance on July 18, 1925, but disappeared sometime in 1927. Between 1927 and 1930, he recorded thirty-six sides for Gennett (and Sears), and he recorded nineteen more for Sears's Conqueror label in 1931. Parker also recorded two sides for Columbia in New York in 1928. One of these, "King Kong Kitchie Kitchie Ki-Me-O," a version of a satirical English ballad commonly known as "Froggie Went a-Courting," was included in the influential *Anthology of American Folksong*, issued in 1952, and was the first introduction of an early National Barn Dance artist to most postwar folk music revivalists.

Beyond these basic facts, little more is known for certain about Chubby Parker, though conjecture is plentiful. Clayton Jackson, a Gennett Records sales manager in Chicago, claimed to have tracked Parker down in a speakeasy to sign him to a Gennett contract after the company had signed its deal with Sears. Charles Wolfe asserted that Parker was a native of Kentucky, that he left WLS out of jealousy over Bradley Kincaid's success, and that in the 1930s he was still living in Chicago but no longer in the music business.[54] There is also some confusion about Parker's banjo playing, as it bears no sonic resemblance to more common traditional styles, clawhammer (down-picking) and two- or three-finger up-picking. My ears hear a plectrum, rather than fingers on the strings, and a picking style similar to early-country guitar playing. Russell and Meade must have heard something similar, for they both list Parker as playing a tenor (or four-string) banjo. But a picture in a Gennett catalog showed him holding a five-string banjo.

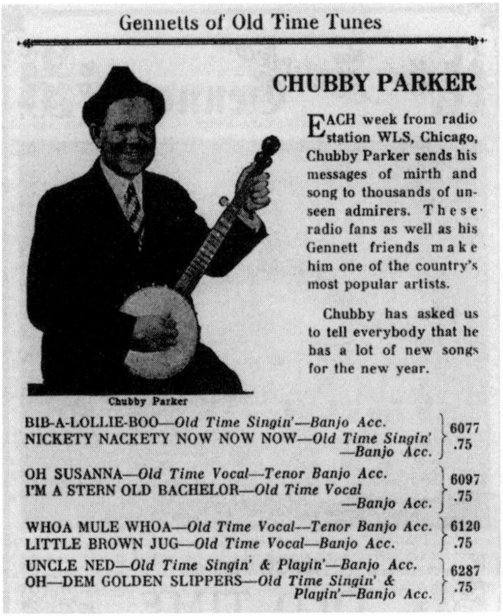
Gennetts of Old Time Tunes

CHUBBY PARKER

EACH week from radio station WLS, Chicago, Chubby Parker sends his messages of mirth and song to thousands of unseen admirers. These radio fans as well as his Gennett friends make him one of the country's most popular artists.

Chubby has asked us to tell everybody that he has a lot of new songs for the new year.

Chubby Parker

BIB-A-LOLLIE-BOO—*Old Time Singin'—Banjo Acc.* 6077
NICKETY NACKETY NOW NOW NOW—*Old Time Singin'—Banjo Acc.* .75

OH SUSANNA—*Old Time Vocal—Tenor Banjo Acc.* 6097
I'M A STERN OLD BACHELOR—*Old Time Vocal—Banjo Acc.* .75

WHOA MULE WHOA—*Old Time Vocal—Tenor Banjo Acc.* 6120
LITTLE BROWN JUG—*Old Time Vocal—Banjo Acc.* .75

UNCLE NED—*Old Time Singin' & Playin'—Banjo Acc.* 6287
OH—DEM GOLDEN SLIPPERS—*Old Time Singin' & Playin'—Banjo Acc.* .75

Figure 19. Chubby Parker and his five-string banjo. Courtesy of Archie Green.

Harry Steele, writing in 1936, claimed that when Parker was pressed into service as a folk singer—he was already singing on WLS—it was a role for which he was ill-suited. Contarily, a more recent critic averred that Parker played the stereotypical role of "backward hillbilly."[55] An aural examination of Parker's recorded repertoire offers a balanced appraisal. The singer was comfortable with a variety of old-time songs, including songs from blackface minstrelsy, abolitionist songs, sentimental songs, and comic songs. On all his recordings, his singing was accompanied by his banjo. On some he added harmonica or whistling. His most famous song, "Little Old Sod Shanty on the Claim," was a remake of Will Hays's well-known "Little Old Cabin in the Lane," first published in 1871. One of the newer compositions Parker recorded, "See the Black Clouds a'Breakin' over Yonder," was evidently written for Huey Long's populist campaign for the governorship of Louisiana. The fifty-six masters recorded by Parker comprised only twenty-nine different songs. He recorded many songs at three or more of his nine recording sessions. Of these twenty-nine songs, only four were not classified by Meade as traditional.

Bradley Kincaid's musical career, on the other hand, has been well chronicled (figure 20). Born in 1895 in Garrard County in the bluegrass region of eastern Kentucky, he was raised in the foothills of the Cumberland Mountains. His family and neighborhood both were full of singers. His father swapped a foxhound for the guitar on which Bradley learned to play. The first phase of his musical education was thus rooted deeply in the folk music traditions of his home and community. The next phase was as well. At age nineteen, he entered the Foundation School at Berea College in neighboring Madison County, where, after serving in the army during World War I, he finished his high school degree at the age of twenty-seven. Berea College is well known for its institutional interest in traditional culture, and Bradley's experiences there certainly solidified his respect for the folksongs he learned at home. Yet when he arrived in Chicago in 1924 to attend the YMCA College (later renamed George Williams College), he busied himself directing glee clubs and church choirs and became a member of the YMCA College Quartet.[56]

The YMCA quartet opened the door for Kincaid to become part of the Barn Dance in 1926. When the quartet performed on a weekday show at WLS, the group's manager told Don Malin, the station's music director, about Kincaid's folksong repertoire. Malin invited him to come back on Saturday and sing a few "old-timers" on the Barn Dance. He did and soon became one of the first big radio stars in the United States. However, Kincaid had in fact aimed his career down a different path, toward formal music education. He even had to borrow a guitar for his Barn Dance debut. But the fifteen-dollar weekly paycheck that came with being on the NBD was too much for a 1920s college student to refuse, and the hundreds of appreciative letters from listeners, which began arriving immediately, convinced him to give radio a try.[57]

Bradley Kincaid, "the Kentucky Mountain Boy" with his "houn' dog guitar," a replica of which was soon offered for sale in the Sears catalog (figure 21), was a big favorite on

Figure 20. Bradley Kincaid. Bradley Kincaid Collection, Southern Appalachian Archives, Berea College.

the Barn Dance for the next four years, until he left for WLW in Cincinnati. During his time at WLS, he discovered—upon urging by station manager Edgar Bill—that a lucrative market existed for his mountain folksongs. In April 1928, he published a songbook, *My Favorite Mountain Ballad and Old Time Songs*, which contained twenty-two songs and proved to be so popular with Barn Dance listeners that it required five additional printings in the next sixteen months. Two additional volumes were printed at WLS, and ten more followed in the next fifteen years, during which Kincaid worked mostly in the Northeast. He also discovered, again to his surprise, that scores of people wanted to hear him in person. He told of arriving in Peoria for his first booking through the WLS Artists Bureau only to see

Figure 21. The 1932 Sears catalog featured a replica of Bradley Kincaid's "Houn' Dog" guitar. From the Sears Archives; used with permission.

people lined up for several blocks outside the theater, having no inkling they were there to see him. He made several hundred dollars that night, and after a few years of radio work, he had achieved a previously unimaginable level of financial comfort.

During his four years on WLS, Bradley Kincaid recorded eighty-five pieces, and another fifty-five before 1942. Like Parker, he recorded many songs at more than one session, often for different labels. In the final count, he recorded ninety-five songs, eighty-five of which are classified as traditional by Meade. His biggest hit was the traditional ballad "Barbara Allen." Several other British ballads were in his repertoire, as well as a broad sample of American ballads, lyric folksongs, frolic songs, sentimental songs, and comic songs. All were recorded with Bradley's spare but solid guitar accompaniment.

Arkansas Woodchopper was the stage name for Luther Ossenbrink, but the Hayloft Gang more often called him "Arkie." Born in 1906 in the town of Knob Noster in central Missouri (not, as often reported, in the Ozarks), Arkie had a thoroughly rural upbringing that introduced him to both the pleasures of country life—hunting, fishing, fiddling, and calling square dances—and the drudgery. "The last real labor I did on the farm was to clear 10 acres of honey locust," he told the *Prairie Farmer*, when he was brand new to the Barn Dance. He started in radio on KMBC, the Sears station in Kansas City, in 1928. He joined the National Barn Dance the next year and stayed through the 1960s. Affable and multi-talented, he was a favorite of both listeners and fellow cast members. A *WLS Family Album* listed his talents as "plunking the guitar to accompany his cowboy or comedy songs; playing 'lead fiddle' in the barn dance orchestra; 'seconding' fiddlers with his banjo or 'calling off' for square dancers."[58] All of Arkie's talents were of a rustic variety. He was pictured playing his fiddle while holding it down against his chest, rather than in a conventional violinist's hold on the shoulder.

Between 1928 and 1931, Arkie, with just his guitar, recorded forty masters, comprising thirty-six songs. Thirty-two of his songs are classified as traditional by Meade, including a smattering of old-time cowboy songs, like "The Cowboy's Dream," and comic songs, for example, "(Who Threw the Overalls in) Mrs. Murphy's Chowder." Most of Arkie's recorded songs were on sentimental themes of home ("Sweet Sunny South"), family ("Write Me a Song of My Father"), and love ("Prisoner at the Bar"). Arkie did not return to the recording studio again for another ten years, when he recorded the eight square dance calls discussed in the previous section.

Mac and Bob were established stars of both radio and phonograph records when they joined the Barn Dance for the first time in 1931. Their initial tenure lasted until 1933, when they moved on to other stations. They returned to WLS in 1939 and stayed until their partnership broke up in 1950. Mac was Lester McFarland, born in 1902 in Kentucky, and Bob was Robert Gardner, born five years earlier in Tennessee. They met in 1915 at the Kentucky School for the Blind in Louisville and embarked upon a full-time career in music in 1922; within three years they were favorites on WNOX in Knoxville, Tennessee. Multi-instrumentalists, their recordings nevertheless featured Mac on mandolin and Bob on guitar. They are often credited as being the first close harmony duet in country music and therefore as pioneering a sound that became prevalent in country music later in the 1930s with the emergence of many popular brother duets, like the Delmore Brothers, the Blue Sky Boys (the Bolick Brothers), the Callahan Brothers, and the Monroe Brothers. (The latter may have performed some vocal duets on the Barn Dance during their time as members of one of the NBD's square dance troupes—a time period that coincided with Mac and Bob's first tenure.) Still, in Charles Wolfe's assessment, "most of their music sounds too restrained and polite to modern ears."[59]

It is true that Mac and Bob's duets clearly lack that intangible vocal affectation that eventually pervaded southern-style country vocals—in recent years it has been dubbed "twang" and is now regarded by many as an essential element of authentic country music. But their stature as broadcast and recording artists before 1942 demands for them a respectful hearing. They recorded 241 separate songs on 282 masters. In addition, McFarland recorded 14 numbers with George Reneau, as the Gentry Brothers, and at least one solo. Mac and Bob were also half of the vocal quartet known as the Old Southern Sacred Singers (for which they also provided instrumental accompaniment), which recorded 30 sides between 1926 and 1929.[60] Meade classified at least 150 of the songs recorded by Mac and Bob, and all but three of those waxed by the Old Southern Sacred Singers, as traditional.

A further analysis of Mac and Bob's repertoire is long overdue but is beyond the scope of the present essay. Still, I would add one observation: there is a noticeable overlap between their recorded body of work and that of the original Carter Family of Maces Springs, Virginia, one of country music's preeminent vocal ensembles. At least thirteen songs made famous by the Carter Family were first recorded by Mac and Bob, including "Are You Tired of Me Darling," "(Bury Me Beneath) The Willow Tree," and "When the Roses Bloom Again." Conversely, only one song the two groups had in common was recorded first by the Carter Family.

Modern Folksong Artists

In 1930, John Lair brought the first southern string band to the National Barn Dance, the Cumberland Ridge Runners. The first lineup—Kentuckians all—included Lair, the group's manager, on jug; Gene Ruppe on fiddle (and perhaps banjo); Doc Hopkins on banjo (and perhaps guitar); Karl Davis on mandolin; and Hartford Taylor on guitar. A year later, Slim Miller, a native of Lizton, Indiana, had replaced Ruppe on fiddle, and Hugh Cross, an established recording artist from Atlanta, took over on banjo for Doc Hopkins. By the time another year had passed, Clyde Julian "Red" Foley had joined the Ridge Runners on bass, and within the next year, Hugh Cross departed, leaving banjo-less this manifestation of the Ridge Runners.[61]

In fact, the Ridge Runners were an umbrella group for a variety of smaller performing units. The most important of these was Karl and Harty—Karl Davis and Hartford Connecticut Taylor, both born in 1905 in Mount Vernon, near the Eastern Kentucky Coal Field—who initially broadcast on WLS and made records as the Renfro Valley Boys. Their close vocal harmony with guitar and mandolin accompaniment followed the same arc that began with Mac and Bob and led to the Monroe Brothers. Red Foley, from Madison County in the Eastern Knobs region of Kentucky, joined the band in Chicago in 1932, when he was only twenty-two years old. Lair quickly paired him with another rookie, nineteen-year-old Myrtle Cooper, to form the comic singing duo of Lulu Belle and Burrhead. Then, perhaps to balance Lulu Belle's gum-smacking, boy-chasing, manic, and sassy persona, Lair added a sweet-voiced, contentedly domestic, and purely virtuous "Sunbonnet Girl," whom he named Linda Parker. Parker's real name was Jeanne Muenich; and though Parker's signature song on the Barn Dance was a gem of Victorian sentimentality, "Bury Me beneath the Willow," Muenich had gotten her start in music as a nightclub singer.[62]

When Linda Parker died tragically from an infection contracted while on a WLS road tour in 1935, the whole Barn Dance family mourned in a sustained public display. Karl and Harty recorded a tribute piece, "We Buried Her beneath the Willow (Ridge Runners' Tribute to Linda Parker)," which was quickly covered by another WLS artist, Sally Foster [Louise Rautenberg], accompanied by the Travelers. Within a short time, the Cumberland Ridge Runners went their separate ways, and even Karl and Harty left WLS for local rival WJJD's Suppertime Frolic. Red Foley became a featured artist, along with Slim Miller and the Girls of the Golden West, on the *Pinex Merrymakers*, a series of transcribed programs perhaps managed by John Lair. By 1937, Lair, Foley, and Miller had relocated to WLW in Cincinnati, where Lair began to develop his own empire, the Renfro Valley Barn Dance. Miller would stick with Lair for the rest of his career. Karl and Harty, on the other hand, returned to WLS and the National Barn Dance in 1941, where they again used the name the Cumberland Ridge Runners for a quartet that included once again Doc Hopkins and added fiddler Buddy McDowell.

Between 1931 and 1942, Karl and Harty recorded a total of seventy masters comprising sixty-six songs. The fourteen recordings made in 1935 and 1936 were issued as by Karl and Harty "Of the . . ." or "Acc. by the Cumberland Ridge Runners." Six additional numbers were issued under the band's name, and four others by the band featured Linda Parker. Of this array, Meade classified as traditional seventeen numbers by Karl and Harty, four by the Ridge Runners (counting Meade's obvious oversight of "Nobody's Darling on Earth"), and only one of Linda Parker's songs. According to Charles Wolfe, the daily grind of radio forced Karl and Harty to hunt up more songs, learning many new pieces from Carter Family records and old hymnals. They also turned to writing their own songs, at which they both proved adept. Karl Davis penned their first big hit, "I'm Just Here to Get My Baby out of Jail," and the later, often-covered "Kentucky." They also had a silent partner in Frank Johnson, who signed his songs with the name "Pat McAdory." He collaborated with the duo on their second hit, "The Prisoner's Dream."[63]

As for Karl and Harty's associates in the Ridge Runners, Doc Hopkins recorded a total of thirty-five songs, in 1931–32, 1936, and 1941. Since Hopkins was later known as "America's Favorite Folk Singer" on his own radio show on WJJD, it is somewhat surprising that Meade classified only a dozen of his recorded songs as traditional. Red Foley recorded five traditional songs, out of the twenty he waxed in the mid-thirties. Hugh Cross made no records while a member of the Ridge Runners.

Lulu Belle and Scotty—Myrtle Cooper and Scott Wiseman—were both born in North Carolina, she in 1913, and he in 1909. But they met in Chicago as fellow cast members of the National Barn Dance, and it was in the Old Hayloft that they became musical partners and, later, husband and wife. Young Myrtle Cooper's family was constantly on the move but settled in Evanston, Illinois, when she was sixteen. Just three years later, Cooper's father brought his big-voiced daughter down to WLS and pestered the station's executives until they auditioned and hired her. She was immediately given the stage name of Lulu Belle—which Myrtle Cooper Wiseman carefully spelled as "Lul*a* Belle" for the rest of her days. Her mother helped design her first costume, which also proved to be long-lasting: a gingham dress with pantaloons and high-topped shoes. John Lair completed the construction of her stage persona by sending her off to a theater to observe the rube starlet in the Weaver Brothers and Elviry, a popular vaudeville act. Following Elviry's lead, Lulu Belle became feisty, smart-alecky, mischievous, and boy crazy. The Barn Dance audiences loved it. In 1936, Lulu Belle was voted "Radio Queen," in a popularity poll run by *Radio Guide* magazine.[64]

Scott Wiseman, on the other hand, was shy, soft-spoken, and serious. He learned to play guitar, banjo, and harmonica, and fell under the influence of Bradley Kincaid. Like Kincaid, Wiseman began to collect traditional songs from mountain singers near his home in Boone, North Carolina. He even met Kincaid on one of the latter's song-collecting trips, and the radio star told him he had a future in radio. But Wiseman wanted to finish his college education first, which he did at Fairmont State College in West Virginia. While a student, he got his first radio job announcing at WMMN in Fairmont and adopted the nickname Skyland Scotty. In 1933, he successfully auditioned for the Barn Dance and joined a long line of traditional folk singers on the show that stretched back through Arkie and Bradley Kincaid to Chubby Parker.[65]

Shortly after Wiseman arrived in the Old Hayloft, Lulu Belle's comic partner, Red Foley, married Eva Overstake of the Three Little Maids. The new wife's jealousy broke up the Lulu Belle and Burrhead team. John Lair instructed Lulu Belle to work up some routines with Skyland Scotty. They clicked with each other and with their audiences, and a decades-long radio partnership was on its way. When they married in 1934, Lulu Belle no longer had to try to catch a man, so the theme of her feistiness shifted to the comic "battle of the sexes," and audiences loved it even more.[66]

In 1933 and 34, Scott Wiseman recorded fourteen sides in Chicago for the Conqueror and Bluebird labels. Meade classified ten of these pieces as traditional. Then from 1935 to 1940, Lulu Belle and Scotty recorded thirty-one more pieces for various labels in the ARC family. Of these thirty-one, Meade classified nineteen as traditional. Many of the newer pieces—that is, modern folksongs, to use George Biggar's label—that worked so well in their act were novelty numbers, such as "When I Yoo-Hoo in the Valley" and "Daffy over Taffy" (which Lulu Belle had originally recorded with Red Foley). Scott Wiseman also proved to be a very capable songwriter. Besides having a hand in composing—along with Bascom Lamar Lunsford of the Asheville area in North Carolina—the classic "Mountain Dew," Scotty's most popular hit from this era is the bittersweet love song "Remember Me," which the duo recorded in 1940.

If ever a group in country music history deserved the serious attention of journalists, scholars, and reissue producers—but was instead almost completely overlooked—it was the

Prairie Ramblers. Formed originally as the Kentucky Ramblers around the talents of boyhood friends Charles "Chick" Hurt and Jack Taylor—both born in 1901—they combined, respectively, mandola and tenor banjo, and guitar and bass. They soon added another musician from their home region of the Pennyrile in south-central Kentucky: Floyd "Salty" Holmes (born in 1909), on jug and harmonica. Perhaps the key addition to the group was the versatile young left-handed fiddler David Shelby "Tex" Atchison, born in 1912 on a farm near Rosine (Bill Monroe's home area) in Kentucky's western coal field. Atchison was an impatient teenager who, because of a broken wrist, learned to play left-handed on a right-handed fiddle. Before his twentieth birthday, Atchison was performing live on radio in Evansville, Indiana. Besides fiddle, he also played clarinet and sax in a band that did both old-time country- and jazz-influenced pop music. He joined the Ramblers in time for that band's radio debut in 1932 on WOC in Davenport, Iowa.[67]

The next year, the Ramblers moved to Chicago, joined the cast of the Barn Dance, and changed their name to the Prairie Ramblers (perhaps in deference to the *Prairie Farmer* company that issued their paychecks). They were initially teamed with a female vocalist, Dixie Mason. Although she recorded two sides in 1933 with just guitar accompaniment, she never recorded with the Ramblers. But by the end of the year, when the band headed to the Victor studios in Chicago for their first recording session, they were joined by Patsy Montana, who would work with them steadily for the next seven years—on the air, on records, and on personal appearances. In 1934, Patsy and the Ramblers headed for New York to make records for Vocalion and the ARC labels.

Looking back, Atchison claimed that their yearlong New York hiatus was quite beneficial to the band: "We left Chicago as an Old-Time string band and we came back from New York as a cowboy band."[68] Perhaps the greatest benefit was that the Ramblers became more professional and were better able to market themselves using their new cowboy image. Did they remake themselves into a western swing band, as some historians have suggested? The western swing sound was emerging in Fort Worth and Tulsa, just as the Ramblers headed off for New York; and the group clearly became one of the first bands east of the Mississippi River to promote a similar merger of swing music and rural sensibilities. However, the swing tendencies had always been present to some extent in the playing of Tex Atchison. Swing was simply an addition to the Ramblers' bag of tricks, for when they returned to Chicago, they picked right up again with the old-time frolic songs, fiddle breakdowns, and gospel numbers they had always played. The biggest change to the sound of the Prairie Ramblers came when Tex Atchison left WLS in 1937—he did his last recording sessions with the Ramblers in 1938—to find work in the music and film industries of California. Atchison was soon replaced by Alan Crockett, a young fiddler who had grown up in the California country music scene as part of the Crockett Family Mountaineers.[69]

The Prairie Ramblers recorded 257 masters that yielded 228 different songs. Meade classified less than half of them as traditional. It is worth noting that a lot of the old-time frolic and gospel songs that they recorded were later covered by the Monroe Brothers, such as "Gonna Have a Feast Here Tonight" and "What Would You Give in Exchange for Your Soul." The Prairie Ramblers also had an alter ego, the Sweet Violet Boys, under which name they cut some rather risqué material that probably was never performed in the Old Hayloft.

The Massey family, known as the Westerners on radio and most often as Louise Massey and the Westerners on phonograph records, arrived at the Barn Dance in 1933 as seasoned veterans. They started out as a family band, led by Henry "Dad" Massey, a fiddler, who soon retired to his ranch in Roswell, New Mexico. The Massey children who carried on included Louise (born 1902), the lead singer and sometimes pianist; Allen (born 1907), on guitar; Curt, also known as Dott (born 1910), on fiddle and trumpet; and Louise's husband, Milt Mabie (born 1900), on bass. After a few years of touring for the Redpath Lyceum Bureau, they landed a radio job in Topeka, and then at KMBC in Kansas City. They stayed at KMBC for five years, added accordionist Larry Wellington to the band, and were heard by George Biggar, who brought them to WLS in 1933. After two years of weekday programs and the Saturday night Barn Dance, the Westerners moved on to New York City, where they joined the cast of NBC's popular variety program *Show Boat.* By 1940, they had come back to Chicago for a second and longer stay in the Old Hayloft.[70]

Between 1933 and 1942, Louise Massey and the Westerners recorded 138 masters of increasingly sophisticated and pop-influenced modern folksongs. Meade classified only twenty-seven of their recordings as traditional, and a large share of these were instrumental dance tunes.

While in New York, they brought Dad Massey into the ARC studios to record seven traditional fiddle tunes (one disc was a medley of two hornpipes). In 1939, they did the same in Chicago, and the senior Massey recorded four more hoedowns, which, sadly, were never issued. The Masseys are best known for their modern folksongs, like "Huckleberry Picnic," "The Honey Song," and, most famous of all, "My Adobe Hacienda," written by Louise.

One of the most distinctive musical acts to join the National Barn Dance was a pair of sisters raised on a farm near Royalton, in the center of the state of Minnesota. Carolyn (born 1919) and Mary Jane DeZurik (born 1917) were part of a musical family of Dutch heritage that included a fiddling father, an accordion-playing brother, and five sisters (out of six) who could sing and play the guitar. While doing chores, the sisters' ears were open to the natural music made by animals around them. They incorporated imitations of these sounds into elaborate trick yodels and novel harmonies that won them many amateur talent contests in central Minnesota. A representative from the WLS Artists Bureau caught their act and invited them to Chicago, where they were hired for the Barn Dance in November 1936. Their stay was lengthened when Carolyn wed Rusty Gill, a staff guitarist and member of the Hoosier Sod Busters, in 1940. Less than a month later, Mary Jane married Augie Klein, a WLS staff accordionist who appeared on the NBD with the Hill Toppers.[71]

But the DeZurik Sisters' stay in Chicago became more complicated when they were engaged by Purina Mills in 1937 for a series of transcribed programs called *Checkerboard Time*, to be broadcast in all forty-eight states. Because of contractual agreements, the DeZuriks appeared on the transcriptions as the Cackle Sisters. Several other NBD artists—the Maple City Four and Otto and the Novelodeons—joined the *Checkerboard* cast as well. In 1938, the DeZurick Sisters recorded six songs for Vocalion, the only commercial records they made before 1942.[72] Meade deemed only one of these songs traditional.

A couple of lesser-known modern folksong artists who were part of the Barn Dance in the mid- to late 1930s should also be mentioned. Eddie and Jimmie Glosup were two brothers from Posey, Texas, who used the stage surname Dean. Eddie came to Chicago in 1926, seeking a career in music. After a sojourn in Shenandoah, Iowa, and radio work in Yankton, South Dakota, and Topeka, Eddie reunited with his brother and returned to Chicago in 1934 to join the National Barn Dance. They stayed in Chicago until 1937, when Eddie left for Hollywood and a new career as a singing cowboy in the movies.[73] In 1934 and 35, the Dean Brothers recorded twenty-nine sides in the Windy City. Only a few of them were western songs. Meade classified even fewer as traditional songs, four (five, if we add in Meade's omission of "Get Along Little Dogies") in all. Fred Kirby, another singer of new country songs, came to the Barn Dance in 1940 from North Carolina, where he had recorded as Fred Kirby and His Carolina Boys. Earlier in the 1930s, he had worked with Cliff Carlisle. Between 1932 and 1938, Kirby recorded forty-eight songs, only five of which were deemed traditional according to Meade's criteria.[74]

Western Song Artists

As should be expected, Gene Autry's name has been mentioned frequently in this essay. He was one of the dominant figures in the field of country music before World War II, and even after the war. Accordingly, he is the most famous performer who was ever a part of the Hayloft Gang. It seems strange, then, that there is so little institutional memory of Autry on the part of WLS and the *Prairie Farmer*. Two pictures of Autry are all that appeared in the *WLS Family Album*. The amnesia was mutual, for in his autobiography, Autry gave only a cursory mention to the show and the station that helped launch him to fame.[75]

Born in Tioga Springs, Texas, in 1907, Orvon Gene Autry was raised in Oklahoma in that state's second decade of statehood. His mother taught him to play guitar, and he learned to sing in the church where his grandfather served as pastor. As a teenager, he traveled with a medicine show; and as a twenty-one-year-old, he undertook a trip to New York City, where his first attempts to record were unsuccessful. Back in Oklahoma, he returned to his job as a railroad telegrapher but also got a radio gig on KVOO in Tulsa. He billed himself as the Oklahoma Yodeling Cowboy, and by 1929 began his very prolific career as a recording artist.[76]

Many of Autry's first records were vocal duets with Jimmy Long, a fellow railroad employee. But what really established his early career was that he could successfully imitate the blue yodel of the early country music giant Jimmie Rodgers. Not only did Autry cover a number of Rodger's pieces, he contributed many blues pieces of his own. Yet, by the time Autry left Chicago to star in Hollywood westerns, he had remade himself into a western singer. Also, during his time in Chicago, because of the incredible success of "That Silver-Haired Daddy of Mine," he was encouraged to focus more on sentimental songs.[77] On many of his sessions during his Chicago days, the Prairie Ramblers accompanied Autry.

Another too-often overlooked gem of the National Barn Dance was a sister act, the Girls of the Golden West (figure 22). The sisters were Mildred and Dorothy Goad, born in 1913

Figure 22. The Girls of the Golden West (Millie and Dolly Goad), shown here with Red Foley, ca. 1939–40, were one of the first major women's acts in popular music. John Lair Collection, Southern Appalachian Archives, Berea College.

and 1915, respectively, on a farm in southern Illinois. By the time Millie was fourteen, the Goad family had moved first to Mount Vernon, in south-central Illinois, and then to East St. Louis. The sisters learned to sing naturally at home, for their mother played guitar and sang and was known to perform in public at church gatherings. Dolly learned guitar from her mother. Harmony also came easily and unstudied, as Millie related in a 1978 interview, explaining that her mother "always had a natural ear for harmony just like I do. . . . When I hear a note, I hear the harmony note to it, so I got that from my mother."[78]

In 1930, after a short time at WIL in St. Louis, the Good Sisters (they changed the spelling) established themselves on the larger KMOX. They started on a morning show and soon joined the Saturday night program called *County Fair*. At some point, they were given the name the Girls of the Golden West and began to focus on traditional cowboy songs and other "western-type songs," even dressing the part with elaborate, homemade western costumes. After a sojourn to Abilene to broadcast programs that, by means of a relay, were aired from XER in Mexico, the sisters were booked by Glenn Snyder to join the Barn Dance in 1933 (though in Millie's memory, it "was about 1931").[79] Whatever the year, at least one of the sisters was still just a teenager. The duo stayed at WLS through 1937, during which time they helped several other young women land roles in the Old Hayloft. As part of the Pinex Merrymakers with Red Foley, they also moved to Cincinnati in 1938 and latched on with the *Boone County Jamboree*, a show started by George Biggar on WLW, "The Nation's Station."

Between 1933 and 1938, the Girls of the Golden West recorded sixty-four harmony duets, always accompanied only by Dolly's guitar. Many of their numbers featured tight harmony yodels. Meade classified seventeen of these songs as traditional, including cowboy ballads such as "Bucking Bronco" and "Lonely Cowgirl." The major part of their recorded repertoire was of newer western songs, like "By the Silvery Rio Grande" and "Take Me Back to My Boots and Saddle." They also waxed some memorable love songs, such as "Roll Along, Prairie Moon" and, perhaps their best known, "There's a Silver Moon on the Golden Gate."

Patsy Montana was a true pioneer. Her self-penned 1935 hit recording "I Want to Be a Cowboy's Sweetheart" was the first disc by a woman in the country music field to sell a million copies. Of greater importance is that her work and success created space for women in a business that, like so many others, had been dominated by men. Robert Oermann and Mary Bufwack capture the essence of her contribution: "In her songs and stage presence she rewrote the myth of the American cowboy to include women, providing a new role option for women country singers, and popularizing an innovative independent female image."[80]

Patsy Montana was born Ruby Blevins in 1912 in Hope, Arkansas, the sole daughter in a family of eleven children. By the time she was a teenager, she had learned to play guitar, studied violin in high school, learned songs from Jimmie Rodgers records, and, most important, figured out on her own how to yodel by singing along with Caruso records left behind by the previous tenant in the family's rented house. In 1929, after graduating from high school, Ruby headed for California, where she planned to live with her brother, enroll at the University of the West (now UCLA), and study violin. These plans were diverted, in part, when she entered and won a talent contest—by singing two Jimmie Rodgers songs—earning the right to appear on the *Breakfast Club* on station KMTR.[81]

In 1933, she came back home with her new stage name and learned that her mother had cooked up quite a plan. Mrs. Blevins had been corresponding with the Girls of the Golden West, stars on her favorite radio show, and told them all about Patsy Montana. Seizing the good fortune of a gigantic, hundred-pound watermelon produced by the family garden, Mrs. Blevins urged two of her sons to take Patsy along and show it off in Chicago at the World's Fair. The three siblings headed north, and while her two brothers took the watermelon into the fair, Patsy went downtown to the Eighth Street Theatre, where she found the Good sisters backstage. Dolly told her, "Honey . . . The Prairie Ramblers are looking for a girl singer. If you're interested, go sign up." She got the job and began the hectic life of a full-time country artist (though she always described herself as a "western" singer and always sewed her own western costumes). Her daily schedule with the Ramblers included broadcasts on *Wake Up and Smile* each morning at 5:30 and 7:30, followed by a road trip to a personal appearance in the station's listening area, followed by yet another drive back home, with hopes for a few hours of sleep before the alarm rang to start it all again. And, of course, there was the Barn Dance on Saturday nights. Even her 1934 marriage to Paul Rose—business manager for Mac and Bob—and the arrival of baby Beverly the following year did not slow Patsy's career. She remembers that in 1936, when she and the Ramblers were first scheduled for the coveted NBC network segment of the Barn Dance, they really had made it, for then they would be heard "coast-to-coast."[82] As noted earlier, the Prairie Ramblers with Patsy Montana were voted one of the three most popular acts on WLS in 1937.

Patsy Montana recorded 87 masters with the Prairie Ramblers between 1933 and 1940. Add in the four pieces recorded in 1932, before she landed her spot on the Barn Dance, and the 13 recorded in Dallas in 1941, after she left Chicago, and her total output on pre-1942 discs is 104 masters, yielding 82 separate songs. Meade classified only three of these as traditional. A large portion of her repertoire was songs she had written. Her earliest signature piece was "Back on Montana Plains," an adaptation of Stuart Hamblen's "Texas Plains." The phenomenal success—slow, steady, and persistent—of "I Want to Be a Cowboy's Sweetheart" led her record label, the ARC group, to urge her to come up with more of the same. She eventually did, with the likes of "I Wanna Be a Cowboy's Dreamgirl." But Patsy proved to be a prodigious and effective songwriter, especially in her use of western themes: "The She Buckaroo," "Cow Boy Rhythm," "Gold Coast Express" (coauthored with Stuart Hamblen), and "Old Nevada Moon" and "My Poncho Pony" (both cowritten with Lee Penny).

Novelty Musicians

From the second week of the National Barn Dance on through 1929, one of the regularly scheduled performers was "Kentucky Wonderbean, harp." By the end of that first summer, the Wonder Bean was clearly identified as Walter Peterson. Not much is known about Peterson himself. His performances featured his "Doubled Barrelled Shot-gun": he cradled a guitar in his arms while simultaneously blowing on a ten-hole harmonica held in a wire rack around his neck. During the same period, Dynamite Jim, a native Hoosier whose real name was Harry Campbell Jr., also performed on WLS with a similar getup, dubbed a "cap and fuse."[83] Between 1924 and 1927, Peterson recorded twenty-two masters; many of them were medleys of old familiar tunes, and all were instrumentals only. Half of them are listed as traditional in Meade. In 1928, the Kentucky Wonder Bean made one final recording, a vocal version of a modern folksong, "My Blue Ridge Mountain Home."

A third NBD musician who paired guitar and harmonica in a rack—his "two cylinder corn cob crusher"—was Pie Plant Pete. In real life he was Claud Moye, born in 1906 and reared on a farm in Gallatin County, Illinois, near Shawneetown. Pete joined the Barn Dance in 1927 and stayed through 1930. In 1929, he headlined a touring unit known as the WLS Show Boat Junior and was seldom heard on the broadcasts. In 1929 and 30, he recorded twenty-six numbers for Gennett, many released under the name Asparagus Joe. In 1934, after he had left WLS for WTAM in Cleveland, Pete recorded another twenty-two songs. All of his Gennett sides, and all but seven of the 1934 sides, were classified by Meade as traditional.[84]

Finally, the National Barn Dance tradition of comic-novelty groups must at least be mentioned, even though those acts cannot be given the attention they deserve. The most famous was the Hoosier Hot Shots, who were formed in 1932 at WOWO in Fort Wayne, Indiana, by remnants from Ezra Buzzington's Rustic Revelers. The next year they came to WLS to join a sponsored program with comedian Uncle Ezra [Pat Barrett]. When they arrived in Chicago, they were still a trio of multi-instrumentalists, all born and raised in Arcadia, Indiana. Charles Otto "Gabe" Ward held forth on clarinet and sometimes saxophone; Paul "Hezzie" Triestch was a wizard of the washboard and slide whistle—"Are you ready, Hezzie?" was their signature salute—and Ken "Rudy" Trietsch was the rhythm section on guitar and tenor banjo. They were soon joined by Illinois native Frank Kettering on bass and guitar. The Hot Shots were a Barn Dance favorite until 1944, when they left for California.[85]

Another longtime audience favorite was the Maple City Four from LaPorte, Indiana. Primarily a vocal quartet, they were also known as cutups who devised a musical instrument out of a shower hose and frequently tried the most outlandish antics to cause Arkie to break into laughter when he was in the middle of his featured number. Most of the other comedy and novelty music groups in the Old Hayloft were instrumental groups, such as the Four Hired Hands from Gary, Indiana; the Novelodeons; and Otto and the Tune Twisters. The latter two were essentially comprised of the same personnel and were led by Ted "Otto" Morse. The Hoosier Sod Busters, who started on WLS in 1933, featured a wide and sometimes weird array of harmonicas played by Reggie Cross, with guitar accompaniment by

Howard Black. In 1939, guitarist and singer Rusty Gill joined them. Apparently, the Sod Busters never made commercial recordings.

SUMMING UP THE BARN DANCE

In spite of having listened to hundreds of old 78 rpm recordings, I find that the actual sounds of the early National Barn Dance remain elusive. Of the four network shows that I have heard, the only artists covered in the previous sections who appeared were the Arkansas Woodchopper, Lulu Belle and Scotty, and the Hoosier Hot Shots—and Arkie did no singing, only a smattering of square dance calls. To be honest, I am pretty disappointed with the music I hear on the air-check recordings. To be sure, it is great to experience the spirit and exuberance of the live broadcasts, to hear the comic sketches of Uncle Ezra and Pat Buttram, and to catch hold of the familiar friendliness of announcer Joe Kelly: "Hello, hello, hello, everybody, everywhere! How's Mother and Dad and the whole family?" But there is a vast dissonance between the music on this small sample of NBC network broadcasts and the vibrant and rustic old-time styles found on the phonograph records by early artists who made "the rafters ring in the old hayloft." Others have tried to deal with this disparity between the image of the National Barn Dance and the preserved broadcast evidence. For instance, Wayne Daniel noted, with a tone of polite objectivity, that "the Barn Dance was a variety show similar in format to other contemporary radio variety shows," and followed with a hopeful suggestion: "Perhaps the non-network broadcast segments of the show featured a higher ratio of 'hillbilly' and 'western' material."[86]

I am convinced that Daniel's latter suggestion is correct, and therein lies the key to understanding the National Barn Dance: it encompassed so much more than the sixty-minute segment heard weekly on the NBC Blue network. It is possible to talk about five overlapping aspects of the Barn Dance. First, all Saturday night programming on WLS, from 7:30 to midnight, was generally understood by listeners as the National Barn Dance. Second, various segments of what went out over the WLS airwaves were plainly titled the National Barn Dance. In the typical program lineup from 1933 quoted earlier, these programs ran from 7:30 to 8:00, and from 11:00 to midnight. Third, beginning in 1932, the National Barn Dance brand was also applied to each of the two-hour-long shows staged before large audiences at the Eighth Street Theatre. The two on-air segments identified in the previous point filled only a portion of the running time of the theater shows. According to Slim Bryant, there were portions of the show at the Eighth Street Theatre that were not broadcast. Fourth, shorter segments of the show aired with the name of a sponsor, like the "Aladdin Barn Dance Frolic" or the "Keystone Barn Dance Party." The most famous of these, the network segment sponsored by Alka-Seltzer, was broadcast live from the Eighth Street Theatre. At least some of the shorter segments, such as those between 9:30 and 10:00, must have originated from the WLS studios. Finally, the National Barn Dance identity also encompassed the active program of artist tours and personal appearances managed through WLS Artists, Inc. For example, the Des Plaines Theater, in the Chicago suburb of the same name, hosted the *WLS National Barn Dance Gang* in 1931 and a *WLS National Barndance* stage show in 1935. The latter featured Rube Tronson and His Texas Cowboys, the Arkansas Woodchopper, Tom Corwine, Bob Gardner, and the Hayloft Trio.[87]

Such size and scope of the National Barn Dance in the 1930s necessitated a prodigious outlay of management and support services. For instance, a radio column in an Atlanta newspaper noted that because each week's program comprised around twenty musical numbers, and because an effort was made to avoid repetition, the WLS music librarian had the monumental task of supplying over a thousand pieces each year. These numbers, however, reflect only the network portion of the broadcast, so the total number of songs and tunes needed was at least four times greater. However, the repetition of songs favored by the audience was, in fact, not avoided, and was carefully monitored through fan mail sent to the station. Helen Loshe of Decatur, Indiana, recalled how, as a teenaged fan of Patsy Montana, she kept a notebook by the radio and each week was able to write down more of the lyrics of Montana's big hit "I Want to Be a Cowboy's Sweetheart." After she had learned the complete song, Helen performed it with a band of her siblings, including fiddler Francis Geels, at a circa 1937 WLS Home Talent Show somewhere in northeastern Indiana.[88]

Besides requiring a large repertoire of songs, the four-and-a-half hours of Barn Dance air time—along with the stage show and the constant demand for personal appearances—presented WLS with a continual need to replenish its talent. The Old Hayloft had its stars, of course, a number of whom stayed at the station for decades. But the show also needed a constant supply of fresh faces and voices, with skills that meshed with those of the rest of the cast and the spirit of the endeavor. Edgar Bill, Glenn Snyder, George Biggar, and John Lair were some of the WLS executives responsible for locating and auditioning performers and, further, for fitting them into the ongoing operation of the programs. Biggar's memoir provides perhaps the best description of how the many parts fit together:

> The National Barn Dance from the stage of the Eighth Street Theatre was primarily divided into half-hour programs—each unit period being built around a "star" with about three other acts—singles, team, trio or instrumental-vocal unit. Each program, usually sponsored, was carefully routined [*sic*] in advance to insure proper pacing. During a typical evening, about twenty entertainment units—singles or larger—appeared during the evening—for a total of between forty and fifty people.
>
> There were always two sets of square dancers of eight members each, with callers.

Future Country Music Hall of Fame member Bill Monroe, for example, got his professional start in show business as an NBD square dancer shortly after he moved north from Rosine, Kentucky, to join his brothers working at an oil refinery in northwest Indiana. Other promising young performers, as Biggar noted, hit the big time of being hired by WLS after a final audition before the audiences at the Eighth Street Theatre. Such was the experience of the Flannery Sisters, who were heard by the Girls of the Golden West (Dolly and Millie Good), when they played a barn dance road show in the Flannerys' hometown of Gladstone, Michigan, in 1935. At Dolly and Millie's recommendation, the Flannery Sisters were invited to Chicago for an audition, and a week later they were touring the Midwest and appearing on the Saturday night Barn Dance.[89]

While perusing the photographs published in the annual *WLS Family Album*, one is struck by the youth of so many of the Barn Dance musicians (figure 23). Yet even many of the youngest were already experienced radio performers when they came to WLS. The Three Little Maids, Smiley Burnette, and Pepper Hawthorne all came from an important downstate Illinois rural-oriented station, WDZ, in Tuscola. Hawthorne, a native of Ramsey, Illinois, and a veteran of a WLS Home Talent Show in nearby Decatur, was just eighteen in 1941 when she joined WLS—her third station.[90] Many of these young artists matured artistically during their tenure in the Old Hayloft, and when they left they found continued success in the entertainment industry. It is worth noting that a phenomenal number of marriages took place among cast members or between performers and members of the support

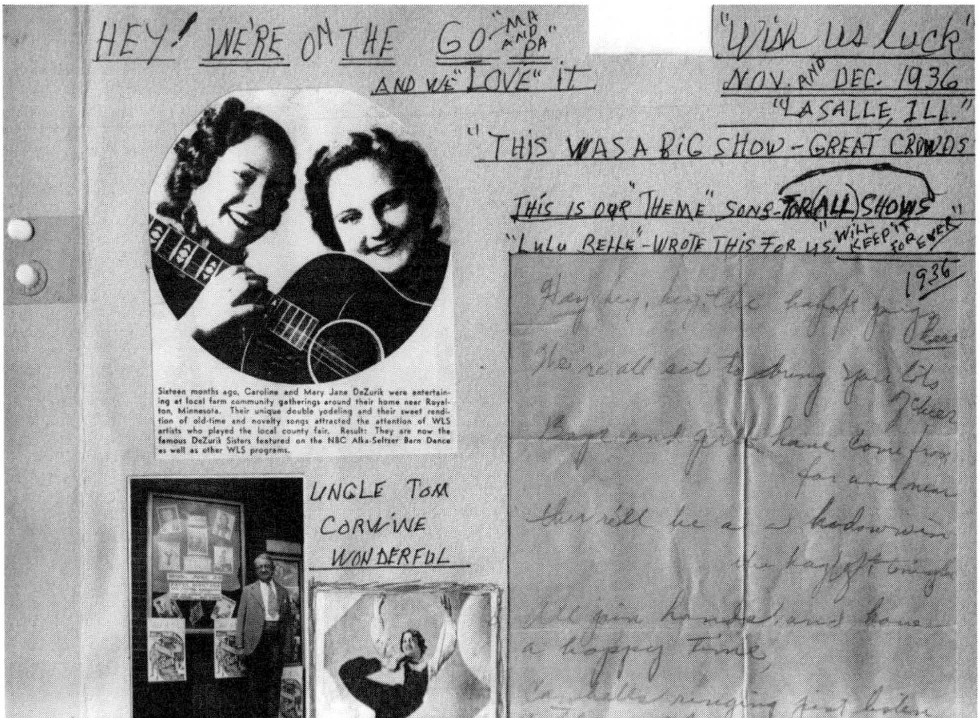

Figure 23. A page from the DeZuriks' scrapbook reminds us that some stars were quite young and pleased with their own stardom. Courtesy of Don Gill.

staff. The number of these marriages reflects the fact that the National Barn Dance was singular in the field of country music for its concentration of featured female artists.[91]

A careful examination of the music of the National Barn Dance, within the context of the developing professionalization of country music during the 1930s, reveals other distinctive aspects of the sounds that rang throughout the Old Hayloft. In one area, the Barn Dance stands practically alone: the pervasive popularity of yodeling. A large number of NBD stars wove solo and harmony yodels into many of their performances. The Arkansas Woodchopper was probably the first Barn Dance artist regularly to incorporate a yodel. Gene Autry also was an early yodeler in the Old Hayloft, but, as noted above, Autry's yodels reflected the bluesier style of Jimmie Rodgers, America's famous "Blue Yodeler." Most subsequent yodeling on the Barn Dance was of a western flavor, and some even contained small traces of Alpine sounds. Solo yodelers included the station's "little Swiss miss" Christine [Endeback], Pie Plant Pete, Red Foley, and the most famous, Patsy Montana. But NBD audiences also often heard team yodels, in a call-and-response pattern, from Lulu Belle and Scotty, and close harmony yodels from the Girls of the Golden West and the DeZurik Sisters.[92]

The Barn Dance can be regarded as an influential leader in the development of a few aspects of style that became important throughout the field of country music. As mentioned earlier, the Old Hayloft always featured vocal duos and trios. Although the sound of many of these groups has not been preserved, it is clear from several groups from the 1930s that Barn Dance audiences appreciated close parallel harmonizing, a style that was distinct from barbershop quartet style. Mac and Bob and Karl and Harty have already been discussed as pioneers in the so-called "brother duet" style. But another important example of close harmony singing was the many harmony duets Gene Autry recorded with his partner Jimmy Long between 1929 and 1937. Autry's vocal duets and trios with Smiley Burnette, who joined him in Chicago in 1933 from downstate Tuscola, should also be considered. However, it is not certain that either Long or Burnette sang with Autry on any of his WLS broadcasts. This is a topic that deserves closer attention and more careful analysis than can be given here. Let it suffice that the key contributions of these duos are related to the fact that they were male—remember that the dominant vocal harmony in country music to that time was provided by the women of the Carter Family—and that they presented carefully crafted, relatively sophisticated diatonic harmonies that relied on parallel, rather than droned, polyphony. Many other important acts in the Old Hayloft built their presentations around similarly crafted harmonies. Besides the yodeling duos mentioned above, this list would include the Three Little Maids (the Overstake Sisters), Jo and Alma, Blaine and Cal Smith, and the Prairie Ramblers.

A second area where the Barn Dance led the way for the rest of the country music field was in the adoption of the plucked, as opposed to bowed, string bass. Basses were rare in the rural string bands that recorded through the early thirties, and those that were brought into the studio were bowed according to a long-established and widespread traditional style.

The plucked bass was an innovation rooted in the newer popular music forms of jazz and blues. So when three rural string bands joined the Barn Dance cast in the early 1930s, all featuring a plucked bass, something new was being added to white, old-time, rural music. These bands ranged from the tenaciously traditional (in sound, more than repertoire) Cumberland Ridge Runners to the progressively modern Westerners (aka the Massey Family). In between were the Prairie Ramblers, as adept with straightforward hoedowns (to be fair, so were the Westerners) and old-time songs as they were with the newer sounds of swing. Another influential string bassist was Ernie Newton, a Californian who came to WLS in 1933 to play with Mac and Bob. He became a versatile member of the staff as part of the Hill Toppers. He left WLS to tour with Les Paul's trio, and after the war he ended up in Nashville, where he became a much sought-after session musician.[93]

Finally, and perhaps conversely, there were several sounds broadly spread throughout country music by 1934 that were noticeably absent, or at least rare, on the National Barn Dance after that date. One is the sound of the Hawaiian guitar, a regular guitar laid horizontally and noted by means of a sliding steel bar. The sound of the Hawaiian guitar was ubiquitous on early radio broadcasts, as the instrument and its music became a fashionable trend in the first decades of the twentieth century. In fact, the alleged "inventor" of the Hawaiian guitar, Joseph Kekuku, was promoting the instrument and teaching at a studio in Chicago as recently as 1928. Kenneth Clark may have been the first to introduce WLS audiences to the instrument in his appearance on the Barn Dance in 1925. The first *WLS Family Album*, prepared in 1929, included pictures of two Hawaiian guitar teams: Cecil and Esther Ward, "barn dance Hawaiian guitar team for a long time," and the Strolling Guitarists. The latter, though not named as such by WLS, was the duo of Jim and Bob—Jim Holstein on harp guitar and Bob Paoli on Hawaiian—who recorded a dozen sides for the Bluebird label in Chicago in 1933.[94] But while the Hawaiian or steel guitar—including its resophonic offspring, like the Dobro and other models that feature metal amplifying cones, and later electric models—became more prominent in country music in the 1930s, the instrument all but disappeared from the country side of the Hayloft Gang. Don Wilson, of the pop-oriented Hill Toppers, at times played an electrified Hawaiian guitar.

The other notable absence on the National Barn Dance, at least after Gene Autry left in 1934, was the blues. Many white southern string bands and songsters had recorded straight blues, or material that was heavily influenced by African American lyrical and musical styles. The foremost white country blues artist was Jimmie Rodgers, whose immense popularity spawned a host of imitators. One of the most famous of these was Gene Autry, who covered a number of Rodgers songs and contributed many blues pieces of his own. After Autry, apparently no white country blues artists were featured in the Old Hayloft. One exception is Kenneth Houchins, who recorded a number of Rodgers- and Autry-styled blues, such as "Mean Old Ball and Chain Blues" in 1933 and 34. By 1937, Houchins had joined the Prairie Ramblers as a replacement for Salty Holmes, and he occasionally performed as a soloist. Yet, though the blues was missing from the Barn Dance (even while it was growing toward its future national prominence in Bronzeville and other African American neighborhoods on Chicago's South Side), the influence of black music styles was still clearly heard. The Prairie Ramblers and the Hoosier Hot Shots were just two of the NBD ensembles that knew how to swing. They had obviously learned a lot from listening to jazz.[95]

Rural rhythm traveled a long and winding road in the first eighteen years of the National Barn Dance. The show started with a nod to rustic simplicity that was both symbolic and pragmatic. The first offerings featured rural performers who were the unnamed, almost generic, "barn dance fiddlers." They were succeeded, but never wholly replaced, by a succession of star singers who accompanied themselves with spare strums on a banjo or guitar. Then came the vocal duets with solid and uncomplicated parallel harmony, and a few string bands for whom the basic melody reigned supreme. As the 1940s drew near, musical arrangements became more sophisticated, even complicated. Instrumental accompanists eschewed earlier values of simplicity and began to weave their sounds around the singer's melody with elaborate counterpoint and many embellishments. Nevertheless, at the end of the period covered by this essay, one of the Barn Dance's most beloved rural artists went back into the studio to record some old-time fiddle tunes that one could . . . well, you could dance to them. Is that not where it all started?

NOTES

Where would I be without my friends who collect ideas, old scraps of information, and 78 rpm phonograph records? I've been able to hear National Barn Dance artists I'd never heard before because tape copies were generously made for me by Kerry Blech, Bob Bovee, Joe Bussard, Wayne Daniel, Paul Gifford, Frank Mare, Jim Nelson, Paul Wells, and the Old Town School of Folk Music's Resource Center. Jim Nelson also loaned me his complete run of *Stand By!* and *WLS Family Album.*

1. *Dallas Morning News,* December 1, 1922, sec. 2, 1; Bill Malone, *Country Music, U.S.A.,* rev. ed. (Austin: University of Texas Press, 1985), 33–34.

2. "A Brief History of WBAP Radio," www.wbap.com/article.asp?id=146501 (accessed October 30, 2007); "You Hear These Every Saturday Night," *WLS Family Album, 1931* (Chicago: Prairie Farmer), 43.

3. Edgar Bill quoted in George C. Biggar, "The WLS National Barn Dance Story: The Early Years," *JEMF Quarterly* 6 (1970): 106; "Jazz Rules City Dance; Old Favorites Hold Country," *Chicago Evening Post Radio Magazine,* May 8, 1924, 16.

4. Boris Emmet and John E. Jeuck, *Catalogues and Counters: A History of Sears, Roebuck and Company* (Chicago: University of Chicago Press, 1950), 623.

5. James F. Evans, *Prairie Farmer and WLS: The Burridge D. Butler Years* (Urbana: University of Illinois Press, 1969), 216, 224.

6. Ibid., 62–72; List'ning In . . . , *Prairie Farmer,* April 15, 1933, 8 (quote).

7. "WLS Foremost in Radio Surveys," in *WLS Family Album, 1930 Edition: The Happy Radio Home* (Chicago: Prairie Farmer, 1930), 35 (first quote); Evans, *Prairie Farmer and WLS,* 202 (second quote).

8. Biggar, "WLS National Barn Dance Story," 110; List'ning In . . . , *Prairie Farmer,* August 5, 1933, 8.

9. *Prairie Farmer*, October 14, 1933, 16.

10. Biggar, "WLS National Barn Dance Story," 109.

11. Ibid., 110; List'ning In . . . , *Prairie Farmer*, September 30, 1933, 8; Evans, *Prairie Farmer and WLS*, 1–2; Patsy Montana with Jane Frost, *The Cowboy's Sweetheart* (Jefferson, N.C.: McFarland, 2002), 124 (quote).

12. "National Barn Dance Tonight," *Chicago Herald and Examiner*, April 19, 1924.

13. Robert Shelton, *The Country Music Story: A Picture History of Country and Western Music* (Secaucus, N.J.: Capitol Books, 1966), 42.

14. Two other Chicago newspapers noted in their program listings, "This will be a regular Saturday night feature." Radio Programs, *Chicago Evening Post and Literary Review*, April 19, 194; Our 23-Hour Program, *Chicago Evening American*, April 19, 1924, pt. 2, 5. See also *Kankakee Daily Republican*, November 18, 1924.

15. Wayne Daniel, "National Barn Dance," in *The Encyclopedia of Country Music*, ed. Paul Kingsbury (New York: Oxford University Press, 1998), 372–73; for the variations in names, see *Chicago Evening Post*, May 3, 1924, November 15, 1924, October 11, 1924, and December 6, 1924.

16. Wayne W. Daniel, "The National Barn Dance on Network Radio: The 1930s," *Journal of Country Music* 9 (1983): 47.

17. Ivan M. Tribe, "National Barn Dance," in *Century of Country*, www.countryworks.com (accessed October 4, 2005; first quote); Douglas Gomery, "WLS Barn Dance," in *The Encyclopedia of Chicago*, ed. James R. Grossman, Ann Durkin Keating, and Janice L. Reiff (Chicago: University of Chicago Press, 2004), 883 (second quote).

18. Tony Russell, *Country Music Records: A Discography, 1921–42* (New York: Oxford University Press), 2004.

19. Ibid., 3. Russell said, "Anyone who was really keen could try counting the recorded masters on each of 31 randomly selected pages and multiplying the total by 30 (since the discography proper occupies 933 pp)"; Tony Russell, personal communication, 2005.

20. D. K. Wilgus, "Country-Western Music and the Urban Hillbilly," *Journal of American Folklore* 83 (April–June 1970): 159; Kristine M. McCusker, "'Bury Me beneath the Willow': Linda Parker and Definitions of Tradition on the National Barn Dance, 1932–1935," *Southern Folklore* 56 (1999): 227–31. The descriptions of Burr and Wilson are from *WLS Family Album, 1941: 10th Anniversary* (Chicago: Prairie Farmer, 1941), 26, and *WLS Family Album, 1930 Edition*, 16, respectively.

21. The descriptions of Arkie, Autry, Vickland, and the Novelodeons are taken from the *WLS Family Album, 1931*, 46; *1933*, 33; *1931*, 14; and *1938*, 27.

22. Quoted in Jeffrey J. Lange, *Smile When You Call Me a Hillbilly: Country Music's Struggle for Respectability, 1939–1954* (Athens: University of Georgia Press, 2004), 27.

23. Bill C. Malone, *Country Music, U.S.A.: A Fifty-Year History* (Austin: University of Texas Press, 1968), viii (first quote); Malone, *Country Music, U.S.A.*, rev. ed., 1 (second quote).

24. D. K. Wilgus, "An Introduction to the Study of Hillbilly Music," *Journal of American Folklore* 78 (1965): 196.

25. Lange, *Smile When You Call Me a Hillbilly*, 27; Charles K. Wolfe, "The Triumph of the Hills: Country Radio, 1920–50," in *Country: The Music and the Musicians, from the Beginnings to the '90s*, ed. by Paul Kingsbury for the Country Music Foundation, 2nd ed. (New York: Abbeville Press, 1994), 50 (quote).

26. Bernard L. Asbel, "The National Barn Dance," *Chicago Magazine*, October 1954, 23; Biggar's discussion, from a unpublished 1967 paper, is paraphrased in Evans, *Prairie Farmer and WLS*, 229.

27. This development was ubiquitous, for though the field of country music emerged in large part from old-time fiddling—a tradition of instrumental music with no lyric content of real importance—country music as heard on the radio and found on hit singles over at least the last fifty years has been almost exclusively vocal and lyrical.

28. "Kenosha Fiddlers Win Honors in WLS Contest," *Chicago Evening Post and Literary Review*, September 27, 1924; "Barn Dance Callers in Contest on WLS," ibid., April 15, 1926; "72 Callers Ready for WLS Barn Dance Contest Saturday," ibid., March 17, 1927.

29. In a similar study of live country music on midwestern radio stations in the 1940s, I learned that radio artists and executives from that era used the terms "legitimate" and "hillbilly" to distinguish two varieties of musicians. I was told that union rules required a station to hire a "legitimate musician" for every country or "hillbilly" musician on their staff. See Paul L. Tyler, "Country Music in the Cornbelt: WOWO–Fort Wayne in the 1920s and '30s," paper delivered to American Folklore Society, Nashville, 1982.

30. Ann and Norm Cohen, "Folk and Hillbilly Music: Some Further Thoughts on Their Relation," *JEMF Quarterly* 13 (1977): 52.

31. A similar symbolic reconfiguration was enacted elsewhere in rural America, as I described in a study of a mid-twentieth-century transition of square dancing from kitchen hops to actual barn dances. See Paul L. Tyler, "Square Dancing in the Rural Midwest: Dance Events and the Location of Community," in *Communities in Motion: Dance, Community, and Tradition in America's Southeast and Beyond*, ed. Susan Eike Spalding and Jane Harris Woodside, Contributions to the Study of Music and Dance 35 (Westport, Conn.: Greenwood, 1995), 38–41.

32. See, for example, the picture of WLS's *Merry-Go-Round* show, where seven of the thirty cast members pictured hold guitars, *WLS Family Album, 1941*, 15; and the three guitars held by the seven musicians pictured with "Here Are Some Folks You Hear Weekly," *WLS Family Album, 1930 Edition*, 43; Thomas Hoyt "Slim" Bryant, telephone interview by author, August 13, 2005.

33. See William Howland Kenney, *Recorded Music in American Life: The Phonograph and Popular Memory, 1890–1945* (New York: Oxford University Press, 1999); and Diane Pecknold, "The Selling Sound: Country Music, Commercialism, and the Politics of Popular Culture, 1920–1974" (Ph.D. diss., Indiana University, 2002), for insightful discussions on the practices of cultural production.

34. *WLS Family Album, 1930*, 12; *1931*, 11; *1935*, 25; and *1939*, 45.

35. Bryant, interview by author.

36. Walter Peterson [The Kentucky Wonder Bean], *Sensational Collection of Mountain Ballads and Old Time Songs* (Chicago: M. M. Cole, 1931).

37. See Bradley Kincaid [The Mountain Boy], *Favorite Old-Time Songs and Mountain Ballads*, Book 2 (Chicago: WLS, 1929); Lester McFarland and Robert Gardner, *Deluxe Edition Mac and Bob: Mountain Songs, Western Songs, Cowboy Songs* (Chicago: M. M. Cole, 1941); *The Arkansas Woodchoppers World's Greatest Collection of Cowboys Songs with Yodel Arrangement* (Chicago: M. M. Cole, 1931), 44, 64.

38. See McFarland and Gardner, *Deluxe Edition Mac and Bob;* Doc Hopkins and Karl and Harty of the Cumberland Ridge Runners, *Mountain Ballads and Home Songs* (Chicago: M. M. Cole, 1936).

39. John Lair, comp., *100 WLS Barn Dance Favorites: Pioneer Songs, Southern Songs, Cowboys Songs, Fiddle Tunes, Sacred Songs, Mountain Songs, Home Songs* (Chicago: M. M. Cole, 1935), 88. I thank Paul Gifford for pointing out to me the historical significance of this Dandurand recording. For further discussion on "singing" versus "patter" calls, see Paul L. Tyler, "'Sets on the Floor': Social Dance as an Emblem of Community in Rural Indiana" (Ph.D. diss., Indiana University, 2002), 177–84.

40. Malone, *Country Music, U.S.A.*, rev. ed., 31–32; Dick Spottswood, "Gennett Records," in Kingsbury, *Encyclopedia of Country Music*, 197–98.

41. This chronology, and others, derives from my analysis of the data in Russell, *Country Music Records*.

42. Charles K. Wolfe, "Autry, Gene," in *Century of Country*.

43. See "Part 3" of Richard A. Peterson, *Creating Country Music: Fabricating Authenticity* (Chicago: University of Chicago Press, 1997); Tyler, "Country Music in the Cornbelt."

44. Biggar, "WLS National Barn Dance Story," 110; Montana, *Cowboy's Sweetheart*, 73.

45. I do not collect 78 rpm phonograph discs, but I have obtained taped copies from other collectors and have scoured LP and CD reissues. However, without the recent reissue projects emanating from the British Archives of Country Music, fewer than four hundred recordings would have been available to me.

46. Guthrie T. Meade Jr., with Dick Spottswood and Douglas S. Meade, *Country Music Sources: A Biblio-Discography of Commercially Recorded Traditional Music* (Chapel Hill, N.C.: Southern Folklife Collection, 2002), xii.

47. See George Biggar, "When the Cowbells Ring Out on Saturday Night: It's National Barn Dance Time," in Lair, *100 WLS Barn Dance Favorites*, n.p.; John Lair, "Foreword," in ibid.; "Radio Programs," *Chicago Evening Post and Literary Review*, April 26, 1924, January 3, 1925; "Fiddlers at Poultry Show This Evening," *Kankakee Daily Republican*, January 3, 1925.

48. "Fiddlers of Past Tighten Strings for WLS Contest," *Chicago Evening Post and Literary Review*, May 17, 1924 (quote); "Real Old-Time Fiddlers Play at Barn Dance," ibid., May 29, 1924.

49. Thanks to Paul F. Wells for suggesting this aural analysis. *Who's Who in Radio* (Chicago: Charles P. Hughes Publishing Co. 1925).

50. "Tommy Dandurand of this city was broadcasting at WLS, Chicago, last Saturday night. He played his old-time fiddle and many Kankakee fans were tuned in for him." Radio, *Kankakee Daily Republican*, October 24, 1924. According to the 1930 U.S. Census, Thomas Dandurand, age sixty-four, lived at 3142 N. Kedzie, Chicago, and was a musician in an orchestra.

51. "Allemande Right!" in *WLS Family Album, 1933* (Chicago: Prairie Farmer, 1933), 38. Brusoe won the big Midwest Fiddle Championship sponsored by the *Chicago Herald and Examiner* in 1926. He was also recorded for the Archive of American Folk Song at the Library of Congress in 1940 by Helen Stratman Thomas, a member of the music faculty at the University of Wisconsin–Madison.

52. McMichen quoted in Charles K. Wolfe, "McMichen, Clayton," *Century of Country*.

53. Russell, *Country Music Records*, 676; Lair, "Foreword," *100 WLS Barn Dance Favorites*, 1 (quote).

54. Cited in Rick Kennedy, *Jelly Roll, Bix, and Hoagy: Gennett Studios and the Birth of Recorded Jazz* (Bloomington: Indiana University Press, 1994), 162; Charles K. Wolfe, *Kentucky Country* (Lexington: University Press of Kentucky, 1982), 47.

55. Harry Steele, "From the Archives: The Inside Story of the Hillbilly Business," *JEMF Quarterly* (1974): 54; Kennedy, *Jelly Roll, Bix, and Hoagy*, 162 (quote).

56. D. K. Wilgus, "Bradley Kincaid," in *Stars of Country Music: Uncle Dave Macon to Johnny Rodriguez*, ed. Bill C. Malone and Judith McCulloh (Urbana: University of Illinois Press, 1975), 87–88.

57. Loyal Jones, *Radio's "Kentucky Mountain Boy": Bradley Kincaid* (Berea, Ky.: Berea College Appalachian Center, 1980), 19–20. For the effect of listeners' mail, see Kristine M. McCusker, "'Dear Radio Friend': Listener Mail and the National Barn Dance, 1931–1941," *American Studies* 39 (Summer): 173–96.

58. List'ning In . . . , *Prairie Farmer*, September 7, 1929, 29; "Here's 'Arkie,'" *WLS Family Album, 1930 Edition*, 48.

59. Charles K. Wolfe, "Mac and Bob," in *Century of Country*; Ivan M. Tribe, "Monroe, Charlie," in *Century of Country*.

60. Some of the Old Southern Sacred Singers discs were released with the name Smoky Mountain Sacred Singers. A group with unidentified personnel recorded by that name in Chicago in 1928. Russell, *Country Music Records*, 852.

61. *WLS Family Album, 1931*, 41; *1932*, 13; *1933*, 20; *1934*, 11.

62. Charles K. Wolfe, *Classic Country: Legends of Country Music* (New York: Routledge), 118–20; Ivan M. Tribe, "Lulu Belle and Scotty," *Century of Country*; McCusker, "'Bury Me beneath the Willow,'" 223–24, 235–38.

63. Wolfe, *Classic Country,* 121.

64. Mary A. Bufwack and Robert K. Oermann, *Finding Her Voice: The Saga of Women in Country Music* (New York: Crown, 1993), 76–79; Tribe, "Lulu Belle and Scotty."

65. Tribe, "Lulu Belle and Scotty."

66. William E. Lightfoot, "Lulu Belle and Scotty," in Kingsbury, *Encyclopedia of Country Music,* 308.

67. Charles K. Wolfe, "Prairie Ramblers," *Century of Country;* Wayne W. Daniel, "The Prairie Ramblers and Their Fiddlers," *Devil's Box* 30 (Fall 1996): 14–16.

68. Quoted in Wolfe, "Prairie Ramblers."

69. Daniel, "Prairie Ramblers and Their Fiddlers," 19–20.

70. Robert K. Oermann, "Louise Massey and the Westerners," in Kingsbury, *Encyclopedia of Country Music,* 329; Wayne W. Daniel, "The Ranch Romance of Louise Massey and the Westerners," *Journal of Country Music* 20 (1999): 38–39.

71. Wayne W. Daniel, "Same Face, Different Names: The DeZurik Sisters and the Cackle Sisters," www.hillbilly-music.com/groups/story/index.php?groupid=12066 (accessed October 30, 2007).

72. Ibid.

73. Ivan M. Tribe, "Dean, Eddie," *Century of Country.*

74. *WLS Family Album, 1941,* 31.

75. *WLS Family Album, 1933,* 33; Gene Autry with Mickey Herskowitz, *Back in the Saddle Again* (Garden City, N.Y.: Doubleday, 1978), 16.

76. Jonathon Guyot Smith, "Gene Autry," in Kingsbury, *Encyclopedia of Country Music,* 22; Autry, *Back in the Saddle,* 14–15.

77. Douglas B. Green, "Gene Autry," in Malone and McCulloh, *Stars of Country Music,* 144; Smith, "Gene Autry," 22–23.

78. Charles Wolfe, "Interview with Millie Good," included with "Two Cowgirls on the Lone Prairie: The True Story of the Girls of the Golden West," *Old Time Music* 43 (1986/87): 7.

79. Ibid., 7–8.

80. Robert K. Oermann and Mary A. Bufwack, "Patsy Montana and the Development of the Cowgirl Image," *Journal of Country Music* 8 (1981): 18.

81. Montana, *Cowboy's Sweetheart,* 11–36.

82. For highlights of Patsy Montana's career in Chicago and the best backstage look at the Barn Dance in 1930s, see Montana, *Cowboy's Sweetheart,* 49–85.

83. "Here Are Some of the Folks You Hear Weekly," in *WLS Family Album, 1930 Edition,* 43.

84. "Pie Plant Pete Pleases," in *WLS Family Album, 1930 Edition,* 46; Tribe, "Pie Plant Pete," in *Century of Country.*

85. Gabe Ward, interview by author, June 30, 1984; "Hoosier Hot Shots," in *Century of Country.*

86. Biggar, "WLS National Barn Dance Story," 105 ("rafters ring"); Daniel, "National Barn Dance on Network Radio," 48 ("a variety show"), 50 ("non-network broadcast segments").

87. Bryant, interview with author; *Daily Herald,* May 8, 1931, and March 22, 1935.

88. Daniel, "National Barn Dance on Network Radio," 50; Helen Geels Loshe, interview by author, June 21, 1979.

89. Biggar, "WLS National Barn Dance Story," 110–11; Charles K. Wolfe, "Monroe Brothers," in Kingsbury, *Encyclopedia of Country Music,* 352; "Girls on Cover," *Prairie Farmer's New WLS Weekly* [*Stand By!*], March 23, 1935, 12.

90. "Pepper," *WLS Family Album, 1942* (Chicago: Prairie Farmer, 1942), 22.

91. See Lange, *Smile When You Call Me a Hillbilly,* 31–33; and Bufwack and Oermann, *Finding Her Voice,* 74–98.

92. See Wayne W. Daniel, "Same Faces, Different Names: The DeZurik Sisters and The Cackle Sisters" (www.hillbilly-music.com/groups/story/index.php?groupid=12066).

93. Walt Trott, "Ernie Newton," in Kingsbury, *Encyclopedia of Country Music*, 360.

94. Ken Kapua [Reece], "Joseph Kekuku: Originator of the Hawaiian Guitar," in *The Hawaiian Steel Guitar and Its Great Hawaiian Musicians*, comp. Lorene Ruymar (Anaheim Hills, Calif.: Centerstream, 1996), 2; Advance Programs, *Radio Digest*, July 27, 1925; *WLS Family Album, 1930 Edition*, 16, 43. Ruymar, in *Hawaiian Steel Guitar*, gives Bob's last name as Paoli, while Russell, in *Country Music Records*, gives it as Kaii.

95. Charles K. Wolfe, "Atchison, Tex," in *Century of Country*.

2 MUSIC OF THE POSTWAR ERA

Wayne W. Daniel

Give me the music of the western range.

—from "Cow Boy Rhythm,"
by Patsy Montana

The majority of the National Barn Dance's early years coincided with the Great Depression, and during the 1930s the show's philosophy, format, and repertoire were influenced by the same social, economic, and aesthetic currents that affected its target audience, the country's rural population, and a bonus audience of urban residents not long off the farm. During the later years of the program, WLS management and Barn Dance entertainers, like other Americans, had to adapt to a society beset by the fears, demands, and sacrifices of a world war followed by a postwar boom that brought a higher standard of living, new consumer mass media technology, altered life styles, changes in musical tastes, and innovative entertainment concepts.[1] No matter how distressful the headlines—whether about soup kitchens or depressed prices at the farmers' markets, military reverses overseas or shortages of consumer goods at home, the potential dangers of the atomic age or the unsettling prospects of a growing generation gap—the troubles of the day could be pushed aside for a while on Saturday nights by the goings-on at the National Barn Dance in Chicago. Whether seated in front of the Barn Dance stage or around the radio at home, Americans found that WLS provided musical entertainment to satisfy a diversity of tastes. Among the nostalgic nineteenth-century pop songs of Grace Wilson and Henry Burr, ballads from the southern mountains rendered by Red Foley and Doc Hopkins, fiddle breakdowns and square dance calls by the Arkansas Woodchopper, songs of the American West by Louise Massey and the Westerners and the Prairie Ramblers, and the novelty high-jinks of Lulu Belle and Scotty and the Hoosier Hot Shots, listeners could find something to their liking.

For the most part, the National Barn Dance experience during its last two decades mirrored the country music scene that unfolded during those years. There was the inevitable turnover of talent. While some Barn Dance veterans left the show in pursuit of greener pastures, new talent vied to replace them in an effort to advance, in ways only Barn Dance membership could, their own careers. Barn Dance artists took advantage of opportunities to supplement their incomes and enhance their careers through movie appearances, record deals, and songwriting. Some of the most popular and widely recorded country songs of the 1940s and 50s came from the pens of Barn Dance performers. Among the numerous cast members who achieved success with their records during the period, one enjoyed the spotlight for several weeks with a number-one chart hit. Many Barn Dance artists appeared in movies, and some achieved success in Hollywood that overshadowed their accomplishments as radio performers. While individual cast members had their career victories and disappointments, the Barn Dance cast as a whole also had its ups and downs. Shortly after the end of World War II, the show lost its network sponsor, a blow that was somewhat softened when WLS management, through other initiatives, succeeded in expanding the listening audience. From the point of view of its artists, one of the greatest mistakes that WLS management made was its failure to enhance the station's outreach through the use of television. Finally, for most of the forties and fifties the National Barn Dance entertainers faced a situation that would have been inconceivable during the prewar era. For some sixteen years, beginning in 1944, WLS talent worked under the shadow of recurring rumors that WLS and its corporate parent, *Prairie Farmer*, were going to be sold. Despite the uncertainties spawned by these rumors, the National Barn Dance, during its last two decades, managed to hold on to a substantial listener base.

The following WLS program log for Saturday evening, January 10, 1942, was typical of the station's Saturday night offerings during and for a time after the war. Names of program sponsors are in parentheses.

6:30	Julian Bentley—News
6:45	"City Cousins" (Quaker Full O'Pep)
7:00	Pinex Ranch—Louise & the Westerners (Pinex)
7:30	Barn Dance Party (Keystone Steel & Wire)
8:00	National Barn Dance (Alka-Seltzer)
9:00	The Murphy Jamboree (Murphy Products Co.)
9:30	101 Years on the Prairie
9:45	Julian Bentley—Commentary

10:00	Hayloft Frolic (Mantle Lamp)
10:15	WLS Barn Dance
10:30	WLS Barn Dance
10:45	WLS National Barn Dance
12:00	Sign off for WENR[2]

The Barn Dance cast entertained from the stage before two audiences each Saturday evening. The first audience watched the show from 7:30 to 9:30, and the second audience watched the 10:00 to midnight program. During most of the postwar years, both shows were broadcast from Chicago's Eighth Street Theatre. The thirty-minute broadcast segment from 9:30 to 10:00, usually consisting of news and other nonmusical features, originated in the WLS studios. Meanwhile, back at the Eighth Street Theatre, the entertainers were taking a break as the first audience exited and the second audience entered the theater.[3]

When the United States entered World War II in December 1941, following Japan's bombing of Pearl Harbor, Burridge D. Butler seized the opportunity to increase the popularity of the National Barn Dance while serving the nation in the massive grass-roots war effort known as the "home front." The rapport that Butler had studiously cultivated during the 1930s between Barn Dance entertainers and their radio audience enabled him to mobilize WLS listeners to become involved in a wide variety of domestic initiatives that made valuable contributions to the war effort and to citizen morale.[4] The sentiments of the Barn Dance cast and management regarding the war were eloquently expressed by emcee Joe Kelly as he introduced the December 5, 1942, program. "Yesterday," Kelly told the audience on that Saturday night, "our president reported to the nation that over one million fighting Yanks will be overseas on foreign soil by the end of the month. . . . All America is proud of our fighting men, and tonight, one year after the war started, our Alka-Seltzer National Barn Dance pays tribute to our one million boys over there. . . . We want them all to know that we're mighty, mighty proud of them and that we are doing our best to back them up here on the Home Front, for we know it's still a hard fight, and we're all in it."[5] Variations on this patriotic message were heard by Barn Dance listeners every Saturday night throughout the war years (figure 24).

Among the contingent of National Barn Dance entertainers, or Hayloft Gang, as they were called, who had established themselves as listener favorites during the 1930s and who were on board during much of the World War II era were Red Foley, the Prairie Ramblers, Grace Wilson, Lulu Belle and Scotty, Pat Buttram (figure 25), the Cumberland Ridge Runners, Louise Massey and the Westerners, Mac and Bob, the Maple City Four, the Hoosier Hot Shots, Doc Hopkins, Patsy Montana, and Arkie the Arkansas Woodchopper. As had been the case during the early years of the Barn Dance, personnel changes among cast members were frequent during the final years. On a regular basis, entertainers left WLS to take jobs at other radio stations, to work in other fields of show business, and, on occasion,

Figure 24. WLS prided itself on its connection with current issues. Note the themes expressed in this *Family Album* cover: concerned motherhood, patriotism, and communication, new and old. Collection of Debby Gray.

to become involved in non-entertainment endeavors. As they departed, other entertainers were always ready and eager to take their places.

The first new voices heard on the Barn Dance after the war began included those of the Linder Sisters, hailed as WLS newcomers and billed as twins by *Prairie Farmer* in its January 23, 1943, issue. Connie and Bonnie Linder, who, as was later revealed, were not really twins,

Figure 25. Alabama-born Pat Buttram came to the National Barn Dance in 1934 and enjoyed several roles as a comic. In the 1960s he landed a role as Mr. Haney on the television show *Green Acres.* Southern Music and Radio Photographic Collection, Southern Appalachian Archives, Berea College.

worked at radio stations in Shenandoah, Iowa, and Yankton, South Dakota, before coming to WLS. Nebraska natives, nineteen-year-old Connie and seventeen-year-old Bonnie were sometimes referred to as the Sunbonnet Girls.[6]

Two groups, the Corn Crackers and the Blue Grass Boys, joined the Barn Dance talent lineup in late 1943. The Corn Crackers, coming to WLS from KMMJ in Grand Island, Nebraska, initially included Jim Colvard, steel guitar; Jim Cottrell, guitar; Lee Lunsford, bass; and Georgia Brown, fiddle. Cottrell was soon replaced by guitarist Eli Haney, and

Joe Maphis became the group's fiddler upon Brown's early departure. The Blue Grass Boys consisted of Chuck Swain, a guitarist, and Langdon Howe, who played accordion, banjo, and guitar. Swain came to Chicago from WLAV in Grand Rapids, Michigan. Howe was previously at WAPO in Chattanooga, Tennessee.[7]

No fewer than five other acts debuted on the Barn Dance before war's end. Two West Virginia natives, Judie and Julie, the Jones Sisters, were on the air by mid-1944. The singing duo had previously worked on stations in Charleston, West Virginia, and Cincinnati, Ohio.[8] A World War II navy veteran, Curley Miller, born in McKeesport, Pennsylvania, introduced his Sage Riders to Barn Dance audiences in fall 1944. Before signing on at WLS, Miller had worked as singer, announcer, and program emcee at various radio stations, including KDKA in Pittsburgh. Other members of Miller's group were his wife, Harriet, and a sister act, Dolores and Pauline Kendall.[9]

Listeners heard the Texas Valley Folks on WLS for the first time on May 21, 1945, on the early morning *Smile-A-While* program. The group was also heard on the daily midday *Dinnerbell* program and the Saturday night Barn Dance. In his *Prairie Farmer* column, Jack Holden described the act as "a most unusual aggregation of musical youngsters . . . four handsome boys! Three lovely girls! And every one of them . . . a true Texan!" Holden told readers that the Texas Valley Folks were "swell kids with a brand of harmony that you'll find most enjoyable."[10] *Billboard* identified the members of the group as Fiddlin' Rook Kirk, the Tatum Sisters, Little Pete Martinez, Chuck Miller, and Penny Whitney.[11]

Joining the Barn Dance cast on July 30, 1945, were three men and one woman who were members of an act billed as the Black Hawk Valley Boys and Penny West. Pete Fall was the emcee and comedian of the group, while George Arthur played guitar and Andy Anderson played accordion. Bass player Penny West had become a member of the group as a replacement for her future husband, Dean Maxedon, when he entered military service. According to WLS publicity, the group played and sang "a great variety of music." Penny West was described as "adept at lending her voice and personality equally well to a folk song, a western ballad, a popular melody or a sacred hymn." Previously the group had been heard on the *Hoosier Hop* program at WOWO, in Fort Wayne, Indiana. After their stint at WLS, the Maxedons became regional favorites as members of the *Midwestern Hayride* television show aired over WLW-TV in Cincinnati, Ohio.[12]

Some two months before the Black Hawk Valley Boys and Penny West arrived on the scene, Rex Allen, destined to become one of the most widely known of the Barn Dance's alumni, made his debut at the Old Hayloft (figure 26). According to the *Prairie Farmer*, Allen stopped the show at the Eighth Street Theatre on Saturday night, June 2, 1945. Born on December 31, 1920, Allen grew up on a ranch near Willcox, Arizona, where, the *Prairie Farmer* story relates, he "learned to herd, brand, dehorn and a million other tasks that go with raising cattle." Such qualifications enabled his WLS bosses to boast that he was "an honest-to-goodness Westerner" who "learned the ballads of the wide-open spaces in their

Figure 26. Singing cowboy Rex Allen came to the NBD in the mid-1940s and spent several successful years before signing on with Republic Pictures. Collection of Debby Gray.

natural setting."[13] Responding to demands for personal appearances, the WLS Artists Bureau assigned Allen to a touring unit with other Barn Dance artists and sent them out to fill show dates throughout the Midwest.[14] Billed as the Arizona Cowboy, Allen became so popular that after thirty-eight on-air offers of his picture, more than forty-seven thousand fans wrote in for one.[15] While Allen's popularity as a guitar-picking singer and yodeler increased, so did his affection for a fellow Barn Dance performer, Bonnie Linder. They were married in WLS's Studio A on August 25, 1946, in a ceremony that was the latest in a long list of weddings between Barn Dance artists whose romances were kindled and nurtured between show dates and radio appearances. Lulu Belle, who had also found romance and a husband on the Eighth Street Theatre stage, served as matron of honor. Longtime Barn Dance ballad singer Doc Hopkins acted as best man.[16] Following in the footsteps of former Barn Dance star Gene Autry, Rex Allen soon succumbed to the lure of Tinseltown, and in early 1949 he signed a seven-year contract with Republic Pictures. He left for Hollywood soon thereafter to begin filming the first of four pictures planned for 1949. The contract also called for the Arizona Cowboy to complete at least six pictures in 1950.[17] The National Barn Dance's loss was Hollywood's gain, as Allen went on to become the last of moviedom's legendary singing cowboys. In addition to appearing in numerous motion pictures, he achieved success as a recording artist and television actor.[18]

While WLS executives were busy hiring new talent and attending to other station business, Butler, spurred on by his populist philosophy, succeeded in inspiring Barn Dance entertainers and their listeners to participate in war bond sales; scrap metal, paper, and rubber drives; and vegetable cultivation as part of the Victory Garden program. WLS officials singled out Chicago-based troops for special treatment on Saturday nights, and Barn Dance artists entertained men and women in the armed services at military bases and at midwestern United Service Organizations (USO) facilities. Within days of the bombing of Pearl Harbor, WLS management set aside five hundred seats in the twelve-hundred-seat Eighth Street Theatre, home of the Saturday night Barn Dance since 1932, for the use of armed services personnel who wished to attend the show on December 20 and 27, 1941.[19] Less than a year later the Barn Dance moved to the Chicago Civic Center to allow use of the Eighth Street Theatre for lectures and entertainment by the Army Air Force Technical Training Command. After having been away since August 29, 1942, the Barn Dancers returned to their old stomping grounds at the corner of Eighth and Wabash on Saturday night, September 11, 1943.[20]

Inured to life on the road during years of making personal appearances throughout the Midwest, Barn Dance artists took extensive trips across the country to entertain the nation's troops. At the end of October 1942, one unit of entertainers completed a personal appearance tour in which they had given a show a day for 139 days, entertaining troops in twenty-five states and traveling ten thousand miles.[21]

The United States financed World War II in part through the sale of war bonds and stamps to Americans who took advantage of that method of contributing to the war effort. Although war bonds and stamps were readily available to purchasers at all times, the government conducted seven special nationwide campaigns between 1942 and 1945 to encourage citizens to dig deeper into their pockets to help keep the country's war chest filled. National Barn Dance entertainers joined other celebrities and patriotic organizations in publicizing and promoting these campaigns. On several occasions admittance to the Barn Dance required the purchase of a war bond, while Barn Dance acts frequently sold war bonds at their personal appearances. Patsy Montana, for example, sold $6,000 in war bonds at a one-day booking in 1943 in the small town of Newton, Illinois.[22]

When it came to collecting scrap materials for use in war-related industries, WLS established itself as the early leader among the nation's radio stations. The Burridge D. Butler machine had aroused the patriotic sentiments of WLS listeners to fever pitch, and the farmers of the Midwest were eager to do their part for the homeland.

Urban residents in close proximity to war plants could find jobs making airplanes and military uniforms. Farmers on remote homesteads had to perform their patriotic duties with the resources at hand. What these agrarian citizens, steeped in a generations-old philosophy of "waste not, want not," found in abundance were vast accumulations of old and obsolete, but long-saved, farm machinery and household items. When WLS announced that tickets for a Barn Dance show scheduled at Normal, Illinois, in summer 1942 could be purchased with scrap materials, 750 listeners jumped at the chance, lugging along old hay binders, junked automobiles, cream separators, and "some things so old-fashioned that the children of [the day had] never even heard of them." The haul for the show was 600,000 pounds of scrap metal and nearly 60,000 pounds of scrap rubber.[23]

By summer 1944, Barn Dance artists, through this and other "see a show for scrap" drives, were responsible for WLS's becoming the first and, at the time, only radio station in the country to receive a U.S. War Production Board Citation for salvage collection.[24] Barn Dance entertainers had assisted in the collection of more than 3,000,000 pounds of scrap metal, rubber, and paper.[25]

Since most of the Barn Dance entertainers had grown up on farms, success came easy to them in another home-front endeavor, the Victory Garden program. Burridge D. Butler turned over his five-acre Burr Ridge farm in suburban Chicago to WLS and *Prairie Farmer* employees for growing vegetables. Among those who took time to plant, tend, and harvest the crops were the Hoosier Hot Shots, Connie and Bonnie Linder, Grace Wilson, Doc Hopkins and his band, Red Foley and family, the DeZurik Sisters, Arkie, and Ted Morse, known to audiences variously as Otto or Little Genevieve. The gardeners not only enjoyed fresh vegetables in season but preserved a portion of their harvest for the winter months. In 1943, for example, they put up for off-season consumption almost two thousand cans of their produce.[26]

When not engaged in home-front activities during the war years, Barn Dance producers and entertainers were making sure that their on-air programs kept listeners aware of the global conflict through their songs and music. From its beginning, the network portion of the National Barn Dance had been structured around a theme, sometimes topical, sometimes nostalgic, and during the war years, often patriotic. The theme of the January 24, 1942, network broadcast, for example, was a musical salute to the countries that were allies of the United States. On Saturday night, May 16, 1942, listeners heard the Hayloft Gang in a "Red, White, and Blue" party celebrating "I Am an American Day." The December 5, 1942, program recognized the first anniversary of the bombing of Pearl Harbor, and featured such war-related songs and tunes as the square dance favorite "Soldier's Joy"; a banjoist's rendition of "Stars and Stripes Forever"; and "Soldier, Will You Marry Me?" sung by Lulu Belle and Scotty. To get the listening audience in a digging, planting, weeding mood, Victory Gardens were the theme of the April 15, 1944, program. Carrying hoes, rakes, spades, and other garden tools, the cast came on stage dressed in overalls, straw hats, and sunbonnets. Songs like "Get Out and Dig, Dig, Dig" and "Plant a Little Garden in Your Own Backyard" urged listeners to become involved in the Victory Garden program.[27]

With the coming of war, Barn Dance performers quickly added patriotic and war-related songs and tunes to their repertoires, and listeners learned to expect weekly doses of musical patriotism on the Saturday night broadcasts. The Dinning Sisters, the Barn Dance's contribution to the then pop-oriented popular singing sister acts, harmoniously assured listeners that "You'll Never Be Blue in a Blue Uniform" and sang of a soldier sweetheart who was "Three Thousand One Hundred and Twenty-One Miles Away." Banjo virtuoso Eddie Peabody plucked away on such flag-waving standards as "Yankee Doodle Dandy" and "Stars and Stripes Forever," while the chorus and orchestra regularly gave rousing renditions of patriotism-inspiring songs and tunes like "Our Old USA," "Marching along Together," "Roll On, USA," and "Marching along to Victory." The Hoosier Hot Shots, true to their novelty-band image, added comic relief to the Barn Dance's serious repertoire with such songs as "She's Got a Great Big Army of Friends" (about a young unattached female who lives invitingly near a military installation); "K. P. Serenade" (an army recruit's frequent mess hall duties are preparing him well for a postwar life as "a wonderful wife"); and "She Was a Washout in the Blackout" (government-mandated dousing of city lights in the interest of security fails to provide the anticipated opportunity for a conniving Lothario to score big with his date).[28]

The hardships of the war years notwithstanding, these were heady times for Barn Dance entertainers. Performers were able to advance their careers through records, movies, personal appearances, and greater on-air exposure resulting from the Barn Dance's expansion to international broadcast outlets. Despite shortages of shellac and other war-related problems, several National Barn Dance acts made commercial recordings during the war. Patsy Montana, who first recorded for the Decca Record Company in 1941, cut "Deep in the Heart of Texas" backed by "I'll Wait for You" in the label's Los Angeles studio in 1942. Having returned to the Barn Dance in 1943 after an absence that included a stint on the Mexico/Texas border station XERA, she entered Decca's Chicago studio on April 10, 1944, to record "Smile and Drive Your Blues Away" and the topical "Good Night, Soldier."[29] In January 1942 Louise Massey and the Westerners cut several sides subsequently released on the Okeh and Columbia labels. The most popular of these were "Gals Don't Mean a Thing (In My Young Life)" and "The Honey Song."[30] During the war the Hoosier Hot Shots recorded for Okeh, Coral, and Decca. Among their most popular recordings were "From the Indies to the Andes in His Undies" (Coral) and "She Broke My Heart in Three Places" (Decca). The three places where the heart had been broken were Seattle, Chicago, and New York. Lucille Overstake, who had joined the National Barn Dance cast in 1932 with her sisters Evelyn and Eva as the Three Little Maids, embarked on a solo career as Jenny Lou Carson on WLS in 1942.[31] A Decca record contract followed, and in 1944 she was in the studio on November 10 and again on November 13. These sessions yielded seven releases, including her own composition, "Jealous Heart," released the following March. This song became a major hit recorded by numerous artists in several genres.[32] Red Foley (figure 27), who was married to Jenny Lou Carson's sister Eva, first recorded for Decca in March

Figure 27. Born and raised near Berea, Kentucky, Red Foley cut his teeth on music learned from customers—black and white—at his father's store. Discovered while at Georgetown College, Foley had a long career in Chicago and Nashville. John Lair Collection, Southern Appalachian Archives, Berea College.

1941. At these sessions he cut such widely recorded songs as "Be Honest with Me" and the prewar draft-inspired "I'll Be Back in a Year Little Darlin'," as well as "Old Shep," a song for which he would always be remembered. Foley's recording of "Smoke on the Water," a song warning that there would be "smoke on the water, on the land and the sea" when the enemy powers were defeated, became the most popular World War II–era recording by a National Barn Dance artist. Recorded on May 4, 1944, the song debuted on *Billboard*'s list of "Most Played Juke Box Folk Records" on August 26 and occupied a spot on that chart for twenty-seven weeks, holding down the number-one spot for thirteen consecutive weeks. Between September 30 and December 16, the record appeared on *Billboard*'s pop music "Most Played Juke Box Records" chart for eleven weeks, during four of which it was in the top ten.[33]

Despite gasoline rationing, tire shortages, and other wartime inconveniences, National Barn Dance fans flocked to the Eighth Street Theatre on Saturday nights in greater than ever numbers. Those without reservations to see the show were frequently turned away from a sold-out house.[34] During the week, the artists also drew large crowds at personal appearances. At the end of November 1942, the WLS Artists Bureau announced that Barn Dance performers had appeared at 127 fairs and expositions during the year.[35] The following year, *Billboard* gave the WLS Artists Bureau credit for probably providing more hillbilly performers for personal appearances than any other talent agency.[36] One of the bureau's biggest coups of 1943 occurred in June when a contingent of Barn Dance performers was booked for a five-day engagement at an amusement park in St. Paul, Minnesota.[37] The popularity of the Barn Dance and its artists did not escape the notice of the print media. The show received national attention in 1943, with a feature article in two mainstream magazines, *Coronet* and *Newsweek*, with a combined circulation estimated at more than five million.[38] A *Coronet* scribe portrayed the Barn Dance as "a homespun conglomeration of sentimental folk songs and guitar strumming, of corn-fed humor and spry square dancing," with crowds jamming the street in front of the theater waiting to get in to see and hear the show. The anonymous author of the *Newsweek* article confided to readers that "probably the closest that radio will ever get to authentic Americana is the National Barn Dance, an unvarnished, though slightly sandpapered group of backwoods talent crowded each week in a Chicago theater for a Saturday night party."[39] With a daily lineup of Barn Dance talent, WLS enjoyed almost sold-out commercial time, with none available at night and very little during the day.[40] In February 1945, WLS's general manager, Glen Snyder, announced that the station reached more than 3,500,000 radio homes in just three states, Illinois, Indiana, and Wisconsin. No mention was made of coverage in other midwestern states and the rest of the nation.[41] To the enormous satisfaction of sponsors and gratification of the artists and management, fans from all over the world flooded the station's mailroom with more than a million pieces of correspondence a year.[42]

In 1942, *Billboard* announced that, beginning March 8, the Alka-Seltzer portion of the

National Barn Dance would be heard via shortwave radio over NBC's international stations WRCA and WNBI, and the Westinghouse station WBOS,[43] which meant that the show would be heard far beyond the borders of the United States. The reach of the National Barn Dance was extended farther when, on January 6, 1945, twenty-six stations of the Canadian Broadcasting Corporation began airing the NBC portion of the show.[44] The Barn Dance had already become known in many parts of the world through the Armed Forces Radio Service (AFRS), which transcribed U.S. radio network programs for rebroadcast to far-flung service personnel and other listeners. The National Barn Dance enjoyed AFRS worldwide exposure from 1942 to 1948.[45]

Continuing a trend that had begun in the 1930s, Barn Dance artists made periodic wartime pilgrimages to the West Coast to appear in motion pictures. Lulu Belle and Scotty appeared in five movies between 1942 and 1945: *Hi, Neighbor* (1942); *Swing, Swing Your Partner* (1943); *The National Barn Dance* (1944); *Sing, Neighbor, Sing* (1944); and the eighth and last film of their career, *Under Western Skies* (1945).[46] The Barn Dance act most frequently commuting between Chicago and Hollywood during the war was the Hoosier Hot Shots. They made the trip six times to appear in *Hoosier Holiday* (1943), *Swing in the Saddle* (1944), *The National Barn Dance* (1944), *Sing Me a Song of Texas* (1945), *Rhythm Round-up* (1945), and *Rockin' in the Rockies* (1945).[47]

For Barn Dance fans and entertainers, the most exciting motion-picture event of the 1940s was the filming and premiere of Hollywood's production *The National Barn Dance.* Readers of the October 27, 1943, issue of *Variety* learned that members of the National Barn Dance cast would be leaving for Hollywood after the November 13 Saturday night broadcast to begin preparations for appearances in a Paramount picture based on the program.[48] On the appointed Saturday night the Haylofters pitched a party before bidding goodbye to the California-bound entertainers. Plans were made for the NBC segment of the National Barn Dance to be broadcast from Hollywood during the filming of the movie.[49] Saturday night, December 25, found the movie veterans back at the Eighth Street Theatre for the network broadcast of the Barn Dance.[50] It would be almost a year, however, before fans would be able to see the movie that had kept NBD performers Pat Buttram, the Hoosier Hot Shots, the Dinning Sisters, Lulu Belle and Scotty, Arkie, and Joe Kelly in Hollywood for the previous six weeks.

The movie, *The National Barn Dance,* premiered at the Eighth Street Theatre on Saturday night, October 14, 1944. *Prairie Farmer* advised readers that the picture would be shown twice, from 8:30 to 9:45 P.M. and from 10:15 to 11:30 P.M., so that the two Saturday night audiences would be able to see the movie as part of the regular Barn Dance stage show.[51] Robert Benchley, humorist, drama critic, and actor, who had been featured in the film, joined the Hayloft Gang on stage, adding his own brand of humor to the program. While musicians, singers, and comedians made merry inside, searchlights illuminated the scene outside the Eighth Street Theatre, made festive with eye-catching banners. Following the night's screenings, Barn Dance personnel, agency and network officials, and newspaper reporters gathered at a nearby hotel for a celebration party.[52] In his review of the *National Barn Dance* movie, *Billboard* writer Nat Green opined,

> The picture should be popular with the hundreds of thousands who have listened to the radio show. Most of it is typical barn dance, with Pat Buttram, Hoosier Hot Shots, Dinning Sisters, Lulu Belle and Scotty, Arkie, and Joe Kelly doing much the same as they do on the Saturday night radio show—and that's what their fans will want. There had to be a story to tie in with the barn dance, and in doping it out the Hollywood crew didn't show too much brilliance. There's a lot of preposterous stuff that marks [*sic*] back to the old Mack Sennett days, but it gets the laughs and gives the barn dance crew ample opportunity to do their stuff, and they come thru with flying colors. Jean Heather and Robert Benchley give the cast excellent support.[53]

Today, the *National Barn Dance* film is not available in VHS or DVD format from the usual sources of old movies. Those who have seen the picture, however, recall that the plot is a fictionalized account of how radio's National Barn Dance got its start. In the movie a Chicago talent agent believes that an advertising executive wants to produce a hillbilly radio program. The agent heads for the South to recruit a crew of musically gifted rustics for the show. He finds that a group of such individuals, who are, of course, the Barn Dance artists appearing in the movie, hold a dance in their barn every Saturday night. The musicians are lured to Chicago only to find that plans for the radio program have evaporated. After a bit of creative maneuvering the musicians prove their competence for the type of show that was originally envisioned, and the "Barn Dance" is born. In addition to Benchley, Heather, and the Barn Dance artists, Charles Dingle and Mabel Paige also appeared in the movie.[54]

But not all news about the National Barn Dance during the first half of the 1940s was good. Both *Billboard* and *Variety* announced in June 1942 that the network portion of the show would soon be cut from a full hour to a half hour. According to *Billboard* the airtime was shortened because of Alka-Seltzer's wish to reduce its advertising budget. The first half-hour show aired on July 4.[55] One can only speculate as to the impact that this change may have had on the program's artists, who likely experienced salary cuts, and on station management, forced to find new sponsors for the lost half hour.

In February 1944 *Variety* reported that an official with the New York City–based Blue Network, the recently sold division of the National Broadcasting Company, had been negotiating with Burridge D. Butler for purchase of WLS.[56] Rumors about the possible sale of WLS began to "fly like snow in a blizzard," according to *Billboard.* Lending credibility to the rumors was the fact that the Blue Network, of which WLS was an affiliate, owned and operated WLS's frequency-sharing WENR in Chicago. Years later, a *Prairie Farmer* editor addressing the subject stated that the impact on *Prairie Farmer* and WLS employees was "distressing." The situation for WLS employees was especially stressful, he explains, because they suspected that if new management took over, a "house cleaning" would follow.[57] Perhaps spirits were buoyed somewhat by statements from Glenn Snyder, WLS vice-president and general manager. "WLS is not for sale," he was quoted in *Billboard* in April. "Anyone saying that it is to be sold to the Blue Network or to any other company or person is merely spreading rumors."[58] But any assurances of stability made by WLS employees may have been short-lived, for the rumors would not go away. Less than three months later, *Billboard* reported that Blue Network officials still wanted to buy the station and that negotiations were likely to be resumed. Again, Butler and Snyder issued statements declaring their intention not to sell WLS.[59] Barn Dance artists were no doubt comforted by news that appeared in the August 30 issue of *Variety*. Miles Laboratories, makers of Alka-Seltzer, announced that its sponsorship of the National Barn Dance had been renewed for another fifty-two weeks. The expiration of this contract would coincide, almost to the day, with the end of World War II.[60]

Rumors that WLS was to be sold resurfaced in 1946. By this time the Blue Network had acquired the name American Broadcasting Company (ABC). Articles in *Billboard* and *Variety* chronicled the ongoing negotiations and attempted negotiations between Butler and ABC officials. According to *Variety*, the two had a meeting of minds as early as mid-October 1947 regarding the price the network would pay for WLS, but Butler, unhappy over the details, had refused to seal the deal.[61] Before any mutually satisfactory agreement could be made legal, fate stepped in. Burridge D. Butler died on March 30, 1948, and future management of *Prairie Farmer*–WLS was placed in the hands of six trustees, "all men associated with him for many years."[62] Butler's will, according to *Variety*, specified that WLS could not be sold before 1958. The article pointed out, however, that WLS had become a less desirable property because it had not aggressively pursued expansion into television and FM radio broadcasting.[63] ABC's craving for a full-time presence in Chicago far outweighed any shortcomings that might be anticipated in WLS ownership, so the network bided its time. National Barn Dance artists and other WLS employees, who may have feared for their future, had been handed a reprieve. They had another ten years in which to plan for the day when WLS might again be up for sale.

With the ending of World War II, more than fifteen million men and women who had served their country began coming home.[64] Among returning veterans were a number of Barn Dance artists, including Frank Messina, accordionist with the Dawn Busters and other WLS groups; Rusty Gill, who would soon be joining the Prairie Ramblers as guitarist and vocalist; banjoist Eddie Peabody; Al Rice, member of the Maple City Four; Frank Kettering of the Hoosier Hot Shots; bass player Lee Lunsford, who had come to WLS in 1943 with the Corn Crackers; comedian Jimmie James; George Goebel, who would become famous as a television comedian; and Augie Klein, former member of the WLS Rangers. In addition, Patsy Montana welcomed home her husband, Paul Rose, one-time booking agent and manager of the WLS act Mac and Bob.

During the years following the war, a steady stream of new voices and faces appeared on Saturday nights in the Old Hayloft. In early January 1946, Dolph Hewitt, vocalist and fiddler, joined the National Barn Dance cast following employment on radio stations in Missouri, West Virginia, and Pennsylvania, his native state. Before establishing himself as a solo act on the Barn Dance, Hewitt was a member of the Sage Riders, an ensemble that also included, at various times, Don White, Ray Klein, Red Blanchard, Cy Rowley, Jimmy Hutchinson, Wally Moore, and Jack Taylor.[65]

At about the time of Dolph Hewitt's arrival at WLS, Donald "Red" Blanchard reappeared on the scene. He had been a WLS performer during the 1930s as a member of Rube Tronson's Texas Cowboys band, with which he was billed as "The Texas Yodeler." Blanchard's return to WLS followed closely on the heels of his discharge from military service. During his first several years back at the station he performed with the Sage Riders as a straight musician, but in 1949 he reinvented himself as a comedian, left the Sage Riders, and embarked on a solo career. In addition to providing comedy on the Barn Dance for the remainder of his stay at WLS, he served as emcee on the station's daily radio programs.[66]

A major talent shakeup at WLS occurred during late 1948 and early 1949. In fall 1948, George Biggar returned to the station as director of the Barn Dance. He had left WLS ten years earlier for a position at WLW in Cincinnati. Shortly after Biggar's reappearance at WLS, the DeZurik Sisters, Doc Hopkins, and the Prairie Ramblers were presented with eight-week termination notices. It is likely that Biggar's contract came with a mandate to bring in new blood. The Prairie Ramblers had been a WLS fixture since the early thirties, and the DeZurik Sisters had been on board since the middle of that decade. Doc Hopkins had first worked at WLS in 1930. Although WLS management had a reputation for resisting change, officials may have felt that new faces and new voices could be more easily sold to postwar sponsors. Station management lost no time in replacing the departing artists. Captain Stubby and His Buccaneers, a novelty act, signed a contract with WLS to join the Hayloft Gang in January 1949. The group came to Chicago following the termination of a long-term gig at the Village Barn, a New York City nightclub that regularly featured country music acts as part of its floor show. Headed by a native midwesterner, whose real name was Tom Fouts, the Buccaneers had worked previously at WDAN in Danville, Illinois, and WLW in Cincinnati. Fouts's trademark musical expertise on a washboard with attached horns, bells, and other gadgets, along with his ability to segue vocally from falsetto to foghorn bass, provided, according to *Prairie Farmer*, "musical comedy that for sheer fun and hilarity is unbeatable." The other Buccaneers debuting at WLS were Dwight "Tiny" Stokes (string bass), Jerry Richards (clarinet), Sonny Fleming (guitar), and Tony Walberg (accordion).[67]

A week after the Buccaneers signed on with WLS, Bob Atcher, a longtime Chicago-based performer, cast his lot with the *Prairie Farmer* station. According to *Billboard*, his contract called for a Saturday, January 29, starting date. He had left Chicago's WBBM six weeks earlier. *Prairie Farmer* advised readers that the new addition to WLS's talent roster had "a warm and winning way of presenting his many lyrics, and a quiet, friendly manner you will like at once."[68] In addition to extensive radio experience, Atcher came to his new job with an impressive background as a recording artist. Drawing from an eclectic repertoire, he had waxed such diverse material as the mainstream country song "You Are My Sunshine"; a comedic rendition of "I'm Thinking Tonight of My Blue Eyes"; the folk chestnut, "Barb'ry Allen"; and the cowboy standard, "Strawberry Roan." Station publicity moguls emphasized his talent as a singer of western songs and exerted considerable effort in building up his image as an authentic westerner. "He is no synthetic cowboy," readers of the annual *WLS Family Album* were told. "He sings traditional and modern western songs with ability and sincerity." He was dubbed the "Top Hand of the Cowhands," and publicity pictures invariably showed him surrounded by horses and other western props and dressed in western regalia, complete with a pair of six-guns.[69] In 1951 and 1952, Atcher was featured in a segment of the Barn Dance described as "a western 'short story' in song," in which he and other performers gathered around a campfire singing western ballads, including the program's theme, "The Night Herding Song."[70]

In summer 1950, *Prairie Farmer* announced that "the nationally famous radio and recording team of Homer and Jethro have been added to the list of special attractions with the WLS National Barn Dance, when the *Prairie Farmer* station show opens the Illinois State Fair at Springfield next Saturday, Aug. 12."[71] From then until 1957 they were regulars on the National Barn Dance. Henry D. Haynes (Homer), guitarist, and Kenneth C. Burns (Jethro), mandolinist, were famous for their irreverent parodies of popular songs.

Other artists who joined the Barn Dance cast after the war included the Sackett Sisters, a vocal duo from Wisconsin; the Beaver Valley Sweethearts, Donna and Colleen Wilson, from South Dakota; singer and guitarist and Illinois native Skeeter Bonn; and Woody Mercer, billed as "a real cowboy from Arizona."[72]

Post–World War II National Barn Dance performers were a part of the explosion in the popularity of country music. Opportunities for career advancement abounded on several fronts. Radio stations continued their longtime tradition of airing live country music, and after the war there were more stations available to country music artists. Whereas, in 1941 there had been 897 licensed AM stations in the United States, there were 961 in 1946. By 1950, the number had reached 2,188.[73] Television, hovering on the postwar horizon, would soon become the main source of home entertainment and a medium through which country music artists would make their presence known.

After the war, the recording industry assumed a dominant role in the careers of country music entertainers. The artistic stature and earning ability of country music performers came to be determined by the number and position of their records appearing on industry charts, rather than the power of the radio station on which they could be heard. There was no lack of recording companies available to the artist in quest of a chart hit. Shortly after the war, more than two hundred firms were in the business of making records, a number that was twice the prewar figure.[74] Before the war, a lion's share of the country musician's income had been derived from personal appearances, but after the war, box office receipts became even more lucrative sources of revenue for the country artist.[75]

National Barn Dance performers were well represented among the ranks of postwar country music entertainers seeking fame and fortune as media personalities, recording artists, and stage-show luminaries. They suffered a blow, however, just a year after the war ended. On September 28, 1946, the Barn Dance, which had enjoyed nationwide radio exposure since becoming a network program in 1933, was broadcast for the last time as an NBC show. As late as 1940 the Alka-Seltzer National Barn Dance was heard on 133 stations nationwide, but effective Saturday night, October 5, 1946, Miles Laboratories was no longer the sponsor of the show that had, according to a contemporary trade publication, "provided a warm, folksy entertainment" with high-caliber talent that brought a high degree of success to the drug company.[76] As a result of the Alka-Seltzer bailout, all segments of the National Barn Dance could be heard only from WLS. This state of affairs lasted until Saturday night, March 19, 1949, when a half-hour segment of the Barn Dance returned to network radio. Sponsored by Phillips Petroleum under a reported one-year contract, the show was aired on sixty-eight stations affiliated with the American Broadcasting Company. The Barn Dance was again heard by millions in the Midwest, Southwest, and far West. In reporting the good news, *Prairie Farmer* waxed ecstatic, informing readers, "There's never an empty seat nor a dull moment on Saturday nights—from the first square dance call to the last. And now, across the nation, there will be millions more tuning in to this all-American favorite each Saturday night." George Biggar directed the new network Barn Dance that showcased Bob Atcher, Captain Stubby and the Buccaneers, Lulu Belle and Scotty, Arkie, the Sage Riders, Red Blanchard, Grace Wilson, and other performers familiar to WLS listeners. The program was emceed by a newcomer, Bill Bailey, of the WLS announcing staff.[77]

Another reason for excitement among Barn Dance performers in 1949 was the prospect of the show's reaching fans via television. Such an eventuality would not result from a WLS initiative, since management was reluctant to become involved in the new entertainment medium.[78] It was left for officials at WENR-TV, owned by the American Broadcasting Company, to move ahead with putting National Barn Dance artists in front of television cameras. Billed as the *ABC Barn Dance*, the thirty-minute show, broadcast Monday evenings over the entire ABC television network on a sustaining basis, went on the air on February 21. The talent lineup included Bob Atcher, Captain Stubby and the Buccaneers, the Sage Riders, Lulu Belle and Scotty, the DeZurik Sisters, Red Blanchard, Ted Morse (Otto, Little Genevieve), Cousin Tilford, and a square dance act consisting of caller John Dolce and twelve dancers. Plans called for a week-to-week rotation of four different casts to avoid performer overexposure.[79]

The televised *ABC Barn Dance* opened to mixed reviews. From *Variety*'s overall negative point of view, the program was "still a radio show, needing more visual attributes than that which the initial session afforded."[80] On the other hand, *Billboard*'s highly laudatory reviewer praised the show as "a television programming natural which includes all the showmanship factors the medium requires. The program has great visual qualities, comedy, top music and talent." In the reviewer's opinion, the show "should become a successful commercial package."[81] The *ABC Barn Dance* lasted thirty-nine weeks, with its final telecast on November 14, 1949. Its demise, presumably, resulted from a lack of sponsorship.[82]

Throughout the history of the National Barn Dance, the show's artists were well represented on American record labels. The postwar era was no exception. Jenny Lou Carson, in April 1946, the month that she left WLS never to return, saw the release on the Decca label of her recording of "Many Tears Ago," another of her compositions. Carson's career as a songwriter, which had been gaining momentum during her last few years on the Barn Dance, skyrocketed after her departure and left in its wake, in addition to "Many Tears Ago" and "Jealous Heart," such country music hits as "Don't Rob Another Man's Castle," "Let Me Go, Lover," and "You Two-Timed Me One Time Too Often."[83]

August 1949 found Dolph Hewitt, backed by the Sage Riders and Smokey Lohman from the WLS Rangers, in the RCA Victor studios for his first recording session. The debut release from this effort was "I Wish I Knew," backed by a novelty song, "I Would Give You Roses, but They Cost Too Much," written by Karl Davis of the Karl and Harty duo. *Billboard*'s record reviewer deemed "I Wish I Knew" a "sincere, warm rendition of a strong sentimentalizer" and stated that "I Would Give You Roses" was "projected with great sympathy and musical intelligence." The record, on the strength of "I Wish I Knew," received considerable air play across the country.[84]

In the mid-1940s, Lulu Belle and Scotty and Patsy Montana were among some half-dozen country music artists who recorded for the short-lived Vogue picture-disc label that featured full-color, full-disc illustrations on each side of a standard-size 78 rpm record. Lulu Belle and Scotty saw six Vogue sides released, including Scotty's composition "Have I Told You Lately That I Love You." Montana had two released sides.[85] During their postwar tenure on the Barn Dance, Lulu Belle and Scotty also recorded for the London and Mercury labels.[86]

Captain Stubby and the Buccaneers, who had seen their records released on the Majestic label before joining the Barn Dance cast, switched to Decca, which released at least a dozen songs and tunes by the group between 1949 and 1951. The Buccaneers' recordings included their typical novelty fare as well as more serious numbers such as the then popular "Beyond the Sunset."[87]

The most prolific recording artist among Barn Dance performers of the postwar era was Bob Atcher (see figure 48), whose contract with Columbia records dated back to the mid-1930s. He continued to record for that label during most of his WLS tenure. During the early 1950s he moved into the long-play vinyl era with several albums, including *Songs of the Saddle*. Released in 1953, this album no doubt enhanced Atcher's cowboy image, which WLS was so carefully cultivating.[88]

Other postwar Barn Dance performers who paid visits to the recording studios include Red Foley, the Maple City Four, Karl and Harty, Phyllis Brown, Homer and Jethro, the Dinning Sisters, the Prairie Ramblers, the Beaver Valley Sweethearts, and Rocky Porter.[89] News stories in *Prairie Farmer* routinely spotlighted new recordings by Barn Dance artists, and listeners were advised to contact WLS if they were unable to obtain the records from their local music stores.[90]

The war was barely over when *Billboard* reported that annual fairs were finding folk artists to be among their top moneymaking attractions.[91] This was hardly news to Barn Dance artists. WLS had been booking its performers at fairs on a regular basis since as early as 1929.[92] Barn Dance artists cited as being in great demand by fairs in fall 1945 were Lulu Belle and Scotty, Red Foley, Otto, and Judie and Julie. WLS performers were booked into almost two hundred fairs that year, and counting appearances at other venues, provided live entertainment for more than six hundred thousand people.[93]

Opening the Illinois State Fair with a Saturday night broadcast of the National Barn Dance, emanating from in front of the grandstand seating twelve thousand or more viewers, had become a long-standing tradition by war's end. Typically, Barn Dance artists also presented on-site daily shows during fair week.[94] Other state fairs that frequently showcased Barn Dance talent were those of Indiana, Wisconsin, and Michigan (see figure 50).[95]

The demand for personal appearances by country music artists was still strong ten years after the war. A writer for the May 21, 1955, issue of *Billboard*, reported that in the United States and Canada combined, receipts from personal appearances by country and western artists were hitting the $50,000,000 per year mark. National Barn Dance artists helped satisfy this robust appetite for country music talent. According to the WLS Artists Bureau, founded in 1931,[96] the station's top crowd pullers for 1954 were Homer and Jethro, Captain Stubby and the Buccaneers, Red Blanchard, and Lulu Belle and Scotty. These four acts alone appeared in twenty-three states and several Canadian provinces, drawing a combined total of four million people. Venues included banquet halls, convention centers, political rallies, and auto and home shows.[97]

In the late 1940s and early 1950s, when square dancing was enjoying a surge of interest, WLS was quick to exploit the trend.[98] Readers were reminded in the July 16 issue of *Prairie Farmer* that "back in 1924, when the very first WLS National Barn Dance went on the air, Midwest folks heard again the music of the old-fashioned square dance," and "it's been part of the program ever since." John Dolce, the Barn Dance's postwar square dance caller, was also a supervisor of recreation with Chicago city parks. WLS announced that he would be calling the dances at the 1949 Square Dance Festival of Chicago, while his fellow National Barn Dance performers would be providing the entertainment. Those scheduled to take part were Lulu Belle and Scotty, Jimmie James, Bob Atcher, Grace Wilson (see figure 32), Arkie the Arkansas Woodchopper, and others. The festival attracted a crowd of twenty thousand people, while many were turned away because of limited seating capacity.[99]

Immediately following the 1949 square dance festival, *Prairie Farmer* and WLS began making plans and priming readers and listeners for the first annual *Prairie Farmer*–WLS International Square Dance Festival to be held in the Chicago Stadium on Saturday, October 28, 1950. The Barn Dance at the Eighth Street Theatre was to be canceled for the evening to allow the show's talent to entertain at the festival. Barn Dance stars slated to perform included Lulu Belle and Scotty, Bob Atcher, Homer and Jethro, the Arkansas Woodchopper, Grace Wilson, Red Blanchard, and Dolph Hewitt. Square dancers from twenty states and Canada took part in the affair, which drew more than eleven thousand attendees. WLS and *Prairie Farmer* set aside October 26–27, 1951, for the second International Square Dance Festival.[100] The postwar square dance revival prompted Columbia Records in 1948 to issue a long-play album of eight square dance tunes and calls that Arkie had originally recorded in 1941 for a four-disc album of 78 rpm records. Caller John Dolce also recorded a square dance record for the Capitol label during the period of heightened interest in square dancing.[101]

For postwar Americans who found square dancing not to their taste, there was the polka. Like square dancing, the polka was a folk dance that enjoyed increased popularity after the war, a fact that did not go unnoticed by the folks at WLS. Beginning on June 23, 1956, polka contests were conducted as part of the Saturday night National Barn Dance programs. Weekly winners competed for the grand championship on December 15. WLS listeners could also tune in the daily *Polka Time*, a program of live polka music directed by Lou Klatt. The artists heard on the program recorded a polka album for Dot Records that was released in January 1958.[102] The popularity of square dancing and polka music provided WLS with a twofold opportunity. The station could boast of offering its listeners its trademark old-time and folk-oriented music while at the same time reaping the pecuniary rewards accruing from involvement in the current musical fads.

Rock 'n' roll was also a popular postwar musical phenomenon, but unlike square dancing and the polka, the new music, popularized by the likes of Elvis Presley and Bill Haley, did not meet with favor among officials at WLS. In the summer of 1957, the year that has been called the first of rock 'n' roll's golden years,[103] a writer for *Prairie Farmer* assured readers that "here at WLS we are out to produce pleasant programs that our listeners enjoy. Our program director Herb Howard does not allow the programming of rock 'n' roll tunes."[104]

After World War II, owners of the Eighth Street Theatre tried to make the Barn Dance's Saturday night home more attractive and comfortable for performers and their audiences. In 1951, *Prairie Farmer* readers were informed that recently the Old Hayloft site, which had opened in 1908 as the Garden Theater, had been "redecorated throughout."[105] In 1955 Barn Dance visitors found that again renovators had been plying their trade at the Eighth Street venue. The results were a new facade and lobby and complete air conditioning, making the home of the National Barn Dance, according to the *Prairie Farmer*, "one of the most up-to-date theaters in Chicago."[106] The new amenities, however, were not to be enjoyed for long by Barn Dancer artists and their fans. The updated facility had attracted the attention of others in search of a roomy, attractive, and comfortable place to stage an event. By 1957, the Hayloft Gang was making Saturday trips to remote locations to entertain and broadcast the National Barn Dance. Residents of places such as Hammond, Indiana, and Harvard, Illinois, found that they did not have to travel to Chicago to see their favorite Barn Dance stars.[107] The coup de grace was delivered in late summer.

Marking the end of an era, the National Barn Dance made its last regularly scheduled broadcast from the stage of the Eighth Street Theatre on August 31, 1957. Except for one year during World War II, the Barn Dance had been a regular Saturday night event at the theater since 1932. Forgetting the year that the Barn Dance was broadcast from the Chicago Civic Center, *Prairie Farmer* called this "25-year engagement . . . the longest stage run in theatrical history." The theater had been purchased recently by the Hilton Hotel for use as a convention site. As for the future of the Barn Dance, *Prairie Farmer* told its readers that "it is planned to take the show on tour more often and it will be appearing in many Midwest communities on coming Saturday nights. When it is in Chicago, it will be presented from the WLS studios. But whether at home or on tour, the WLS National Barn Dance will be broadcast over WLS every Saturday night from 7:30 to midnight to keep its thousands of devoted listeners happy." Through the August 31 show, 2,617,375 people had paid to see the Saturday night broadcast from the stage of the Eighth Street Theatre.[108]

Three of the entertainers on stage for the last broadcast of the Barn Dance from the Eighth Street Theatre had been present at the first broadcast. They were Grace Wilson, a regular performer since 1924; Arkie, who signed on in 1929; and Red Blanchard, who had joined the 1932 cast as a member of the Rube Tronson and His Texas Cowboys act.[109]

The year 1957 also saw the end of another WLS tradition—the publication of the annual *WLS Family Album*. This picture book, which provided photographs and information about WLS artists and staff, was first published in 1930. Over the next twenty-seven years it was eagerly awaited by thousands of fans wanting to become better acquainted with the artists they heard on the radio, as well as the employees behind the scenes who made it all possible.[110]

The Hayloft Gang was dealt another blow in 1959. As the state fair season approached that year, midwesterners learned that the Grand Ole Opry had been booked to open the Illinois State Fair on Saturday, August 15. For the first time in two decades, visitors to this fair would not be entertained by National Barn Dance artists.[111] By now, the cast realized that the Barn Dance was on a roller coaster ride to oblivion. "They've been threatening us for so long, keeping us on pins and needles," Grace Wilson told a newspaper reporter, "that we'll probably breathe a sigh of relief when it's all over."[112] Any shred of doubt that a Barn Dance cast member may have clung to was surely erased the following spring. In March 1960 WLS was finally bought by its longtime suitor, which had merged with United Paramount Theatres, Inc., to become American Broadcasting–Paramount Theatres Inc., or as it was known in business circles, AB–PT.[113]

Following the sale of WLS to AB–PT, one of the most glorious eras of broadcast history came to a speedy end. On Saturday night, April 30, 1960, the last National Barn Dance show was broadcast from the studios of WLS. Among the performers on the last broadcast were Bob Atcher and his wife, Maggie; Grace Wilson; Lee Morgan and the Midwesterners; Lou Klatt and his polka band, the Klatts and Jammers; and Dolph Hewitt and the Sage Riders. Bob Atcher served as emcee. Grace Wilson sang several of the songs that, over the years, had endeared her to Barn Dance listeners: "Everywhere You Go," "April Showers," "Always," and "Bringing Home the Bacon." Wilson reminded listeners that she had also sung "Bringing Home the Bacon" on the first National Barn Dance program. Dolph Hewitt sang his hit of a few years back, "I Wish I Knew." Lee Morgan evoked memories of onetime Barn Dance favorite Patsy Montana with a spirited rendition of "I Want to Be a Cowboy's Sweetheart." Bob Atcher, true to his Top Hand of the Cowhands image, sang "The Place Where I Worship (Is the Wide Open Spaces)," "Ghost Riders in the Sky," and, accompanied by Maggie, "My Adobe Hacienda." To listeners unaware that this was the last broadcast of the National Barn Dance, most of the evening's program no doubt sounded pretty much the same as it had in recent months. It was not until the final minutes of the show, when Bob Atcher assumed the role of obituarist, that listeners were told that they were hearing the last broadcast.

"This is our last National Barn Dance in this big, long series," Atcher announced. He continued,

> The show as you know was, up until tonight—and it will still hold the record for quite a while before any other show can catch up to it—was the oldest, the longest continuously broadcast program of any kind anywhere in the world. There's a reason for that. It wasn't the oldest show for any reason other than the fact that so many people throughout the nation loved to listen to it. It's you people, who have been tuning in Saturday night after Saturday night for some thirty-six years, who have made this a great show and have kept it on the air for so long. You've heard it before, I'm sure, that a thing is not good because it's old. It's old because it's good. Throughout the years this show has been personally in front of millions and millions of people. And those millions have said so many times the way they have felt about this particular kind of music.

Grace Wilson, the acknowledged Queen of the National Barn Dance, closed the show with "You Go to Your Church and I'll Go to Mine" and "It Is No Secret." As the music faded, she uttered the last words to be heard on the National Barn Dance, "Good night friends; not goodbye, but just so long and God bless."[114]

With the close of that April 30, 1960, show, the ethereal signal—which had wafted to eager listeners in the vast Midwest and the world beyond the rural-oriented songs and tunes of Gene Autry, Patsy Montana, the Hoosier Hot Shots (figure 28), Louise Massey and the Westerners, the Prairie Ramblers, Bob Atcher and many others—became the medium for disseminating a new urban music. The radio station that a mere three years earlier had

Figure 28. When they heard "Are you ready, Hezzie?" WLS listeners knew the zany Hoosier Hot Shots were about to perform their "midwestern jazz" routine. Right to left: Paul "Hezzie" Trietsch, Ken "Rudy" Trietsch, Frank Delaney Kettering, and Charles Otto "Gabe" Ward. Southern Music and Radio Photographic Collection, Southern Appalachian Archives, Berea College.

eschewed the sounds of rock 'n' roll became, on Monday morning, May 2, 1960, a leader in purveying that genre to a new generation of listeners.

True to "the show must go on" tradition, the National Barn Dance artists who were thrown to the wolves by the new owners of WLS wasted little time in getting their careers back on track. In his final words on that fateful April night, Bob Atcher hinted at plans of the artists who had just received their walking papers. "Now, for the same reason that the show has been around for so many years, it will continue," he told listeners, "not necessarily as the National Barn Dance, not here at WLS. But these bright stars that have grown to such high, high glory here on this big old show are not going to lose their glimmer. They're going to go right on. I wouldn't be the least bit surprised to find that in a few weeks, possibly, you'll hear a show made up possibly of some of the boys and girls who are right here tonight," he continued. "We kinda hope that you'll watch the program listings in your newspapers because, eventually, you're going to see it pop up."[115]

Atcher's predictions were realized. Within the year, Chicago's WGN began airing the Saturday night WGN Barn Dance, first as a radio and stage show, and later as a program seen on television as well. During its tenure the WGN Barn Dance featured, among other talent, such former NBD entertainers as Dolph Hewitt, Red Blanchard, Bob Atcher, Arkie the Arkansas Woodchopper, Cousin Tilford, and the Sage Riders. The WGN Barn Dance went off the air in 1969.[116]

The WLS National Barn Dance was taken off the air a scant five years after rock 'n' roll captured the allegiance of many of the music fans who otherwise would have supported country music. The rock 'n' roll juggernaut has been blamed for much of the erosion of country music's post–World War II popularity, which had been strong up to the mid-1950s. Considering the action in April 1960 by the new owners of WLS, one is tempted to lay blame for the demise of the National Barn Dance on the shoulders of Elvis Presley and his followers. In a sense, such a conviction is justified. But the issues surrounding the termination of the National Barn Dance are too complex for hasty judgment. Bob Atcher points out in his closing remarks during the show's final broadcast that the new owners of WLS were merely in the business to program the kind of entertainment that they knew how to merchandise. Management at AB–PT had not been recruited from the ranks of those steeped in rural tradition. There was no Burridge D. Butler among them. But, according to James C. Thomson, a *Prairie Farmer* editor from 1950 to 1978, WLS did not have to be sold.

The picture at WLS–*Prairie Farmer* headquarters that Thomson paints is one of a profitable but floundering operation ruled by a "triumvirate" of powerful executives who had long ago abandoned the philosophy and ethics espoused by Butler. They were nearing retirement, and, against the protestations of less powerful staff members and company stock holders, they saw the sale of the broadcasting and publication holdings as an opportunity to "take the money and run."[117]

Thomson's revelations, along with the appearance of the dismissed artists on another barn dance show, suggest that if WLS had not been sold, the nine years that former WLS performers spent at WGN might have been spent at WLS, extending by almost a decade the life of the National Barn Dance. The popularity and likely durability of WLS performers at the time of the sale is further substantiated by Thomson, who states that when WLS was sold, the station-operated booking agency was a profitable one that consistently sent hundreds of WLS artists and other performers to entertainment venues throughout the Midwest. According to Thomson, entertainers in some instances were given minor roles on the Saturday night WLS broadcast so they could be sold as performers on the still-revered National Barn Dance.[118] The profitability of a booking agency catering to National Barn Dance artists suggests that rock 'n' roll had not seriously eroded the fan base of these performers. Although data are not readily available regarding the personal appearance experiences of members of the WGN Barn Dance, it is likely that the program, like country music generally, was an important source of revenue. If the immediate cause of the National Barn Dance's death was rock 'n' roll, it was an indirect cause, made possible by the sale of WLS. The in-house maneuverings of the *Prairie Farmer* "triumvirate" prior to the sale of WLS as described by Thomson have to be taken into account and viewed at least as a contributing factor. However, as the almost ten-year success of the WGN Barn Dance attests, whatever brought the National Barn Dance to an end did not, across the board, immediately terminate the careers of the individual performers.

NOTES

1. For insight into the various aspects of the decades during which the Barn Dance was heard on the radio, I recommend the following books. For the 1920s, Frederick Louis Allen, *Only Yesterday* (New York: Bantam, 1959); William E. Leuchtenberg, *The Perils of Prosperity, 1914–1932*, 2d ed. (Chicago: University of Chicago Press, 1993). For the 1930s: Don Congdon, ed., *The Thirties: A Time to Remember* (New York: Simon and Schuster, 1962); Edward Robb Ellis, *A Nation in Torment: The Great American Depression, 1929–1939* (New York: Coward-McCann, 1970). For the 1940s: Mark Jonathan Harris, Franklin D. Mitchell, and Steven J. Schechter, *Homefront: America during World War II* (New York: Putnam, 1984); Richard R. Lingeman, *Don't You Know There's a War On? The American Home Front, 1941–1945* (New York: Putnam, 1970). For the 1950s: Douglas T. Miller and Marion Nowak, *The Fifties: The Way We Really Were* (Garden City, N.Y.: Doubleday, 1977); J. Ronald Oakley, *God's Country: America in the Fifties* (New York: Dembner, 1986).

2. *Prairie Farmer*, January 10, 1942, 23. WENR was a Chicago station that shared the broadcast frequency with WLS.

3. Ibid.; e-mail from Dale H. Shimp, former WLS engineer, September 26, 2005.

4. For a detailed discussion of the National Barn Dance during World War II, see Wayne W. Daniel, "Hayloft Patriotism: The National Barn Dance During World War II," in *Country Music Goes to War*, ed. Charles K. Wolfe and James E. Akenson (Lexington: University Press of Kentucky, 2005), 81–101.

5. Audio tape of National Barn Dance program for December 5, 1942, in author's collection.

6. *Prairie Farmer*, January 23, 1943, 11; ibid., February 20, 1943, 28; ibid., April 1, 1944, 22.

7. *Billboard*, October 16, 1943, 65; *Prairie Farmer*, January 8, 1944, 30.

8. *Prairie Farmer*, May 13, 1944, 22; ibid., August 18, 1944, 24.

9. Ibid., October 14, 1944, 30; ibid., November 11, 1944, 30.
10. Ibid., May 26, 1945, 25.
11. *Billboard*, June 30, 1945, 75.
12. *WLS Family Album, 1946* (Chicago: Prairie Farmer, 1946), 28 (first quote); *Prairie Farmer*, August 4, 1945, 24 (second quote); obituary, Penny Maxedon, www.kypost.com/2005/02/28/kobits022805.html (accessed November 29, 2007).
13. *Prairie Farmer*, June 9, 1945, 22.
14. *Billboard*, December 15, 1945, 84.
15. Ibid., 11.
16. *Prairie Farmer*, September 14, 1946, 36.
17. *Billboard*, February 5, 1949, 30.
18. Douglas B. Green, *Singing in the Saddle: The History of the Singing Cowboy* (Nashville: Country Music Foundation and Vanderbilt University Press, 2002), 266–68.
19. *Variety*, December 17, 1941, 31.
20. *Prairie Farmer*, September 5, 1942, 30; ibid., September 4, 1943, 29.
21. *Variety*, October 28, 1942, 34; *Prairie Farmer*, June 27, 1942, 9; ibid., November 14, 1942, 28.
22. *Prairie Farmer*, August 7, 1943, 25.
23. Ibid., July 11, 1942, 16.
24. *Variety*, August 30, 1944, 28.
25. *Prairie Farmer*, August 5, 1944, 22.
26. Ibid., October 2, 1943, 29.
27. Information on the content of National Barn Dance programs comes from recordings of the show and previews in the *Atlanta Journal*, January 24, 1942, and May 16, 1942.
28. These songs may be heard on extant tapes of various National Barn Dance broadcasts made during World War II.
29. Cary Ginell, *The Decca Hillbilly Discography, 1927–1945* (New York: Greenwood, 1989), 222–23.
30. Ronnie Pugh, Country Music Foundation, personal communication, February 9, 1998.
31. *Billboard*, August 8, 1942, 8.
32. Arnold Rogers and Jerry Langley, *Many Tears Ago: The Life and Times of Jenny Lou Carson* (Madison, Tenn.: Nova/Nashville Books, 2005), 325–28.
33. Ginell, *Decca Hillbilly Discography*, 180–81; "Most Played Juke Box Folk Records" and "Most Played Juke Box Records," *Billboard*, individual issues between September 30, 1944, and January 6, 1945.
34. *Prairie Farmer*, November 13, 1942, 29; February 19, 1944, 29; July 22, 1944, 17.
35. *Billboard: Cavalcade of Fairs*, November 28, 1942, 22.
36. *Billboard: 1943 Music Year Book*, September 25, 1943, 102.
37. *Variety*, June 16, 1943, 36.
38. J. Percy H. Johnson, ed., *N. W. Ayer & Sons, Directory of Newspapers and Periodicals* (Philadelphia: N. W. Ayer, 1942), 669; ibid., 1944, 639; John Tebbel and Mary Ellen Zuckerman, *The Magazine in America* (New York: Oxford University Press, 1991), 187.
39. Bernard Lewis, "Square Dance Roundup," *Coronet*, August 1943, 80–84; "And That Is Hay," *Newsweek*, May 3, 1943, 64, 66.
40. *Billboard*, September 25, 1943, 9
41. *Variety*, February 14, 1945, 38.
42. Ibid., January 12, 1944, 38.
43. *Billboard*, March 7, 1942, 6.
44. *Variety*, January 17, 1945, 34.
45. Harry Mackenzie, *The Directory of the Armed Forces Radio Service Series* (Westport, Conn.: Greenwood, 1999).

46. Alan G. Fetrow, *Feature Films, 1940–1949* (Jefferson, N.C.: McFarland, 1994), entries 1559, 2501, 3322, 3636, 3977.

47. Ibid., entries 1635, 2501, 2977, 3052, 3321, 3629.

48. *Variety*, October 27, 1943, 28; the planned trip was also mentioned in *Billboard*, October 30, 1943, 66.

49. *Billboard*, November 20, 1943, 7, 63.

50. *Variety*, December 22, 1943, 36.

51. *Prairie Farmer*, October 14, 1944, 30.

52. *Billboard*, October 28, 1944, 64.

53. Ibid.

54. Several plot synopses can be found online. One, written by the motion picture historian Les Adams, is at http://poll.imdb.com/title/tt0037119/summary (accessed November 1, 2007).

55. *Billboard*, June 27, 1942, 6; *Variety*, June 24, 1942, 39.

56. *Variety*, February 23, 1944, 26.

57. *Billboard*, April 8, 1944, 5; James C. Thomson, *The Prairie Farmer Story: 1950 to 1980* (n.p: n.p, 1987), 101.

58. *Billboard*, April 8, 1944, 5.

59. Ibid., June 24, 1944, 13.

60. *Variety*, August 30, 1944, 28.

61. Ibid., October 15, 1947, 27.

62. *Prairie Farmer WLS Family Album and Almanac* (Chicago: Prairie Farmer, 1948), 2.

63. *Variety*, April 14, 1948, 21, 34.

64. Joseph C. Goulden, *The Best Years: 1945–1950* (New York: Atheneum, 1976), 9.

65. *Prairie Farmer*, September 3, 1949, 36; ibid., December 3, 1949, 26.

66. Ibid., October 1, 1949, 36; ibid., December 3, 1949, 26.

67. *Variety*, October 13, 1948, 36; *Billboard*, January 8, 1949, 26; *Prairie Farmer*, March 5, 1949, 42.

68. *Billboard*, January 29, 1949, 30; *Prairie Farmer*, February 19, 1949, 44.

69. *WLS Family Album, 1953* (Chicago: Prairie Farmer, 1952), 19; *WLS Family Album, 1954* (Chicago: Prairie Farmer, 1954), 24.

70. *Prairie Farmer*, June 16, 1951, 31 (quote); ibid., April 19, 1952, 49.

71. Ibid., August 5, 1950, 34.

72. Ibid., September 14, 1946, 36; ibid., May 17, 1952, 56; ibid., June 7, 1952, 38; ibid., January 2, 1954, 36; ibid., May 15, 1954, 54; ibid., December 16, 1950, 28.

73. Federal Communications Commission, *Eighth Annual Report*, Fiscal Year Ended June 30, 1942, 65; ibid., *Sixteenth Annual Report*, Fiscal Year Ended June 30, 1950.

74. Neil F. Harrison, "The Role of the Independents in Today's Record Picture," in *Record Retailing Yearbook and Directory* (New York: M. and N. Harrison, 1946), 92–95.

75. *Billboard*, December 27, 1947, 1, 18.

76. "The Alka-Seltzer Story," *Sponsor*, January 29, 1951, 26–27, 84.

77. *Billboard*, February 5, 1949, 6; *Prairie Farmer*, March 19, 1949, 42.

78. Thomson, *Prairie Farmer Story*, 146–52.

79. *Variety*, February 2, 1949, 26; *Billboard*, February 12, 1949, 14, 30.

80. *Variety*, February 23, 1949, 28.

81. *Billboard*, March 12, 1949, 14.

82. James F. Evans, *Prairie Farmer and WLS: The Burridge D. Butler Years* (Urbana: University of Illinois Press, 1969), 224.

83. Rogers and Langley, *Many Tears Ago*, 324–35.

84. *Billboard*, August 8, 1949, 31; ibid., September 24, 1949, 112; *Prairie Farmer*, September 3, 1949, 36.

85. Edgar L. Curry, *Vogue: The Picture Record* (Everett, Wash.: Edgar L. Curry, 1990), 10–11.

86. *Prairie Farmer*, March 18, 1950, 44; Michel Ruppli and Ed Novitsky, *The Mercury Labels: A Discography*, vol. 1 (Westport, Conn.: Greenwood, 1993), 301, 305, 311, 316.

87. Ruppli and Novitsky, *Mercury Labels*, 301, 305, 311, 316.

88. Willem Agenant, *Columbia 78 RPM Record Listing 20001 thru 21571 Plus Okeh Records 18001 thru 18059* (Zephyrhills, Fla.: Joyce Record Club, n.d.), 1, 4–7, 10, 12–16, 18, 20, 21, 23, 25; www.billboard.com/bbcom/discography/index.jsp?pid=123794&aid=192597 (accessed November 29, 2007).

89. *Prairie Farmer*, March 18, 1950, 44; ibid., August 16, 1952, 38.

90. Ibid., May 19, 1951, 41.

91. Folk was then the current designation of the type of music and performer previously called hillbilly. The term "hillbilly" was later replaced by the term "country and western," which was eventually shortened to "country."

92. *Prairie Farmer*, August 17, 1929, 4.

93. *Billboard*, September 8, 1945, 87; ibid., July 6, 1946, 12.

94. *Prairie Farmer*, August 1, 1953, 18–19; ibid., July 20, 1957, 38.

95. Ibid., August 4, 1951, 48; ibid., September 1, 1951, 46; ibid., July 19, 1952, 34–35; ibid., August 1, 1953, 18.

96. Ibid., April 21, 1956, 66.

97. *Billboard*, May 21, 1955, 1, 15, 48.

98. Jim Mayo, *Step by Step through Modern Square Dance History* (Bloomington, Ind.: 1st Books Library, 2004); Joseph Stocker, "The Turkey's in the Straw Again," *Nation's Business*, September 1950, 46.

99. *Prairie Farmer*, July 16, 1949, 28; ibid., August 20, 1949, 30.

100. Ibid., April 15, 1960, 42; ibid., October 7, 1950, 6; *WLS Family Album, 1951* (Chicago: Prairie Farmer, 1951), 26; *Prairie Farmer*, September 15, 1951, 54.

101. *Prairie Farmer*, March 18, 1950, 46.

102. Victor Greene, *A Passion for Polka* (Berkeley: University of California Press, 1992), 1, 4, 135, 249; *Prairie Farmer*, August 18, 1956, 40; ibid., July 7, 1956, 36; ibid., February 15, 1958, 6.

103. Paul Du Noyer, *The Story of Rock 'n' Roll: The Year-by-Year Illustrated Chronicle* (New York: Schirmer, 1995), 26.

104. *Prairie Farmer*, June 15, 1957, 30.

105. Ibid., February 3, 1951, 44.

106. Ibid., March 19, 1955, 58.

107. Ibid., April 20, 1957, 63; ibid., June 1, 1957, 48.

108. Ibid., August 17, 1957, 54.

109. Ibid., September 21, 1957, 32.

110. Ibid., February 15, 1958, 46.

111. Ibid., August 1, 1959, 10.

112. Terry Turner, "Exit Radio's Oldest Show," *Chicago Daily News*, April 30, 1960, 38.

113. *Variety*, March 30, 1960, 50.

114. *The Best of Chuck Schaden's Those Were the Days, WLS National Barn Dance 70th Anniversary Salute*, audio tape. This two-cassette package containing the last broadcast of the National Barn Dance is available from the Audio File, Box 93, Glenview, IL 60025.

115. Ibid.

116. The history of Chicago's WGN Radio 720 is outlined at http://wgngold.com/programs/barndance.htm (accessed, December 14, 2006).

117. Thomson, *Prairie Farmer Story*, 107–16.

118. Ibid., 111–12.

3 CHICAGO AS FORGOTTEN COUNTRY MUSIC MECCA

Lisa Krissoff Boehm

Chicago, the economic and cultural capital of the state of Illinois and indeed the entire Great Lakes region, offered a home to the National Barn Dance (NBD) radio program. In the 1930s and 40s, the NBD, broadcast on Chicago's 50,000-watt station, WLS, reigned as the most important national radio program featuring rural music. Yet, by the late twentieth century, when the bulk of the history of American rural music and broadcasting had been written, the NBD had been virtually forgotten.

Many scholars and fans of rural music have overlooked the NBD's role as an important component of the history of rural folk music (later repackaged as "country and western" and then as "country"). Similarly, urban historians have failed to integrate the history of the NBD with their studies of Chicago. The NBD has much to tell us about the city and even informs us about the Midwest generally. Although the NBD remained on the radio in various guises for decades, and in its later years made its way to television, in a varied form, as *ABC Barn Dance*, the program garnered only a few sentences in the 2004 *Encyclopedia of Chicago*.[1] Most other publications on general Chicago history omit it altogether. The NBD has remained only an interesting side note for country music fans, who might know it simply as a starting point for Gene Autry or as a precursor to the Grand Ole Opry. But the NBD carries more historical significance than previously accorded it. The other essays in this volume address the NBD's importance to the history of rural-oriented music. This chapter seeks to better situate the NBD in the general history of Chicago and to explore some of the reasons for our seeming collective amnesia regarding the show's historical value.

CHICAGO, SETTING OF MIDWESTERN CULTURE

The National Barn Dance billed itself as the best source of authentic, rural, midwestern music available to the national audience. And in many senses, in the show's initial days, Chicago offered the perfect home for this portrayal of the homespun life. Chicago was, and arguably remains, the cultural and economic capital of the Middle West. The city grew out of geographical possibility. Although actually a bog—thick with mud and a far-from-solid building site for the soaring skyscrapers that came to be built there—the setting of the city could not be surpassed in terms of regional position. Sitting near the southernmost curve of Lake Michigan, Chicago had access to the Great Lakes and the trade that would bring. The city sat just a short portage from the Illinois River and, ultimately, the Mississippi River, the port of New Orleans, and the Gulf of Mexico. With the opening of the Illinois and Michigan Canal in 1848, and with the arrival of the railroad shortly thereafter, Chicago secured geographical preeminence in the region. The residents of St. Louis could scoff, but the battle had been won. In later years, bustling O'Hare Airport (designed in 1963) solidified Chicago's role as a hub for travelers and freight in the modern age.

Chicago was the setting of business, but it was a thoroughly midwestern business, with strong rural connections. Cyrus McCormick launched the strongest early manufacturing plant in the city, his McCormick Reaper Works. McCormick arrived in the city in 1848 and soon had the largest factory in Chicago—one hundred twenty employees using the power of the plant's awe-inspiring thirty-horsepower engine to produce thousands of shiny red reapers a year. The McCormick reaper of Chicago harnessed the true power of the midwestern farm; now farmers would not have to watch their crops decay because they lacked the ability to harvest them fast enough. McCormick's "mechanical man" allowed for a swifter harvest.[2]

Chicago went on to welcome the great business of meatpacking. With the confluence of railroads in Chicago, excellent access to the animal farmers of the Midwest, and the invention of the refrigerated railroad car, the city had a lock on the meatpacking business for much of the twentieth century. As Upton Sinclair's *The Jungle* of 1906 would show, however, the stockyards and the adjoining neighborhoods were teeming with immigrants, but the nature of the business itself tied Chicago solidly with midwestern farm life.

Even design connected Chicago with the surrounding prairie landscape. Frank Lloyd Wright, perhaps Chicago's most famous architect, came of age artistically in the city. Originally an employee of the architect Louis Sullivan, Wright learned early on to try to make his buildings' embellishments and overall style mesh with the surrounding landscape. Wright's designs—with their low lines; thick, overhanging roofs; and expanses of glass offering inviting views of the outside—echo the relentlessly flat landscape of the Midwest. Wright's windows, featuring leaded-glass imprints evocative of indigenous forms, lend regional distinctiveness to the designs. The Robie House, designed in 1909 for a bicycle manufacturer, now serves as the home of the alumni association of the University of Chicago. It remains one of the most outstanding examples of regionally expressive design in the city. As George A. Larson and Jay Pridmore explain, "The house begins with relentlessly horizontal lines, mammoth overhanging eaves, and long banks of glass, all of which tend to sever strict boundaries between inside and out." The home embraced its native landscape. The architects of the Prairie School, inspired by Wright, also expressed a design mentality that could be termed authentically midwestern.[3] Chicago offered a comfortable home to midwestern-based design and midwestern-type business, and it also came to offer a comfortable and long-term home to the authentic musical style of the region.

The National Barn Dance marketing materials billed the show as authentic, "old-time" midwestern music. And the music featured did represent a midwestern sound, true to the city and the region. The music grasped at something that was being lost—a connection with the rural—as Chicago grew outward across the landscape of Illinois (and in effect on into Wisconsin and Indiana) at an alarming rate. In reality all of America was urbanizing, as urban culture and urban jobs increasingly lured Americans to the cities. And if one could not live in the city, one might partake in urban culture through the mass media. Provocatively, the rural-focused NBD offered entrée into urban life for rural dwellers while simultaneously providing a recreation of rural life for urban dwellers. For rural Americans, the musical types seemed familiar, but the fact that the program was broadcast live from Chicago gave it an urban connection. For the urban dwellers tuning in, the show's rural imagery connected them to a supposedly simpler time, an imagined life of fewer complications and more easily won pleasures. For the hundreds of thousands of rural-to-urban migrants who tuned into the show, the show could evoke meaningful memories.

The NBD featured a midwestern style strongly flavored by the flow of white southerners coming into the region. The show tried to downplay the southern aspects of the culture, but such distillations could not be perfectly achieved. *Prairie Farmer* newspaper and WLS station owner Burridge Davenal Butler aimed to keep the Barn Dance from becoming "a showcase for hillbillies or a slick Hollywood act."[4] Butler wanted a midwestern show. This emphasis on country over southern was seen as especially important for the national audience. Butler envisioned a distinction between a midwestern rural style and a southern rural style that he tried to adhere to tightly. While NBD can be characterized as a more midwestern product than the Grand Ole Opry, the line between what constitutes the style of the rural Midwest and that of the rural South cannot be drawn with indelible ink. The futility of such categorization proves even more obvious when one considers the numbers of rural southern migrants flowing into the Midwest's major and minor cities. These migrants formed a significant portion of the listenership of NBD and influenced the culture of their new region. Yet, antisouthern sentiment raged in the Midwest, especially in the show's later years, and southern style was not considered wholly fitting for the middle-class wrapping applied to the NBD. Butler's task of categorization is one undertaken by radio programmers today. Is John Mellencamp country or rock? Where to put the black country musician Charley Pride? It is a matter of packaging an idea rather than a tangible difference. Note that when Butler and the *Prairie Farmer* took over WLS in 1928, the budding Grand Ole Opry was three years old. WLS needed to differentiate the NBD as effectively as it could, but the distinction between the midwestern rural sound and that broadcast from the southern United States was imprecise at best.

Butler's attempt to distinguish midwestern from southern proves more interesting when one considers his own origins. Butler was born February 5, 1868, in Louisville, Kentucky, so he himself was a southern migrant, albeit from the upper South. A shrewd businessman, Butler acquired the *Prairie Farmer* newspaper, headquartered in Chicago and serving readers around the Midwest, in 1909. Butler took over the regional farming papers of his rivals, absorbing them into the *Prairie Farmer*, and won the confidence of the region's farm families with such wholesome publicity events as corn-husking contests. Butler purchased WLS and its flagship program, NBD, in 1928.[5] Clearly Butler envisioned WLS as a highly related product, a radio version of the farm periodical. Complete with live reports from the Union Stockyards, WLS management claimed to consider its listeners as family. Throngs of visitors, ranging from groups of farm women to 4–H clubs from Michigan, testified to the strong ties listeners had with the station (figure 29). The editor of the 1932 *WLS Family Album* claimed, "You who are regular listeners to WLS will understand the family feeling between us and our listeners. We like our friends and are glad to have them call."[6]

While the barn dance musicians played for hours every Saturday night, the nationally broadcast show featured only an hour of the festivities and kept the southern elements more muted. Still, southern accents and a country flavor were evident in these broadcasts. As noted, those responsible for the NBD highlighted the midwestern sound more directly than its southern spinoff, the Grand Ole Opry. Clearly, however, the offerings mixed a rural, midwestern sound with an imported western and southern-born music. A solid distinction cannot be drawn between midwestern, rural sensibility on the one hand and southern culture on the other. It is unclear whether the distinction was really necessary. Listeners who were longtime residents of the rural Midwest would have known that millions of southern migrants had contributed to the building of the Midwest and had settled around them. Chicago and other midwestern cities had neighborhoods where southern white migrants struggled, and these areas garnered considerable press, especially in the late 1950s. But, as the historian James N. Gregory has shown in *The Southern Diaspora: How the Great Migration of Black and*

Figure 29. Cast members' visit to a brewery in 1934 would not have made WLS marketers happy, since it was contrary to the carefully constructed, wholesome image of the NBD. In the picture, Christine Holmes holds a beer in the front row on the right, and Salty Holmes is to her left, with beer in hand. Patsy Montana appears to be in the second row, wearing a beret. Jack Taylor (?) is directly behind Patsy, and a woman identified as Millie Goad (Good) is directly to her right. Paul Rose, Patsy's husband, stands behind and to the right of Goad. The cowboy in the front row is thought to be Gene Autry. Grace Wilson appears to be in the back row on the far left, with the light-colored head scarf. Thanks to Debby Gray and Wayne Daniel for assistance with identification. Courtesy of Michael Montana.

White Southerners Transformed America, southern-born white migrants (as well as southern black migrants) achieved far more economically than previous historiography has led us to believe. Many long-settled midwesterners had friends, workmates, and neighbors who had made the migration successfully.[7]

There was also an affection for the West throughout the United States, a sentiment that played particularly well in the upper Midwest. The region had once been known as the Northwest Territory, and natives remembered the area's role as the frontier. The Midwest itself was an amalgam. Midwesterners, at best, did not celebrate "hillbilly" culture, although some distinguished what they saw as an isolated, mountain culture from general southern culture, especially one with western elements. Yet the rather late settlement of the region in comparison with that of the East Coast led to fewer worries about family origins among midwesterners than among residents of the Northeast. After a generation, the regional origins of white residents were often forgotten. And despite Butler's protestations about keeping away any "hillbilly" aspect, NBD performers did not hide their southern roots. As Butler kept a close watch on his radio station, we can assume he felt comfortable with this cultural fusion, as long as it still played as middle class to his urban and rural audiences.[8]

The names of the musical groups featured on the program betray this mixed musical legacy. Although some of the claimed "authenticity" was actually an identity invented for the stage, the names illustrate the marketability of southern, western, and midwestern origins to WLS listeners. Unlike other regions, the Midwest claims no single defining historical moment beyond the connection of its settlers with the land; no Plymouth Rock, Appomattox, or California Gold Rush structured the region's view of itself. Hence, midwesterners were open-minded about what they embraced as their own.

The NBD featured acts like the Prairie Sod Boy, the Prairie Ramblers (the latter were previously known as the Kentucky Ramblers and accompanied Patsy Montana), the Hoosier Hot Shots, and the Hoosier Sod Busters. The frequent emphasis on the show's rich Indiana roots reveals this southern-midwestern mix, because southern elements feature prominently in the culture of the state. Performers Joe Kelly, Hezekiah and Kenny Trietsch, Gabe Ward, Fritz Meissner, Art Janes, and "Pat" Petterson all claimed Indiana as their home. Some historians claim that the term "Hoosier" itself stems from pride in the state's high level of connection with the South and high percentage of southern settlers.[9] The *Prairie Farmer* maintained a regional office in Indianapolis, and thus connections with this state loomed large. Acts like Patsy Montana and Arkie the Arkansas Woodchopper (from the western gateway state, Missouri) also performed. Bob Atcher hailed from Kentucky and North Dakota, and the comedian Pat Buttram (see figure 25) from Winston County, Alabama. WLS billed the Cumberland Ridge Runners as a distinctly southern group, and WLS marketing materials claimed that the Girls of the Golden West, Mildred and Dorothy Good, came from Texas when they were actually from Mount Carmel, Illinois.[10] If antisouthern sentiment had truly ruled at the station, such personas never would have been created for these performers. Listeners in Chicago and coast to coast felt comfortable with the wide range of regional influences in NBD's musical styles.

The National Barn Dance began at a time when highlighting a rural identity rather than an urban one was likely enough to differentiate oneself within American culture. In the seemingly rapid evolution of the early twentieth century, the distinction between southern and midwestern rural roots meant little when compared to the greater disparities between the poles of rural and urban identities. The NBD packaged and sold rural identity on its weekly shows and brought it to the people in local performances at state fairs and other events. Chicago was a natural staging ground for this radio program. Marketing materials for the show highlighted the NBD's Chicago location, mentioning it frequently. WLS did not need to hide the show's urban broadcast location, for listeners knew Chicago as a city with solid connections with the countryside. Yet the show itself and the materials made little of the setting apart from including the city's name; the show yearned to recreate an authentic barn dance, and the rural feel was highlighted at every opportunity. Remember WLS's roots as a station serving a rural listenership. Although determining exactly who was listening to a radio broadcast is an inexact science, in these years WLS clearly catered more to an overtly rural or rural-oriented listenership than did many radio stations.[11]

Government officials from Chicago enjoyed the connection with the Barn Dance and things rural. The 1933–34 World's Fair featured a Farm Week and performances by WLS stars. In 1937, city officials declared September 12 to 18 "Farm Week Festival." Mayor Edward J. Kelly proclaimed, "During Farm Week Chicago will pay tribute to the farmers of the Middle West, whose industry and prosperity have contributed in so important a measure to Chicago's importance as a trading center. Everything in the city's power will be done to make Farm Week interesting, stimulating and inspirational for our rural guests and neighbors." A farm parade featuring leading figures in agricultural life and live farm animals marched down the city's famous boulevard, Michigan Avenue. The celebration on Friday, September 17, 1937, featured performances by Barn Dance stars in the city's Soldier Field.[12] In the 1930s and 40s, Chicagoans thought of their city as a hub for agriculture-based business and delighted in a celebration of rural culture. As the years passed, however, this fondness for the rural would wane.

CHICAGO'S IMAGE VS. REALITY

Despite the many connections between Chicago and a homegrown midwestern agricultural business and culture, Chicago became known as a city with a foreign-born population. Chicago's foreigners were seen as harboring the potential to threaten an American way of life. The city was a symbol for an antiurban sentiment that carried a lot of weight in national popular culture. The symbolism of the city did not preclude all other readings of the city, but most Americans who consumed popular culture understood the symbolism. It is important to understand that one can hold two views, even contradictory ones, of a place simultaneously. Often we understand place from two perspectives—our own personal conception of it, and the role of that place in national culture. For WLS listeners, the name of Chicago evoked thoughts of the comfortable sounds emanating from the Barn Dance program through the family radio on Saturday nights. But surely most listeners understood

Chicago had another reputation as well. In Chicago, according to national popular culture, chaos often reigned.

Chicago's image in popular culture did not arise entirely from reality. The young city did not have a long history. The city was not incorporated as a town until 1833 and did not officially become a city until 1837. In 1831, when the East Coast of the United States was already industrializing, the settlement that would become Chicago had only two hundred residents and was probably outside of the thoughts of most Americans. Given this blank slate, it took just a few incidents for the city to gain a dark reputation. The city first burst into the national consciousness with the scandals surrounding the Great Chicago Fire in 1871. Before the flurry of media stories centered on the fire, Chicago garnered very little national press. When considered at all, the city was imagined as a frontier location where alcohol flowed freely and real estate speculation figured as the central concern of business. With the Great Chicago Fire, however, Chicago's role as a central antiurban symbol in the national consciousness emerged.

In my book *Popular Culture and the Enduring Myth of Chicago*, I assert that the city played the role of "infamous city," or leading antiurban symbol, in American popular culture from the time of the fire up through the late 1960s. Today we have forgotten the power of this aspect of Chicago's popular image because the city has largely shed this infamous image. During the heyday of Butler's National Barn Dance in the 1930s and 40s, however, other producers of popular culture cast Chicago as a symbol of urban turmoil. A deluge of such material reduced the power of any alternative readings of the midwestern urban center. This image shift occurred even though WLS broadcast its wholesome musical offerings to a wide and eager national audience. The NBD was an important cultural offering; its safe programming ran counter to most of the messages the national audience received about Chicago. While WLS listeners certainly knew that this particular rural musical form originated in Chicago, they were undoubtedly aware of the city's darker image as well.

The Great Chicago Fire turned out to be just the beginning of the challenges to Chicago's image. In 1886, strikes related to organized labor's national movement for an eight-hour workday led to intense violence in the city. Police monitoring a workers' rally near the city's Haymarket Square became the victims of a bomb let loose in the crowd. The instigator of the violence remains unknown even today. After the bomb went off, the police fired their weapons in fear. Seven policemen and several civilians died in the melee. In 1894, workers at the Pullman Palace Car Company went on strike. The protest soon turned violent: workers set railroad cars on fire and the government called in troops to restore order. Both the Haymarket riot and the Pullman strike caught the nation's attention, again offering up Chicago as a symbol of urban unrest. And there was more: the events fueled xenophobic sentiments held by native-born Americans. For much of the early twentieth century, Chicago reigned as the home of an urban culture that challenged the longstanding Anglo-Saxon authority of the nation. Like New York City, Chicago drew great numbers of immigrants to settle in its neighborhoods. Chicago at times had a higher percentage of immigrants and their children than did New York; in 1890 this group composed 87 percent of Chicago's population, while in New York City it constituted 80 percent of the population. In New York City, mitigating factors such as a longstanding history and unparalleled offerings in high culture—art, music, theater, and the like—partially offset American fears about the influence of immigrant newcomers to the city. But for youthful Chicago, the impact of the immigrants weighed more heavily on the conception of the city in national culture.

The World's Columbian Exposition of 1893 was the official U.S. celebration of the arrival of Columbus in the New World, four hundred and one years earlier. The pomp and circumstance of the fair awed its twenty-seven million visitors, and the event received intense press coverage. But the carefully orchestrated event and the beautifully designed, sparkling white, temporary buildings of the Court of Honor contrasted strikingly with the teeming streets of the actual city of Chicago. Visitors compared the fair's "White City" negatively with the "Grey City" of the metropolis beyond the fairgrounds. Visitors wondered why the real city could not impress as the fantasy city had. To strengthen Chicago's infrastructure, Daniel Burnham, the exposition's head architect, devised his "Plan of Chicago" in 1909, bound the plan in a text complete with beautiful watercolor illustrations, and launched a publicity campaign for his ideas. The plan showed what Chicago could look like with increased planning. Much of Burnham's plan was implemented, forming the basis of Chicago's present-day appeal for visitors. But the mixed reviews of the city during the exposition of 1893 remained; the shock of the city, filled with jostling pedestrians, crisscrossing trolley routes, the smell of the South Side stockyards, and the soot of the industrial plants, remained in the memories of fair goers. Many of them left the city with stronger memories of the circus-like attractions of the exposition's Midway than of the highbrow attractions of the fair's central exhibits. Instead of art, architecture, and the industrial innovations displayed inside the fairgrounds proper, many visitors spoke most passionately about the Great Ferris Wheel, the first of its kind in the world, or the mesmerizing "danse du ventre" (belly dance) offered at many of the Midway's sideshow attractions. The impact of the World's Columbian Exposition remained decidedly mixed; not all of the Chicago boosters' marketing dreams were realized.

Part of the city's negative reputation came, ironically, from the publications related to the innumerable progressive public service activities designed to clean up Chicago. In the Progressive era, Chicago became a laboratory of social action, with groups such as Jane Addams's Hull-House, the Chicago Civic Federation, and the Chicago Secret Six crime fighters gaining press inside the city and beyond. Chicago led other cities in the invention of methodologies to improve urban life. The city's premier site of higher education, the University of Chicago, launched the formal study of the field of social work. Media focus on Chicago's leadership in these areas skewed the nation's view of the city, however. The public perceived Chicago to be in special need of such ameliorative activities, rather than just as a leader in the techniques necessary to upgrade the urban environment.

THE NATIONAL BARN DANCE, GANGSTERS, AND THE 1933–34 WORLD'S FAIR

A cartoon by the famed Chicago cartoonist John T. McCutcheon from the early 1930s sums up Chicago's reputation at the time (figure 30). Ironically, the launch of the National Barn Dance as a national radio program in 1932 perfectly coincided with the heyday of Chicago's sordid reputation. The wholesome musical sounds of the program were little match for the outpouring of popular culture materials that soured the national conception of the city. The bulk of the rhetoric focused on the exploits of the city's gangsters, especially the deeds of Chicago's Public Enemy #1, Alphonse Capone.

McCutcheon's cartoon features three horizontal strips. The top layer depicts the city of Chicago as a frightened old man, shielding himself from the onslaught of gangster activity, including the Valentine's Day Massacre of 1929 (the brutal deaths of seven men in a rival gang most likely instituted by Capone), racketeering, machine gun warfare, and intimidation. In the second layer, we again see a harried man personifying Chicago, this time literally tied up by local government waste, corruption, and city governmental scandals. Finally, in the bottom layer of the cartoon, we see a younger man—an unabashed booster representing the new Chicago, smiling from ear to ear, as he welcomes A Century of Progress, the World's Fair of 1933 and 1934, to the city. Clearly, the city's hopes for a change to its dark national reputation lay with the fair, as did its own private hopes for a more peaceful, livable city.

Chicago was not the only city to fight organized criminal activity, but one might not know that from a cursory look at the national papers. In the late 1920s and 30s, Chicago became so closely linked with the actions of Al Capone and other gangsters that it reigned as the national center of urban crime. Influential Chicagoans fought back against this perception, noting that while their city surely did have a criminal element, the types and frequency of the coverage of its crime in the national press manufactured the city's sordid image. Interviewed by a reporter from the *Saturday Evening Post* in 1930, Robert I. Randolph proclaimed, "Millions of people living in cities having a higher homicidal [*sic*] rate than ours regard Chicago with holy terror because the editors of their papers bury their own crime news in the back pages while giving the latest reports from Chicago gangland front-page positions."[13]

City leaders' desire to improve Chicago's national image fueled the plan to hold a second world's fair in Chicago. Chicagoans looked back fondly at the World's Columbian Exposition of 1893, although it had not been an unmitigated success in terms of public relations. Boosters hoped a second fair, marking the city's hundredth birthday, would bring status to Chicago on the national front, finally giving it credit for being the cultural

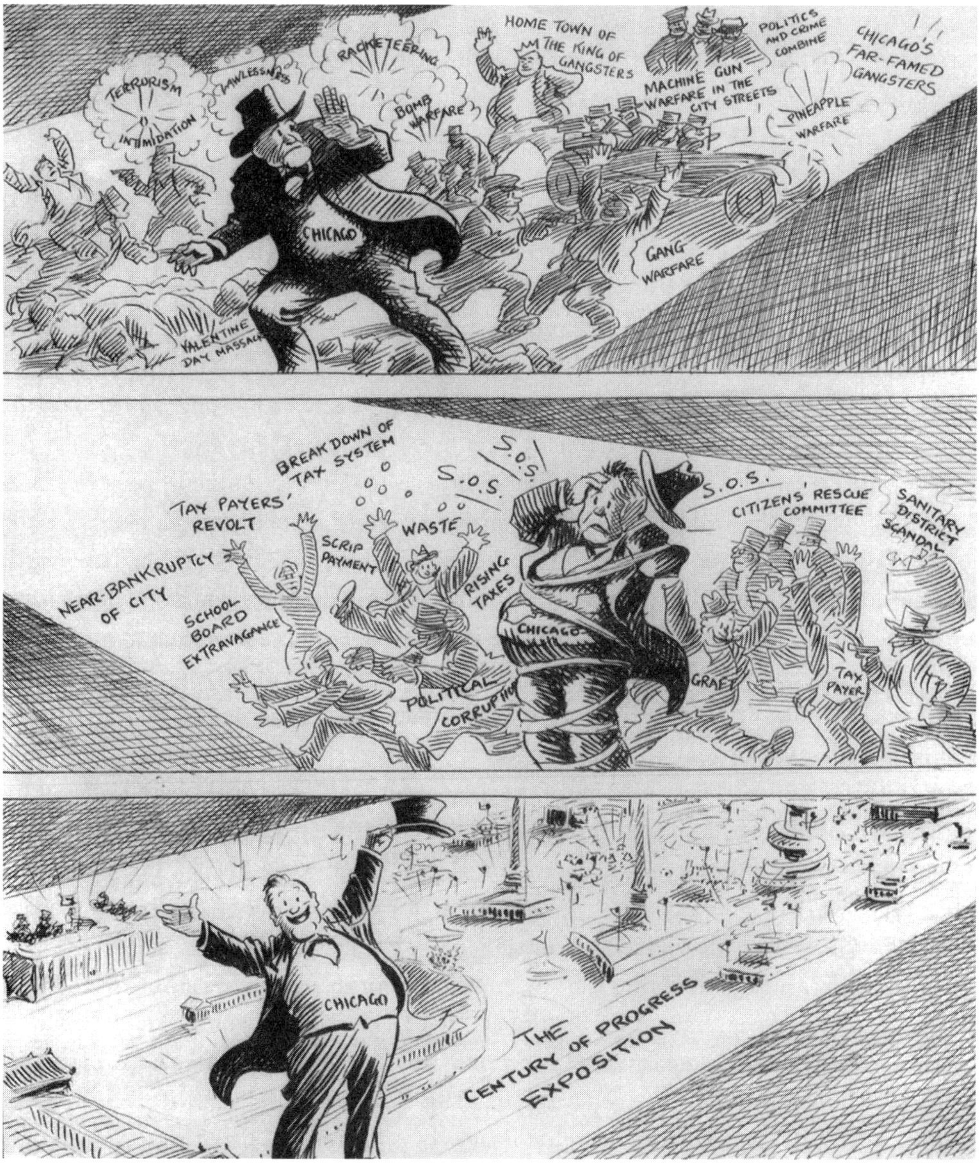

Figure 30. John T. McCutcheon's cartoon contrasts the assaults on Chicago's public image with the dream that A Century of Progress would bring the city positive press. ICHi-11692, Chicago History Museum.

center it had been since the late nineteenth century. Certainly, they hoped, the events would make the nation forget about the gangsters. Harriet Monroe, the famed Chicago poet, spoke directly to the fair planners' intent in an article in the *New Republic*, saying that the fair organizers hoped to "adorn Chicago's reputation with something more decorative than grafting politicians and murdering racketeers."[14] Working with the National Research Council, fair organizers came up with a scientific theme for their endeavor. The fair's title, "A Century of Progress," advertised the event's commitment to showcasing the most recent scientific technology. Among other exhibits, fairgoers could learn about television, air-conditioning, and cutting-edge home design at the architect George Fred Keck's House of Tomorrow.

Despite the hopes of Chicago's boosters, A Century of Progress left fair goers with mixed memories. For some, the fair's highbrow offerings beckoned, but others found longer-lasting connections with the exposition's lowbrow attractions. Despite the best intentions of those who conceptualized the scientific theme, the educational displays could not compete with overt, sexually oriented exhibits at the Century of Progress. The fair opened in 1933, the height of the Great Depression, and many attendees were hungry for diversion (figure 31). Fair organizers feigned distress at the immorality of the offerings of their concessionaires but fought back only weakly. The sexually charged exhibits certainly made money for the fair, a must in time of economic depression. Visitors could view fully or partially undressed women in "artist studios," live portrayals of famous works of art (mostly nudes), and a variety of sexual dancing acts. Sally Rand's fan dance at the 1933 fair became a legend.

Many connections exist between A Century of Progress and the National Barn Dance. WLS covered the fair, especially the aspects of broad appeal to a rural audience. The fair pulled into Chicago visitors who undoubtedly then attended the live NBD performances at the city's Eighth Street Theatre, home of the show after 1931. The fair also lured at least two future NBD stars to Chicago. National Barn Dance star Patsy Montana came to Chicago to see the Century of Progress and audition with WLS; because of the fair her legend was born. Pat Buttram, later a character on the television sitcom *Green Acres*, landed a place on WLS after he was "discovered" in an audience-participation event broadcast from the Century of Progress.[15] Jenny Lou Carson, an NBD favorite, performed at the fair.

A Century of Progress and the National Barn Dance offered another conception of Chicago to a nation of onlookers. Both competed with the images portrayed in that top level of McCutcheon's cartoon—the gangster and gang violence in Chicago. The lively, warm music of the NBD and even the naughty images of A Century of Progress were really no match for the materials related to Chicago's criminal underworld. The outpouring of these materials shaped the public's conception of place to such an extent that a single individual, Al Capone, is often the first to be named when people are asked to cite the major figures in Chicago's history. A brief list of popular depictions of Chicago's gangster life speaks to the popularity of the subject in its day; it includes Armitrage Trail's 1930 novel *Scarface*, the 1932 film *Scarface*, and Warner Brothers' 1931 film *Public Enemy*. Al Capone remained the name most strongly linked with Chicago history. Works such as the 1957 book *The Untouchables* and the 1959 television show of the same name perpetuated the dark side of Chicago history.

Figure 31. Technology of the air combined with that of the airwaves in a 1933 remote broadcast from a plane flying over Chicago. Left to right: Check Stafford, Red Foley, unknown, WLS engineer William T. (Andy) Anderson, Thomas Hoyt "Slim" Bryant (with hat in hand), Clayton McMichen, unknown, and WLS announcer Hal O'Halloran. Southern Music and Radio Photographic Collection, Southern Appalachian Archives, Berea College.

WHY NASHVILLE AND THE GRAND OLE OPRY?

It is puzzling that the National Barn Dance, the first national program featuring this rural-born sound, failed to establish Chicago as the premier city for the musical genre. Why did Nashville, whose own Grand Ole Opry began after the National Barn Dance, evolve into the premier setting for country music? The issue cannot be easily resolved. In his book *The Social Origins of the Urban South: Race, Gender, and Migration in Nashville and Middle Tennessee, 1890–1930*, Louis M. Kyriakoudes deftly paints a picture of Nashville as a regional center and shows that the establishment of the Opry was central to the city's rise as the urban cultural hub of its region. The Opry not only launched Nashville's reign in a cultural sense, but it also brought the South to the nation. As Kyriakoudes claims without a trace of hyperbole, "Few institutions in modern America so completely reflect the culture and sensibilities of the white rural South as the Opry." George D. Hay began the program in November 1925, just one month after the National Life and Accident Insurance Policy Company started radio station WSM in Nashville. Born in Attica, Indiana, and raised in Chicago, Hay came to the Opry by way of the National Barn Dance, where he had worked briefly. The Opry was an open recreation of the NBD's success on southern soil and was originally broadcast to a southern-only listening audience. Kyriakoudes refers to the NBD as "the first major radio review and the model for the WSM Barn Dance."[16] (The WSM Barn Dance was the original name of the Grand Ole Opry.)

Why did the Grand Ole Opry endure when the National Barn Dance did not? Part of the answer lies in the story of how the NBD receded from public view in the late 1950s. The audience for the NBD dwindled in these years, forcing it out of the television market where it had found a home briefly, then off the national radio airwaves, and finally off the air in Chicago. For WLS, rock music proved more profitable. Ultimately, the wholesome sound of the previous version of WLS appealed to a shrinking listenership. The change does not indicate a lack of cultural importance for the NBD or its musical type to the history of Chicago. Even blues, perhaps the musical product most linked with Chicago history, is featured in only scattered programming on the city's radio stations today. In 1960, ABC purchased WLS from *Prairie Farmer*, and quickly brought the station over to a new style. The reformatted WLS catered to the growing market for rock 'n' roll. Like most radio stations, WLS was now aimed at a younger demographic cohort, whereas *Prairie Farmer*'s WLS had offered programming for the entire family. With the popularity of television, most families no longer clustered around the radio on Saturday nights. The previous NBD listeners did not disappear, but their market dollars were not as sought after as those of the young crowd. Although WLS remained a powerful station (in the 1970s and 80s, it could be heard across the lake in Michigan), most radio listeners no longer sought out stations in faraway locales. WLS, begun as a way for Sears to reach out to its rural clientele of all ages, had metamorphosed into a popular urban radio channel aimed at teenagers and young adults.

The wholesome flavor of the previous style of WLS could not be sustained into the end of the century, despite the NBD's important history and strong connection with the city. In its final years, the National Barn Dance failed even to retain its cachet as midwesterners' favorite form of rural music; Wayne Daniel notes the watershed moment in which the Illinois State Fair hired performers from the Grand Ole Opry over NBD talent in 1959.[17]

The Grand Ole Opry itself was also not without its lean years. The Opry's music theme park, Opryland, opened in 1972 and closed in 1997. While Opryland had welcomed fifty-four million visitors over those years, its popularity lagged in the late twentieth century. Gaylord Entertainment, the developer, replaced Opryland and its tribute to country music with a shopping complex, the Opry Mills Mall.

Nashville's self-identity and national image rested more centrally in the Grand Ole Opry and country music than Chicago's ever did in the National Barn Dance. The NBD was just one musical type among many that found a home in Chicago; the city also hosted an electrified form of the blues, gospel, Irish ballads, the polka, and other musical forms. These other musical expressions also had limited radio access. As a listenership for the NBD tapered off, the city did not have a burning need to keep the form alive. If the NBD billed itself as "old-time" music in the 1930s, it could hardly claim to be au courant in the 1950s. As personal memories of this rural music faded in the midwestern countryside, listeners turned to other radio programs.

But like the third-generation Americans who now want to learn the languages spoken by their ancestors, a new generation of adults feels compelled to learn about the music of their grandparents. With the growth of the audience for new country music in the last few decades, our interest in the past of rural music has grown. More of us know how to appreciate this musical form. Now, we are ready for the Hayloft Gang and this particular history. We are witnessing a new flowering of historical interest in rural music.

CHICAGO AS A HOME OF THE BLUES

In many ways, Chicago's connection with the blues echoed the city's link with the music of the National Barn Dance. Like the NBD-style music, the blues was the product of a mixing of the cultures of southern-born migrants and native midwesterners. Chicago had been a city for less than one hundred years when the southern migrants arrived. The influence of those migrants proved strong. The migrants fostered the blossoming of the blues in Chicago in a relatively brief period. This musical style has become intertwined with the current conception of the city. This did not happen with the music of the National Barn Dance. It was in Chicago that Muddy Waters, Howlin' Wolf, Memphis Minnie, Big Maceo, and other big blues names found their sound. In Chicago a new type of blues was born.

A few key differences distinguish the migration of African American southerners from that of white southerners and may help to explain why popular memory has embraced

Chicago's blues heritage but not its rural, white musical forms. For one, African American migrants did not carry the "divided heart" historian Chad Berry speaks about in his book *Southern Migrants, Northern Exiles.* While black migrants held some dear memories of their southern homes, especially the positive aspects of rural life, deep racism and violence fueled their move northward. The North was far from the "promised land" some had hoped for, but black migrants were not in a hurry to resettle in the South. White migrants, however, often yearned to return home and carried a "divided heart" with them in their travels. For these sojourners, the South remained home. Berry explains that "shuttle migration" (movement between the regions) was typical for white migrants. Some African American migrants, on the other hand, vowed never to return to the South again.[18]

Assimilation into mainstream midwestern culture proved an option for the white southerners who remained settled in the North. For black southerners, assimilation was not usually possible, nor was migration within the city. Throughout the twentieth century, black Chicagoans remained highly clustered in south and west Chicago, the areas in which they first settled. This geographic clustering makes their history visible. When Chicagoans document their past, they pay attention to the history of black Chicago. The fact that the city's first nonnative resident, Jean Baptiste Point Du Sable, was the son of a Quebec merchant and a former slave from Santo Domingo, also reminds historians and social scientists about Chicago's African American history.[19] The southern whites who decided to remain in the region could settle into mainstream culture with greater anonymity.

In the 1930s and 40s, the National Barn Dance enjoyed great national success. By its later years, the NBD could not claim this kind of resonance in national culture; it became the music of older Americans and did not have the cutting-edge feel that the blues would hold for many. In the 1940s and 50s, with the beginnings of the Second Great Migration, the movement of southern blacks from the rural South to the urban North, hundreds of thousands of black migrants streamed into Chicago. The blues that had most likely been born in the Mississippi Delta were transformed in their new urban home; Chicago blues highlighted the electrification of the guitar, the addition of drums, and the use of larger ensembles, rather than the lone singer and acoustic guitar featured in southern forms. The Chicago blues also emphasized a faster rhythm, a pace that in effect resembled that of the noisy el trains shaking their way through the city.

THE NATIONAL BARN DANCE REMEMBERED

Chicago provided an inviting home to the National Barn Dance in its early years, but the city was not the appropriate base for country music in the latter part of the twentieth century. Nashville's nuturing of its homegrown musical form trumped Chicago's support for rural-based music. Nashville rightfully reigns as the modern urban center of country music. As Chicago aged, its citizens lost their conception of the city as a capital of the vast prairie. Although once home to the packing plants and the reaper factory, Chicago saw its rural-oriented businesses move on. Chicagoans proved more concerned with measuring their culture against that of New York and other eastern cities than with boasting of rural connections. Their conception of their city no longer contained overt connections with agriculture.[20] White southern migrants flocked to the city in the twentieth century, but they primarily assimilated or returned to their southern homes. The NBD, or even a modern descendant, most likely would not find a home in today's Chicago. This is not to say that there are not country music fans in the city, but the form does not find an organic home there. The city has hosted its own country music event, the Chicago Country Music Festival, for years, in conjunction with the famed Taste of Chicago eating festival. The musicians featured in 2007 included Kenny Rogers, Sara Evans, Craig Morgan, and Lisa Hewitt. The list of performers for this two-day event remains decidedly shorter than the lineups for the city's annual four-day jazz festival or its four-day blues fest.[21]

The line between blues and country is not always clear; if we acknowledge that the two forms have intertwined roots, many of them growing out of southern soil, it may be easier to reintroduce Chicagoans and those interested in Chicago's past to the city's historic role in country music. Chicago's importance in the history of the blues is now well accepted, although acceptance came only with time. Jazz, considered a "highbrow" and urban musical form, gained acceptability more quickly than did its country cousin, the blues. The blues of Chicago and other northern cities formed the basis for the rock 'n' roll sound of the black and, increasingly, white musicians of the mid-twentieth century. The strong connection of blues with rock 'n' roll led to a revival of interest in the musical form in the last decades of the twentieth century. And in the late twentieth century, the United States experienced a flowering of country music. Millions of listeners now buy the albums billed as country released by major music labels. As this musical interest grows, so too does the interest in the musical roots of the form. We review the more obvious characteristics in depth and then turn to the more obscure stories. As we draw out these stories and then tell them to each other, our memories are reworked. The National Barn Dance emerges as a significant part of Chicago's past; it may become part of our national conception of Chicago as a place, as it should, and perhaps even of Chicagoans' sense of their own urban history.

NOTES

1. See Douglas Gomery, "WLS Barn Dance," in *Encyclopedia of Chicago*, ed. James R. Grossman, Ann Durkin Keating, and Janice L. Reiff (Chicago: University of Chicago Press, 2004), 883.

2. Donald L. Miller, *City of the Century* (New York: Simon and Schuster, 1996), 103–4.

3. George A. Larson and Jay Pridmore, *Chicago Architecture and Design* (New York: Abrams, 1993), 87.

4. See *The History of WLS Radio*, www.wlshistory.com (accessed November 2, 2007).

5. Susan Sessions Rugh, "Prairie Farmer" and "Biographical Dictionary," in Grossman, Keating, and Reiff, *Encyclopedia of Chicago*, 645, 960.

6. *WLS Family Album, 1932*, www.richsamuels.com (accessed November 2, 2007).

7. James N. Gregory, *The Southern Diaspora: How the Great Migrations of Black and White Southerners Transformed America* (Chapel Hill: University of North Carolina Press, 2005), 81–108.

8. Religious differences remained between those descended from white southern migrants and other white midwesterners, but they would not necessarily have been tied overtly to southern ancestry.

9. See David Hackett Fischer, *Albion's Seed: Four British Folkways in America* (New York: Oxford University Press, 1989), 757–58.

10. See WLS resources at www.richsamuels.com (accessed November 2, 2007).

11. For more on this subject, see Susan Smulyan, "Early Broadcasting and Radio Audiences," in this volume.

12. *WLS Family Albums* and *Stand By!* the fan periodical, from the personal collections of Steven Parry, Hayloft Gang producer, director (the Kelly quote is from *Stand By!*). Also see "National Barn Dance" at www.wlshistory.org (accessed November 2, 2007).

13. Robert Isham Randolph, quoted in Forrest Crissey, "Business Fights Crime in Chicago," *Saturday Evening Post*, August 16, 1930, 12. See also Lisa Krissoff Boehm, *Popular Culture and the Enduring Myth of Chicago, 1871–1968* (New York: Routledge, 2004).

14. Harriet Monroe, "Defending the World's Fair," *New Republic*, July 19, 1933, 265.

15. *WLS Family Album, 1941*, and curator's note, collection available online at www.richsamuels.com (accessed November 2, 2007).

16. Louis M. Kyriakoudes, *The Social Origins of the Urban South: Race, Gender, and Migration in Nashville and Middle Tennessee, 1890–1930* (Chapel Hill: University of North Carolina Press, 2003), 7, 14. See also Louis M. Kyriakoudes, "The Grand Ole Opry and the Urban South," *Southern Cultures* 10.1 (Spring 2004): 67–84.

17. See Wayne W. Daniel, "Music of the Postwar Era," in this volume.

18. See Chad Berry, *Southern Migrants, Northern Exiles* (Urbana: University of Illinois Press, 2000), and Mike Rowe, *Chicago Blues: The City and the Music* (New York: Da Capo, 1975).

19. See Richard Lindberg, *Ethnic Chicago: A Complete Guide to the Many Faces and Cultures of Chicago* (Chicago: Passport Books, 1994). While claiming to be complete, this book has no chapter on southern migration to Chicago.

20. A personal memory may prove informative. When I was growing up in the urban upper Midwest of the 1970s, square dancing was a common pastime. We danced in gym class for exercise and in the evening for special events. Few youngsters in the urban Midwest would partake in such a pastime today.

21. See "Mayor's Office of Special Events," www.CityofChicago.org (accessed December 4, 2007).

4 EARLY BROADCASTING AND RADIO AUDIENCES

Susan Smulyan

Lulu Belle and Scotty, two popular singers on the National Barn Dance, introduced a collection of their music by acknowledging their radio roots: "We gratefully dedicate this collection of our songs to our many Friends of the Airways, to the loyal listeners of WLS, and to Radio Station WLS itself, all of whom have made this book possible."[1]

The dedication reminds us that the National Barn Dance was first and foremost a wildly popular radio program whose history and strategies explain a lot about the development of American broadcasting. The radio history of the National Barn Dance helps explain the program's success.

The National Barn Dance may have been even more important to radio history than it was to the development of country music; its history provides a glimpse of early broadcasting and how radio changed over time. More abstractly, the National Barn Dance catapults us into an interesting discussion among historians of radio. Was radio a nationalizing influence, building a homogenized American community through a networked and commercialized system, or was the system more fragmented, with individual stations and groups of listeners having power over what was heard on the airwaves? The evidence from the National Barn Dance sometimes supports one side of the argument, and sometimes the other, and helps historians understand the competing roles of the national, regional, and local in broadcasting and U.S. history.

The National Barn Dance, at each step in its development, illustrated how radio grew. One of the first radio stations in the country, WLS began broadcasting on April 12, 1924. Sears, Roebuck started the station, as a public service, under the direction of its nonprofit Agricultural Foundation. Like many different institutions, Sears began broadcasting uncertain where radio was going but eager to dive into the new technology. Many stores, big and small, started radio stations to get publicity but didn't foresee direct advertising as either a source of income or a way to reach customers with product information. In the early 1920s, if you wanted to send your message over the radio, you founded a radio station and traded programming (mostly by amateurs) for the goodwill of listeners. In his history of the *Prairie Farmer* newspaper (which later owned WLS), James Evans wrote, "Widespread talk about the potential value of radio for farm people led Sears to house the new station in its Agricultural Foundation and devote most programming to agriculture."[2]

From the beginning, farmers and radio seemed made for each other. The radio press enthused often about how useful radio could be to farm listeners. A 1926 *Radio Age* article noted, "Radio recognizes no snow blockades, is not averse to penetrating the lowly log cabin, is immune to the blasts of winter, is unafraid of darkness, and robs isolation of its terrors. Truly, radio brings the countryside nearer to the city and will answer in truth and reality the words of the popular song, 'How Are You Going to Keep Them Down on the Farm?'"[3] Farmers found economic as well as social benefits from radio. Stories abounded about farm families able to compete more successfully against city slickers because radio brought prices and weather forecasts into their homes.[4]

WLS provided weather forecasts, market information, and agricultural education to farmers with some programs the station generated and others sent from the United States Department of Agriculture. Chicago proved a great venue, with the radio station able to reach a large audience of midwestern farmers. The first radio listeners wanted to hear faraway stations, finding the search for distant places part of the fun of radio. In the case of farmers, the urban stations brought important information only available in the city and so gave an added impetus to the search for stations. Just as important, farm families now had access to urban performers and the professional entertainment they provided.

Chicago quickly became an important broadcasting center. At least one of the other stations provided programming very different from that of WLS. The first station in town, owned by Westinghouse (founder of Pittsburgh's KDKA), broadcast the Chicago Opera Company to great acclaim by all kinds of listeners. Later, Chicago became an important source of radio serials—dramatic, comic, and soap opera—to the national networks.[5] The National Barn Dance grew within a diverse and experimental broadcasting scene with an audience of both urban and rural listeners eager to hear what the new technology could bring into their homes.

The NBD began within two weeks of WLS's going on the air and continued throughout the station's changes in ownership, programming, and economic structure. In the late 1920s, many of the first radio stations went out of business or were sold as listeners demanded better, and more expensive, programming, and merchants decided that broadcasting called for a different set of skills than running a store. Local and regional newspapers stepped in and added radio stations to their operations as an extension of their advertising, news gathering, and entertainment operations. In addition, the news services (such as the Associated Press) gave newspapers familiarity with combining local and national content, just as national radio networks began with a similar model.

The biggest change in broadcasting between the founding of WLS and its sale to the regional newspaper was that WLS could now pay for itself. The *Prairie Farmer* planned to finance the purchase price from station revenues, unlike Sears, which had envisioned the radio station as a publicity and service organization.[6] By 1928, both NBC and CBS were beginning to plan programs, and selling advertising time on the airwaves, not considered earlier, became more of a reality. Properly run radio stations generated profits, in addition to providing community service and goodwill for their owners.

The new owners of WLS wanted to continue broadcasting the National Barn Dance, both because of its popularity and because it fit their mission of providing information and entertainment to farmers. Even when the Federal Radio Commission forced WLS to share a frequency with another station—a common practice in early radio—WLS insisted on keeping the Saturday evening slot for the National Barn Dance.[7] Programming remained a problem, with most early stations finding it difficult to fill available air time. National Barn Dance stars, looking for full-time jobs, also began performing on the morning and noon shows. As George Biggar noted, "there was no way to hold the better acts and individuals except by paying them a living weekly wage and using them on more programs."[8] Radio networks grew, at least in part, to provide high-quality programming, mostly sent from New York, to local stations that lacked access to professional performers or the money to pay them.

Within a short time, the National Barn Dance also became part of the new network system. WLS first carried network programs in exchange for sharing time with an NBC-owned station on the same frequency. Less than a year later, WLS became unusual when it contributed the National Barn Dance to network programming, first as a half-hour unsponsored program and then, in 1933, as an hour program sponsored by Alka-Seltzer. Most stations accepted network programs and maintained some local programming, with the network programming originating primarily in New York. The Barn Dance became an anomaly, one hour on the network from Chicago and the rest broadcast locally over WLS, at least until the Alka-Seltzer sponsorship ended in 1946.[9] The program often placed among the top ten in network radio polls, attesting to its popularity.[10] And the bifurcated nature of the National Barn Dance, as both a national and a local program at the same time, illustrated the tightrope that radio walked throughout its early history.

The performers on the Barn Dance shared backgrounds with other radio stars. Early radio called on amateur performers, then on professional recording artists, and finally on professional minstrel show performers and vaudevillians, who were looking for work in the 1920s as their genres faded. The Barn Dance first featured amateurs who quickly became professional musicians; then recording artists who had been working with the early southern recording studios and knew how to sing into microphones; and finally minstrels and vaudevillians who brought with them a knowledge of specialized acts, presented in a variety format.[11] Because early recording artists were accustomed to pushing the song, not themselves, they worked well on radio where they often performed under different names in order to change their acts or to advertise a variety of products. The Happiness Boys, popular on 1920s radio as performers for a candy company, were also heard as the Tastyeast Jesters and the Interwoven Pair (for Interwoven Socks). Linda Parker appeared as the Sunbonnet Girl on the National Barn Dance but under a range of different names for other WLS shows.[12] As radio became more popular, and advertising succeeded in making it more profitable, performers sang under their own names and became the reason people turned on the radio. Using their own names, and depending on their celebrity, vaudeville stars such as Eddie Cantor, Burns and Allen, and Jack Benny discovered new fame and fortune on network radio as vaudeville was dying. On the National Barn Dance, Grace Wilson (figure 32), "a faded vaudevillian . . . found new life . . . singing the golden oldies of the turn of the century. She parlayed nostalgia for these numbers into the longest career of any Barn Dance performer."[13]

Just like other radio programs in the early 1930s, the National Barn Dance constructed its program on a vaudeville model. The National Barn Dance took from vaudeville the idea of using star performers to attract an audience. The stars joined an array of specialty acts, and each performed short "sets" designed to stave off listener boredom and to work against static and interference.[14] Listeners fiddling with dials to bring in the Chicago station might miss one act but would be sure to catch the next, and static would not obliterate any important narrative cues. The audience could keep track of the well-defined performers even if they couldn't hear part of their song due to interference or problems in tuning.

The success of the National Barn Dance might be traced to its ability to build up stars, especially women, each with a definite personality and talent. As Kristine McCusker notes, Linda Parker's early and brief career presented a wonderful case study of how National Barn Dance producers constructed and promoted a traditional persona for the singer. Parker's early death saddened listeners who had come to love her music and personality.[15]

Like many other radio stars, the National Barn Dance singers and comedians often performed in front of live audiences, both during the radio program and on promotional tours. Early radio performers sometimes dressed in costumes for their personal appearances and even for their live broadcasts, despite the lack of in-studio audiences. On the National Barn Dance, the costumes added authenticity. The *New York Times* explained that the Coon Creek Girls got help to make "up their high-necked gingham dresses—simple patterns of

Figure 32. Grace Wilson successfully negotiated the transition between vaudeville and the radio era. Courtesy of Don Gill.

tiny flowers with one or two horizontal bands of rickrack braid" and added that "white stockings are another item in Coon Creek's wardrobe of glad rags for barn dances and vaudeville and county fair appearances."[16] Eddie Cantor, coming from vaudeville, began the tradition of having a studio audience for his radio program both so that listeners could tell the show was performed live and in order to have an audience with whom the performers (used to the vaudeville stage) could interact. The live performances of the National Barn Dance became attractions in themselves, and the performers traveled extensively to promote the show, meet the audience, and earn extra money.[17]

The large live audiences reassured early broadcasters, who worried constantly about whether anyone was listening. Transmitters and receivers proved unreliable, and broadcasters found listeners fickle, liable to be so offended by commercials that they turned off their radios for good. Listener letters helped assuage the worries. Broadcasters urged people to send letters and cards, at first to see the strength and coverage of the signal, and then to prove there were eager listeners for advertisements. Radio shows got a lot of mail. The first listeners got into the habit of writing radio stations to report signal strength and passed the custom along to new listeners as programming came to depend on commercials. Sponsors wanted to know who was listening and, before ratings, audience mail proved that radio time was worth buying.[18] When President Franklin Roosevelt used the radio to communicate with the country, in his Fireside Chats, listener letters poured in as citizens told the president they were listening and expressed their hopes and fears.[19]

The National Barn Dance generated audience mail (figure 33) and built listener loyalty by creating individual stars; by sending performers across the Midwest to meet listeners in person; by turning the radio broadcast into a very popular show that listeners could attend; and by moving the National Barn Dance into a range of media, including sheet music, recordings, film, and eventually television. But letters remained important. Kristine McCusker

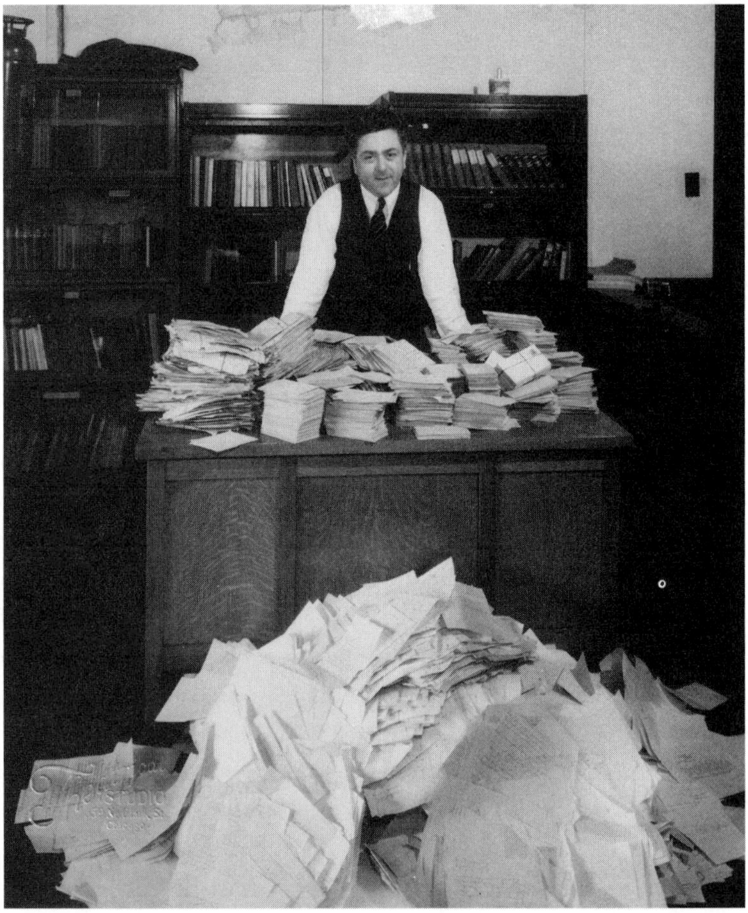

Figure 33. John Lair looks proudly into the camera, grateful to have voluminous fan mail from WLS listeners. John Lair Collection, Southern Appalachian Archives, Berea College.

has written with great insight about the letters sent to National Barn Dance performers, particularly Bradley Kincaid and John Lair. McCusker used the letters to explore how the audience incorporated the new entertainment media of radio into their everyday lives. Listeners turned the performers into friends, McCusker showed, and in the process managed "radio's place in their homes."[20]

Historians have the same problem as early broadcasters in figuring out who was listening and why. The National Barn Dance presents a wonderful conundrum. Several historians, myself included, believe that the popularity of the National Barn Dance stemmed in part from its appeal to hidden or ignored audiences. The National Barn Dance worked hard to address the white middle class that broadcasters had early identified as their target. The interpolated advertisements and the use of stars to sell themselves as products provided a commodified (and soon familiar) approach to middle-class listeners. In addition, the program's emphasis on family, with the performers presented as surrogate members of the listeners' families (as shown in the listener letters), added to the middle-class tone of the National Barn Dance.

Network programmers had a clear idea of their audience and ignored large groups who didn't fit their image of middle-class consumers. In his book *Fireside Politics: Radio and Political Culture in the United States*, Douglas Craig explained how national radio left out women, farmers, and African Americans (exactly the three groups of listeners sought by the Barn Dance) because they supposedly lacked purchasing power. Craig wrote that, despite "promises of a more inclusive community united and educated by radio," broadcasters viewed listeners "through an economic prism, which valued audiences only in terms of their attractiveness to advertisers."[21] Radio treated the three groups differently, and so did the National Barn Dance. Radio had been a male preserve but, with the beginnings of national radio and a commodified audience, networks saw a need to include women in the audience. Despite the early claims about how radio would change rural life, national networks ignored farmers. And radio worked hard to construct a white audience, keeping African American performers off the airwaves and allowing jazz only when played by white performers.

One way to account for the success of the National Barn Dance is to understand that not much broadcast on the national airwaves aimed at rural folks. Derek Vaillant notes that radio began just as the pace of urbanization picked up. Vaillant writes that "histories of early radio have underreported the extent to which tensions between rural and urban ways of life structured dynamics and listener reactions to early radio."[22] Vaillant's depiction of Wisconsin's WHA shows that regional stations that programmed to farmers (like WHA and WLS) filled in the gaps left by the national networks' urban focus. Both stations, WLS and WHA, operated on the belief that farm families, as well as urban dwellers, had money to spend and thought of themselves as middle class.

During the late 1920s, American broadcasting worked to attract women listeners. The addition of women to entertainment audiences helped give a new entertainment medium a middle-class aura of respectability. Both vaudeville and movies cleaned up theaters, for example, to ensure that middle-class women felt comfortable. On radio, at first considered a male preserve because of the technical skill supposedly needed to operate the receiving set, new programs and new structures (such as daytime broadcasting) soon made women part of the audience.[23] The National Barn Dance's focus on female singers signaled its intent to appeal to women listeners. The women performers on the National Barn Dance can be seen both as part of radio's vision of itself as an entertainment form with a mixed audience, and as a means of increasing the number of listeners.

Finally, as I've argued elsewhere, the music heard on the National Barn Dance, tied as it was to both the white and black southern traditions, may have been familiar to a host of African Americans who had moved from the rural South to northern and southern cities. Almost no African American music, not even blues or jazz, was heard over the early radio waves, with only two exceptions. Some early radio stations, including those in Chicago, broadcast from hotels and clubs to save money on performers. As stations began to be profitable, these "remote pick-ups" were dropped because of their unpredictability, and thus African American performers disappeared from radio. Derek Vaillant has written brilliantly on the ways in which Chicago's ethnic immigrants used radio to claim whiteness, in part by ensuring that radio banished black performers and African American music.[24] Some jazz, performed by white musicians, crept onto the airwaves, but the southern music of the barn dance programs may have been the closest to the black vernacular available on the radio.

Other scholars have argued that the National Barn Dance excluded black audiences or at least constructed and reinforced the whiteness of its listeners. I'm saying something a little different. The Barn Dance simultaneously upheld early broadcasting's commercial imperative to program for those with buying power—urban, white, middle-class men—and pushed against those narrow limits without alienating either its audience or sponsors. The National Barn Dance maintained broadcasting as a racialized and gendered middle-class preserve, while also broadening its appeal. Audiences excluded from usual network radio programming (women, farmers, African Americans) understood the National Barn Dance as a place where they might hear something of interest while still not holding full radio "citizenship," in Craig's phrase. By making only the slightest of efforts, the National Barn Dance may have taught otherwise excluded listeners how to hear radio as a medium that, at least marginally, included them. The program's popularity can be explained by the way it maintained a middle-class white and male audience while also attracting farmers, women, and African Americans, all of whom had been overlooked by national networks, and even by urban local broadcasters.

The National Barn Dance also appealed to both national and regional audiences, an unusual juggling act. Historians have traditionally looked at radio, especially in its golden age with the rise of the network system, as a national medium. Early radio historians, myself included, talked about how national radio networks allowed the country to think of itself as connected. Michele Hilmes, in *Radio Voices: American Broadcasting, 1922–1952*, went further in calling radio "the nation's voice" and described how radio helped create what the anthropologist Benedict Anderson termed an "imagined community" for the United States. Susan Douglas, in her book *Listening In: Radio in the American Imagination*, made a similar point.[25] Recently, scholars have challenged the view of radio as primarily a national and nationalizing phenomenon, with the networks acting as important constructers of American identity. Even the titles of the books tell us that we have entered a different paradigm, as Clifford Doerksen calls his history of this period *American Babel: Rogue Radio Broadcasters of the Jazz Age* and Jason Loviglio writes *Radio's Intimate Public*.[26] Young historians at two international conferences on the emerging field of "radio studies" have made the case that local and regional radio flourished even at the height of network power.[27]

The National Barn Dance holds a unique position in the argument over whether radio was a hegemonic "voice" imposed on an unruly nation or a babble with many individuals and broadcasters remaking the medium in their own image. "National" in name and carried over a major network, the Barn Dance presented a rural voice to the whole country, reminding urban and rural listeners alike that farmers still existed and were an important part of the national imaginary. Yet, perhaps we can most usefully see the National Barn Dance as an expression of a way of life, a hybrid of southern, midwestern, nostalgic, and rural cultures that opposed a national imaginary which, by the late 1920s, thought of the United States as urban. Scholars can use the National Barn Dance to prove both positions, as radio remained simultaneously a national, a regional, and a local medium.

In May 1963, *Newsweek* explained the varying audiences for, and appeals of, the National Barn Dance in an article titled "And That is Hay":

> Probably the closest that radio will ever get to authentic Americana is the National Barn Dance, an unvarnished though slightly sandpapered group of backwoods talent crowded each week into a Chicago theater for a Saturday night party. So close has the 9 to 9:30 EWT broadcast grown to the hearts of its 10,000,000 NBC listeners that any attempt by the sponsor to slick up its style immediately brings an avalanche of protest. This week's performance, its 500th on a national hookup, follows virtually the same pattern as the first show on April 24, 1924.[28]

Despite *Newsweek's* contention that it had stayed the same, the National Barn Dance changed as radio changed. What remained constant was the program's ability to juggle appeals to the middle class, women, farmers, and African Americans, as well as to national, regional, and local audiences. Such successful juggling made the National Barn Dance a perennial favorite.

NOTES

I would like to thank Aslihan Tokgoz for her research help.

1. Lulu Belle and Scotty, *Lulu Belle's and Skyland Scotty's Home Folk Songs* (S. Wiseman), 1937, Harris Collection of American Poetry and Plays, John Hay Library, Brown University.

2. James Evans, *Prairie Farmer and WLS: The Burridge D. Butler Years* (Urbana: University of Illinois Press, 1969), 106.

3. S. R. Winters, "Radio on the Farm" *Radio Age* 5 (May 1926): 14.

4. Robert H. Moulton, "Linking the Farmer with His Market," *Radio Broadcast*, July 1924, 261–65; for a slightly later review of farmers and radio, see Edmund de Schweinitz Brunner, *Radio and the Farmer* (New York: Radio Institute of the Audible Arts, 1935); Mary Neth, *Preserving the Family Farm: Women, Community, and the Foundations of Agribusiness in the Midwest, 1900–1940* (Baltimore: Johns Hopkins University Press, 1995); and Ronald Kline, *Consumers in the Country: Technology and Social Change in Rural America* (Baltimore: Johns Hopkins University Press, 2000).

5. George P. Stone, "Radio Has Gripped Chicago," *Radio Broadcast*, October 1922, 503–11; Larry Wolters, "Report from the Loop," *New York Times*, February 7, 1943, X9, as found in ProQuest Historical Newspapers, *New York Times* (1851–2001), www.umi.com/proquest (accessed December 17, 2007). For other accounts of Chicago radio see Derek W. Vaillant, "Sounds of Whiteness: Local Radio, Racial Formation, and Public Culture in Chicago, 1921–1935," *American Quarterly* 54 (2002): 25–65; and Nathan Godfried, *WCFL, Chicago's Voice of Labor, 1926–78* (Urbana: University of Illinois Press, 1997).

6. Evans, *Prairie Farmer*, 174.

7. Ibid., 182.

8. George Biggar, "The WLS National Barn Dance Story," *JEMF Quarterly* 7 (August 1971): 109; see also Richard Stockdell, "The Evolution of the Country Radio Format," *Journal of Popular Culture* 16 (Spring 1983): 145.

9. Evans, *Prairie Farmer*, 183, 224; Biggar, "WLS National Barn Dance Story," 111.

10. For two exemplary mentions of the ratings, see "News and Gossip of the Studios," *New York Times*, October 3, 1937, 180; "News Acts Flash down the Wave Lengths," ibid., September 11, 1938, 194, both as found in ProQuest Historical Newspapers, *New York Times* (1851–2001), www.umi.com/proquest (accessed December 17, 2007).

11. On recording artists, see Timothy Patterson, "Hillbilly Music among the Flatlanders," *Journal of Country Music* 6 (Spring 1975): 12–18. On minstrels, see an obituary that mentions performances in minstrel shows and on the National Barn Dance, "Joseph M. Parsons," *New York Times*, December 24, 1947, 21, as found in ProQuest Historical Newspapers, *New York Times* (1851–2001), www.umi.com/proquest (accessed December 17, 2007); on use of microphones, see Richard A. Peterson, *Creating Country Music: Fabricating Authenticity* (Chicago: University of Chicago Press, 1997), 106.

12. Peterson, *Creating Country Music*, 112.

13. Mary A. Bufwack and Robert K. Oermann, *Finding Her Voice: Women in Country Music, 1800–2000* (Nashville: Vanderbilt University Press, 2003), 69.

14. For a listing and analysis of National Barn Dance content, see Wayne W. Daniel, "The National Barn Dance on Network Radio—The 1930s," *Journal of Country Music* 9 (1983): 47–62.

15. Kristine M. McCusker, "'Bury Me beneath the Willow': Linda Parker and Definitions of Tradition on the National Barn Dance, 1932–1935," in *A Boy Named Sue: Gender and Country Music*, ed. Kristine M. McCusker and Diane Pecknold (Jackson: University Press of Mississippi, 2004), 3–23; for analysis of other National Barn Dance performers, see Bufwack and Oermann, *Finding Her Voice*, 63–91.

16. Robert Allen, "Coon Creek Girls from the Kentucky Hills," *New York Times*, June 4, 1939, X6; found in ProQuest Historical Newspapers, *New York Times* (1851–2001), www.umi.com/proquest (accessed December 17, 2007).

17. Evans, *Prairie Farmer*, 222–24.

18. For a dazzling review of listener mail to radio stations and performers, see Elena Razlagova, "The Voice of the Listener: Americans and the Radio Industry, 1920–1945" (Ph.D. diss., George Mason University, 2004).

19. See the discussion in Douglas B. Craig, *Fireside Politics: Radio and Political Culture in the United States, 1920–1940* (Baltimore: Johns Hopkins University Press, 2000); Jason Loviglio, *Radio's Intimate Public: Network Broadcasting and Mass-mediated Democracy* (Minneapolis: University of Minnesota Press, 2005).

20. Kristine M. McCusker, "'Dear Radio Friend': Listener Mail and the National Barn Dance, 1931–1941," *American Studies* 39 (Summer 1998): 192; for letters from other rural listeners see Derek Vaillant, "'Your Voice Came in Last Night . . . But I Thought . . . It Sounded a Little Scared': Rural Radio Listening and 'Talking Back' during the Progressive Era in Wisconsin, 1920–1932," in *Radio Reader: Essays in the Cultural History of Radio*, ed. Michele Hilmes and Jason Loviglio (New York: Routledge, 2002): 63–88.

21. Craig, *Fireside Politics*, 257.

22. Vaillant, "'Your Voice Came in Last Night,'" 66.

23. On radio as male, see Susan Douglas, *Inventing American Broadcasting, 1899–1922* (Baltimore: Johns Hopkins University Press, 1987); on constructing a female audience, see Richard Butsch, "Crystal Sets and Scarf-pin Radios: Gender, Technology, and the Construction of American Radio," *Media, Culture and Society* 20 (October 1998): 557–72; and Susan Smulyan, "Radio Advertising to American Women in the 1920s: A Latchkey to Every Home," *Historical Journal of Film, Radio, and Television* 13 (1993): 299–314.

24. See Vaillant, "Sounds of Whiteness."

25. See Michele Hilmes, *Radio Voices: American Broadcasting, 1922–1952* (Minneapolis: University of Minnesota Press, 1997); Susan J. Douglas, *Listening In: Radio and the American Imagination* (New York: Times Books, 1999).

26. See Clifford J. Doerksen, *American Babel: Rogue Radio Broadcasters of the Jazz Age* (Philadelphia: University of Pennsylvania Press, 2005); Loviglio, *Radio's Intimate Public.*

27. See "The Radio Conference: A Transnational Forum," July 2003, Madison, Wisconsin, http://commarts.wisc.edu/radioconference/; and "The Radio Conference," July 2005, Melbourne, Australia, *Radio in the World: Radio Conference 2005*, online juried proceedings, RMIT Publishing, December 23, 2005, http://search.informit.com.au/documentSummary;dn=039259077654193;res=E-LIBRARY (accessed January 2, 2005).

28. "And That Is Hay," *Newsweek*, May 3, 1963, 64, 66.

5 RACE AND RURAL IDENTITY

Michael T. Bertrand

In fall 1938, *Rural Radio*, a monthly fan magazine published in Nashville, Tennessee, posed a question to its readers: "Do rural audiences demand a different kind of radio show than urban ones?" Like most who took the time to write, a Michigan correspondent answered in the affirmative. Evoking Jeffersonian imagery and the ideology of a rapidly vanishing era identified more with agri*culture* than with agri*business*, he emphasized that the farmer "lives simply and works close to nature." While rural and city folk might have appreciated some of the same programs and performers, he suspected that their respective environments produced differences in taste that were difficult to reconcile. "The farmer's time to enjoy radio is limited. So when they do listen to it, they want entertainment and information that can be quickly absorbed, and music that will bolster their spirits, such as western songs and yodels, and good old home folk tunes that live so near to their hearts." Most important, the letter writer pronounced, "Farmers want to hear the features and folks that are most nearly like themselves."[1]

This raises an interesting question: *Why* did farm folks want to hear radio personalities and people who were most nearly like themselves? For those who have habitually tuned in to the electronic medium, an explanation may seem unnecessary. Further scrutiny, however, promises to reveal much, not only about listening habits, but also about the multifarious ways consumers "use" popular culture. In her analysis of early national radio programming, for instance, Michele Hilmes aptly concluded that popular culture as manifested through the airwaves has the power to assure us of "who we are and who we are not." For historians, many of whom have generally ignored or marginalized commercial or popular entertainment, Hilmes's assessment might seem a bit strong. Yet if, as she suggests, popular culture resides more at the center of individual consciousness than on an exiled periphery, this compels us to take seriously the opening statement of the WLS Creed written by Burridge Butler: "To me radio is far more than a mere medium of entertainment." Indeed, rural radio listeners arguably were engaged in something more than frolicsome recreation when they "cut loose with an old-fashioned hoedown" or "set their feet a-tapping and their hands clapping in time with the music." They were constructing, or perhaps reiterating, a particular identity through their choice of radio programs. They were, so to speak, making a statement as to who they were and who they were not.[2]

The WLS National Barn Dance provides us with an opportunity to explore how this process of self-definition through popular culture worked. WLS, one of approximately seventy radio stations to emerge in Chicago during the 1920s, hit the airwaves in April 1924 with a fairly inclusive agenda: "Every distinctive American type of music has a part in WLS programs. Mountain Ballads, Cowboy Songs, Barn Dance Tunes, Negro Spirituals, Plantation Songs, Work Songs, Indian Chants and American popular music."[3] One week following its debut, the station inaugurated its version of the radio barn dance. In doing so, WLS, although never completely abandoning its original wide-ranging musical outlook, had carved out a niche, one that would attract rural listeners. The station's ensuing emphasis on the timelessness and racial exclusivity of the midwestern agricultural experience would prove especially appealing to a specialized audience and market.

Understanding who WLS consistently targeted as a listening audience would help historians to identify who listened. As a "farm" station set in a major northern metropolitan area, however, WLS has posed special problems pertaining to audience identification. Unfortunately, until recently there has been little scholarly interest in the station, the composition of its audience, or its larger social and historical impact. A major exception has been country music studies. Given the rural nature of much of WLS programming, this is not surprising. The work of country music historians has certainly shed much light on WLS and radio culture in the years before World War II. In many ways, however, this scholarship has been problematic.

In emphasizing the art form's southern origins, conventional interpretations of country music have struggled to account for the major contributions WLS, the National Barn Dance, and Chicago made to country music's early development and dissemination. A common explanation is that Chicago served as the destination for a large influx of southern migrants, displaced dixiecrats who eventually became the core audience for country music programming in the Windy City. Yet the folklorist D. K. Wilgus has argued that the success of WLS and the barn dance cannot "be explained solely by the presence of southern migrants." Further examination likewise might discover that urban dwellers played less of a role than rural residents in the program's evolution. On the surface, this may seem like a needless and redundant distinction. Nonetheless, it is an important one. The station seems to have played primarily to farm families attached to the land, not uprooted ruralites reminiscing about the land they had abandoned (although such listeners obviously tuned in). "It was but natural that we booked in old-time music on Saturday night," program director George Biggar explained. "We leaned toward the homey, old-time and familiar tunes, as we were primarily a farm station." Despite being located in the nation's second largest city, then, WLS was a "farm station," and as Wilgus maintained, its "essence was of rural America"—and, he might have added, a rural America under siege. "We have given city folk a different picture of the people they call 'hicks,'" one so-called provincial declared in defending the agenda of barn dance radio. "We have shown them that country people get more out of life, are more content and generally live a more wholesome life."[4]

Perhaps. Yet the 1920s (and later, the 1930s) represented a tough time for American farmers. Although agriculture had enjoyed a boom during World War I when demand outraced supply and commodity prices accordingly skyrocketed, the years after the armistice witnessed an economic downturn for those who worked the land. By 1925, due to crop overproduction, farmers watched in dismay as the prices of their goods plummeted while their farm mortgage payments did not. Such circumstances only anticipated the larger general depression that would envelop them in the 1930s. Full recovery for the agricultural sector would not occur until 1939. For many, however, it would be too little, too late. In 1920, there were 31,614,269 people living on 6,448,343 farms across the country (1920 also marked the first time in the nation's history that a majority of Americans were city dwellers—51 percent; farmers constituted 30 percent of the whole population). By 1940, those numbers had dropped significantly. Twenty-three percent of the nation's population stayed steadfastly tied to the soil (with the country remaining 44 percent "country" or rural) during the twenty-year span, while more than 350,000 farms simply disappeared. Statistics, however, could never fully capture the instability and uncertainty that plagued many farmers and rural inhabitants in the years between World War I and World War II.[5]

To add insult to injury, farmers and rural residents found themselves in a cultural minority, a bumper crop of perceived hayseeds and yokels satirized by reporters and authors seeking to measure and trumpet their own sophistication. Indeed, the fifty million "unenlightened" Americans who lived in what F. Scott Fitzgerald labeled "that vast obscurity beyond the city" anxiously gazed over the distant horizon only to see hordes of literati and industrial, commercial, and urban forces in a stampede to stamp out the agrarian way of life.[6] Tradition, it seemed, stood embroiled in a life-and-death struggle with modernity. Cultural conflict certainly permeated the air, materializing seemingly everywhere. In the 1920s alone, it took the form of the Eighteenth Amendment, which codified Prohibition, as well as the open and clandestine criminal defiance that the law inspired. Or it made headlines in a "Monkey Trial," where religious fundamentalists lost dramatically on the stage of public opinion in their battle against science and the theory of evolution. Fear of the future and insecurity within the present brought out the worst in individuals and groups, as the National Origins Act and the "new" Ku Klux Klan demonstrated all too well. The world was changing, and not everyone sought to embrace the impending upheaval associated with cultural renovation. Country folk in particular appeared poised to resist. In doing so, not unsurprisingly, they turned to music.

The rise of radio barn dance programs in the 1920s and 1930s represented a process whereupon tradition adapted to modernity and traditionalists adopted commercial or popular culture for their own purposes. The agenda of these traditionalists included, but was not exclusive to, disassociating themselves from the Jazz Age and all that it symbolized. In implementing their design, they put forward a vision of the American past and present that emphasized morality, harmony, and community. And above all, whiteness. It will not be argued here that barn dance enthusiasts were racists; such an assertion would oversimplify a midwestern rural reality in which African Americans were invisible not because they were overlooked or excluded, but because they simply were missing. Yet the conflation of images within the national popular culture and music of the period that equated jazz, urban life, and black culture with immorality and wantonness no doubt influenced rural listeners of the region. That they thereby chose an entertainment form that excluded African Americans (except for the standard yet very significant inclusion of whites in blackface) hardly seems accidental. It is suggested here that through their choice of "local" radio activities, specifically the barn dance, many such consumers were reassuring themselves of who they were, and, perhaps more important, who they were not.

Some may think that this is placing too much significance on a fancy piece of furniture that happened to emit sound. Yet is it a coincidence that the radio barn dance emerged at a time when cultural conflict and upheaval compelled many to fear the permanent demise of traditional values and mores? Does it matter that these old-fashioned frolics over the air "were designed to create the atmosphere of wholesome family fun and entertainment associated with village or rural life" during an era when rural residents fretted that the countryside had surrendered to the city and that the sacred had given way to the profane? In January 1923, as national newspaper headlines highlighted the licentious activities of gin swillers, bootleggers, and gangsters, radio station WBAP in Fort Worth, Texas, aired, without fanfare, the first barn dance, an hour and a half of square dance music and fiddle playing. According to legend, telegrams and telephone calls inundated WBAP with requests for more old-time material. Other stations across the country with signals that reached rural areas took notice. They immediately appreciated the potential of the barn dance format to attract audiences and sponsors. By the late 1920s and 1930s, such programs were "spreading like kudzu." Since radio previously had catered exclusively to urban listeners whose tastes gravitated toward jazz and popular or classical music, a forgotten, neglected, and ostensibly outdated audience (and an unexploited market) had literally been rescued and, in various ways, empowered. For as many recognized, modernity did not necessarily sound a death knell for traditionalists; in the guise of technology, it paradoxically held the key to their preservation.[7]

Ironically, no one grasped or personified this conundrum better than Henry Ford, the automobile titan whose innovative notions on mass production, mechanized labor, factory organization, workers' wages, consumerism, and mass culture cast him as the leading architect of American modernity. Despite his obvious role in shaping an industrial society made for the future, however, the mature Ford seemed desperate to steer American culture through a U-turn back to its agrarian past. The son of midwestern Irish immigrant farmers, Ford as a young man yearned to work with machines and did not seem temperamentally suited for agricultural labor. He left the farm as soon as he could to make his mark on the larger world. Only after gaining success as a car maker and industrialist did the autocratic antiquarian publicly hark back to that which he had left behind. But when he did set out to turn back the clock, he did so with a vengeance. Throughout the 1920s, one observer later noted, "it was a queer day when Henry Ford's antique collection or his concern for *McGuffey's Readers*, ancient inns, old-fashioned dancing, and old-time fiddlers was not mentioned in the daily press."[8]

Ford's attempts to square the progress of the present with a reverence for the (not so) distant past mirrored the struggles of a rural population endeavoring to comprehend the historical changes going on so rapidly around it. Like that of other "plain folks," the self-styled and popular "people's tycoon's" respect for tradition found expression in music and dance. An amateur violinist—he possessed a collection of violins worth over $500,000—Ford had learned to play (and not so well) the instrument as a boy. His tastes then, as they would be half a century later, veered toward rustic fiddle tunes. Later in life he took great enjoyment in entertaining guests by pulling out a $75,000 Stradivarius and scraping out songs he was fond of in his youth, such as "Turkey in the Straw" or "Home, Sweet, Home." By the early Jazz Age, however, Ford's favorites were, to say the least, no longer in vogue. Yet he put great stock in the moral value of the musical activities of his rural upbringing. Old-fashioned barn raisings, quilting bees, outdoor barbecues, public assemblies, and religious revivals came equipped with harmonious soundtracks, he recalled nostalgically, and his melodious memories evoked images of community, respect, and conjectured order. Conversely, much of what he heard and saw in relationship to modern popular music proved disturbing. Jazz, and particularly the sensual dancing that supplemented the syncopated rhythms, such as the Black Bottom and the Charleston, degraded Ford's vision of American culture. According to the Fordian perspective, these foreign imports were "dances that originated in the African Congo, dances from the gypsies of the South American pampas, and dances from the hot-blooded races of Southern Europe," and they epitomized "the racial characteristics of the people who dance them." In contrast, the automaker insisted, "Old American dancing was clean and healthful."[9]

The solution, it seemed clear, was to bring back the older styles of music and dance. In such a way Ford hoped to substitute upright agrarian values for downright urban depravity. Consequently, he led a campaign to revive old-time square and round dancing and old-fashioned fiddle playing. He began, significantly, by holding a dance in the barn of the old Ford home place in rural Michigan. Later, in utilizing car dealerships that spanned the nation, he organized a highly publicized series of local, state, and national fiddle competitions. In 1923, he crowned an eighty-year-old performer from Michigan as the "King of the Country Fiddlers" and presented him with the "Henry Ford Gold Cup." ("It is fine to see how those old fiddlers come to life through their music," a pleased Ford exclaimed.) Several years of such contests followed, culminating in 1926 with a multiround battle involving more than 1,875 contestants. At least one historian has argued that the Ford fiddle phenomenon led to the emergence, at least indirectly, of commercial country music. More important, perhaps, Ford's very public interest in nostalgia sounded a note of apprehension comprehensible to a large number of people. As a familiar friend (despite his wealth and prominence) who successfully negotiated between the past and the present, however, Ford was able to assuage the fears and uncertainties wrought by modernity. Indeed, the backward-looking industrial colossus proved that innovation and tradition could happily coexist.[10]

Like Ford's revivals, radio barn dance programs of the 1920s and 1930s also attempted to recreate a particular version of the past so as to reassure those in the present (and like Ford himself, the radio shows embodied both technological progress and a time-honored outlook). The WLS National Barn Dance was no exception. An account of the inaugural broadcast could have been describing Henry Ford's memories as they were played out in his Historical Greenfield Village Museum: amidst clanging cowbells and fired-up fiddles crying out what sounded like an old-fashioned hoedown, the studio announcer spoke to an invisible audience of the air as if they were all sitting together on farm fences and communal hay bales. "This program is to be sincere, friendly and informal—planned to remind you folks of the fun and fellowship of the barn warmings, the husking bees and the square dances in our farm communities of yesteryear and even today."[11]

As with Ford's "village of yesterday" museum, where he went to great lengths to recreate a living and useful version of the past (the automaker even went so far as to dismantle, transport, and reassemble at his spruced-up antique mall the Stephen Foster and Noah Webster Houses, Thomas Edison's Menlo Park laboratory, the Wright Brothers Bicycle Shop, and a courthouse where a young Abraham Lincoln had argued several cases), so too did the "past" animate the National Barn Dance. Listen in for a moment, as John Lair introduced the Barn Dance radio audience to "Bunk House and Cabin Songs" in spring 1936: "Howdy Folks. Less set down an take it easy, now, as the boys an girls bring you the good old-time songs of long ago from hill an plain, from cabin an bunk house—the songs yer daddies an mammies grew up with." Significantly, Lair may have been referring to parents, songs, and a time buried in the past, but the message he promoted was timeless. Such scripted dialogue evoked not only a sentimentality for what their "mammies and daddies" had achieved yesterday, but a feeling of pride in what the descendants of their predecessors were doing today. In the words of one listener,

> As we saw it, and as we *still* see it, the 48% of America's population that lives in rural communities represent both the backbone and the breadbasket of the nation. We believe that one of the greatest things that ever happened to this group was the invention of radio. We believe that, as a group, this audience likes local station programs better than the more sophisticated type of entertainment. And we further believe that with these local stars lie score after score of stories just as *interesting*, just as *dramatic*, and just as *helpful* as anything that Hollywood or Broadway has to offer.[12]

Launched only one week after Sears-owned WLS made its on-air debut, the National Barn Dance aimed its signal at the "backbone and breadbasket of the nation." It was "dedicated to the men and women, boys and girls, of the farms and homes of America." In other words, it explicitly targeted rural residents/customers who received Sears' mail-order catalog. For while its signal undoubtedly could be heard elsewhere, the station's primary coverage area became the Midwest, where approximately 42 percent of the population was classified as rural (with whites comprising 98 percent of those who lived in the countryside). Significantly, almost half of the farm families in the region owned radios (a rather large percentage, particularly when compared to the South, where only 5 percent of farm families could say the same as late as 1938). The Agricultural Foundation and Farm Service Division of Sears, Roebuck, which already had the responsibility of translating scientific and statistical information relevant to crop cultivation and animal husbandry into "dirt farmer's language," gained the additional assignment of operating the radio station. Accordingly, WLS, recognized by staff members and listeners as "the shirt-sleeve station," professed that its mission called for assisting farmers "with crop and weather intelligence, marketing information, education, and entertainment."[13]

The station's commitment to the agricultural sector was genuine; when given the opportunity to sell WLS to the utilities magnet Samuel Insull, for instance, Sears, Roebuck refused to do so, primarily because Julius Rosenwald, the company's president, did not feel that Insull would maintain the station's rural identity. The department store giant eventually did sell WLS to the Illinois-based Prairie Farmer Publishing Company, but only after assurances that its pastoral programming would continue. Almost immediately the company had the opportunity to reiterate its agrarian commitment. In contesting a decision of the Federal Radio Commission that limited the airtime of WLS, the *Prairie Farmer* phrased its petition in terms that Henry Ford would have understood: "Is there a place on the air for the voice of the country—for the songs of the prairies and the hills, for the barn dance fiddlers, for the homely virtues of the everyday folks who have made America? We believe that there should be. We are fighting for that place. It is not our fight, but the fight of agriculture."[14]

Without skipping a beat, the station under its new management retained or inaugurated a scheduling and programming format favorable to farmers: the 5:30 A.M. wake-up *Smile-A-While Show;* the *Dinnerbell,* a highly popular noon program which "operated on the basis that it owned part of every farm, every steer, and every chicken within its signal"; a *Homemaker's Hour* geared to farm women and rural service, *Hymn Time* and *Little Brown Church of the Air* for the devout; "live" corn-husking contests; periodic productions on pioneer life in the Midwest; and the *Little Red Schoolhouse* and *School Time,* programs that served as supplements for rural schools "besieged with low budgets, poorly qualified teachers, aging facilities, and declining numbers of students." Off-the-air goodwill activities sponsored by the station included disaster relief contributions, the WLS Community Kitchen, Christmas Giving Parties, and a Middle West Farm Sports Committee that focused on outdoor competition and camaraderie as experienced through baseball, horseshoes, hog calling, chicken calling, trapshooting, milking, plowing, and horse pulling. Significantly, Sears, Roebuck remained a major sponsor of the station, with International Harvester, Red Brand Farm Fence, and Murphy's Feeds and Corn signing on as well.[15]

WLS certainly possessed the necessary credentials to host a barn dance program. As a continuous stream of correspondence to "The Voice of Agriculture" intimated, farmers appreciated the many services the station provided and thought of the station in terms that transcended the usual business-sponsor-customer relationship. "We feel that we know members of your radio family just as we do those of our own family" represented a common refrain found in mail dispatched to the station. "Listener's Mike," a letters-to-the-editor feature that appeared in *Stand By! Prairie Farmer's Radio Weekly* during the mid- to late 1930s, underscored the rural, family, and neighborly nature of WLS audiences. It commonly contained missives from listeners that described life on the farm and how they eagerly welcomed wholesome WLS "stars" into their homes. "I must tell you in my own words just what we like," one regular listener pronounced. "First, this is an old-fashioned home. Supper with us is done early on Saturday night—a big pan of popcorn and a dish of shiny red apples—a good fire and the radio dialed on WLS at 7 o'clock—we stay with you until you sign off." And as one grateful letter writer explained, "I have laughed, cried, sung, and prayed while listening to your varied programs. Your men, women, boys, and girls are the cleanest and finest talent that I have heard over the air. God bless you all."[16]

Listeners also frequently presumed "ownership" of the station's operations, not only in requesting particular songs or genres ("Don't get too much up-to-date music on the program. The good old songs are best"; "Let's have more of the old-time songs and ballads with old-time music"), but likewise in asking the station to accommodate work rituals and routines like planting, gathering, canning, cooking, sewing, and slaughtering. Such was the case, for instance, when two dairy farmers from Illinois inquired about the possibility of shifting the station's start time from 5:30 to 5:00 A.M. They had recently altered their milking schedule but subsequently discovered that their cows would not cooperate. Avid fans of the *Smile-A-While Show*, which aired at 5:30, the cows refused to give milk until they had heard the opening strains of their favorite program transmitted from the barn radio. As was the case with other radios stationed in living rooms, kitchens, bedrooms, tool sheds, and front porches throughout the rural Midwest (according to letters addressed to the station), the radio dial in this particular cow barn was set permanently at WLS-870 kHz.[17]

Although we may never know exactly why cows loyally listened to the WLS *Smile-A-While Show*, we can reflect upon the human appeal of the WLS National Barn Dance. In one sense, the attraction could be attributed to familiarity. As George Biggar insisted, "It was only natural that the Barn Dance should become popular. Here were thousands of farm families in the audience who knew first-hand the fun and informality of this type of entertainment." The stress on intimacy as reflected through the connections between families likewise created a sense of communal solidarity that proved appealing, if not essential. Responding to requests for pictures of their radio "friends," the station further solidified its "imagined community" by publishing annually the *WLS Family Album*, "a book of pictures and stories that will enable you to get better acquainted with the Prairie Farmer Station folks who come to you through your loudspeaker." A *Behind the Scenes* souvenir booklet similarly emphasized that the radio station's various personnel were more than simply anonymous strangers or disembodied voices; they were "just plain folks" who might one day happen to drop by for real. So, as the booklet explained, "we thought it would be a good idea to tell you what some of their favorite foods are, in case the time for entertaining ever comes . . ."[18]

The presumption that barn dance performers were just "plain folks" who might informally drop by someone's home and have a meal at any time went a long way to explain the show's popularity. As with the annual *Family Album* that visually connected people by their appearance ("I feel I know you all, for I refer to my *WLS Family Album.* I can just picture each artist"; "You seem just like home folks"), there was a strong implication of inclusion, the feeling that a group of people who may not have been related by blood nevertheless shared certain experiences, viewpoints, and leisure activities (figure 34). In emphasizing the past, the program insinuated that this "kinship" transcended time. Listeners well understood this point of view because it reiterated what they already believed, no matter how hackneyed or clichéd: "To the average unsophisticated city dweller, born and raised in a gas-choked atmosphere and artificial surroundings, it is doubtful if the Barn Dance program means anything," one fan disclosed. "But if the listener—like myself—has away back in his boyhood days worked on the farm in summer, and in the winter trudged through the crunching snow on his way to school—with the little miss at his side, who in after years walked him down the long road of life, you can safely wager your last inflated dollar that the WLS Barn Dance will raise him off his feet!"[19]

Figure 34. Barn Dance publications connected fans and performers. The original owner of this 1953 *Family Album* jotted down notes about the radio personalities, as one might do in a yearbook. Collection of Debby Gray.

As the above testimonial indicated, not only did the barn dance experience emphasize *inclusion*, it simultaneously implied *exclusion*. City folks, it seemed, automatically were viewed as different or alien, as not being able to understand or appreciate that which rural folks both endured and enjoyed. They surely were not going to be celebrated very often within the pages of the *Family Album* or on the barn dance stage. Also obvious by their omission were African Americans. On the surface, this might not seem unusual; after all, African Americans comprised less than 3 percent of the midwestern rural population. And they probably constituted an even smaller percentage of the WLS listening audience, thus drawing little interest from all-important sponsors (see figure 6). As George Biggar once stated in the pages of *Stand By!* perhaps hinting at why blacks did not frequent the National Barn Dance airwaves, "We northerners like negro [*sic*] spirituals, but we do not love them as does a southern audience, comprised of people who truly appreciate the richness of their folk hymns that come from the souls of a race in bondage." This ambivalence, however, did not prevent Biggar and the Saturday night Barn Dance from regularly showcasing (on the network portion of the program) an "old-time Dixieland minstrel show," in which the Hayloft's resident rube character, Uncle Ezra, coached "certain members of the crew who aspire toward blackface proficiency." That proficiency, of course, equated with the ability, in Biggar's words, "to extract laughable wisecracks." And as one veteran entertainer familiar with the minstrel format and audience proclaimed, an aptitude for "burnt cork entertainment" produced side-splitting hilarity and few dull moments (figure 35). "If properly produced," he explained, "the antics of these loveable, easy-going, irresponsible colored people would make a 'hit' show."[20]

Apparently Uncle Ezra succeeded in his coaching capacity, for the Hayloft's blackened crew was so popular with the radio audience that it took its antics on the road. Playing to packed houses in towns like Peoria, Edwardsville, Galesburg, Alton, Aurora, Quincy, Bloomington, Danville, Vincennes, and DeKalb, the WLS Minstrels customarily broke attendance records at every stop. The thirty-performer cast specialized in putting on a "real revival of an old-time minstrel" and featured the standard set of comical characters: corked-up end men (comprised of one "who is sarcastic in nature, another who is droll and slow in speech, one

Figure 35. In an earlier time, white people worried little about stereotyping African Americans, as shown in this 1920s picture of John Lair (left) in blackface; also pictured are Bob Fish, Bill Davis, and Ramey Richard. John Lair Collection, Southern Appalachian Archives, Berea College.

who is fat and jolly," and another "who is well qualified for recitations") and a white-faced middleman or interlocutor (one who possessed "a great deal of dignity" and who spoke "in a clear distinct voice"). The company followed a traditional minstrel format, establishing the tone early with an Old South stage set and a chorus production either of "Dixie" or "Old Folks at Home." The layout for the evening's entertainment included the "First Part" (the "backbone" of the program, and consisting of musical numbers and gags between the end men and the interlocutor sitting in a semicircle), the "Olio" (following a brief intermission, an interlude that comprised blackface skits, musical numbers, and dancing exhibitions), and a "Grand Finale by the entire cast." The road show could last between two and a half and three hours, and reflected a full-fledged version of the truncated one included on the radio Barn Dance. (It seems that the WSM Grand Ole Opry also featured blackface performers in its road shows. *Billboard* reported in 1935, for instance, that the veteran minstrel Al Tint had joined a Grand Ole Opry tour in Memphis. The trade paper then passed along a message from a couple of Tint's friends who were performing with Max "Sambo" Trout's Minstrels: "Howdy to Al Tint and all the cork-opry boys.")[21]

Whites in blackface or using minstrel dialect represented regular components of local and network radio in the pre–World War II era. The "Amos and Andy" characterizations, for instance, which began in Chicago, were extremely popular during this period. Stories on blackface performers, including "Amos and Andy," maintained a persistent presence in rural radio magazines, including *Stand By! Billboard* featured a regular minstrel column called "Minstrelsy" all through the 1920s and 1930s and routinely reported on activities occurring in the world of "burnt cork." Significantly, much of the news emanated from the Midwest (the columnists, who depended on correspondence from the field, had a Cincinnati, Ohio, office and mailing address). It was not unusual, for instance, to read accounts of sold-out minstrel shows in old opera houses and vaudeville theaters in small towns in Ohio, Illinois, Indiana, Iowa, Michigan, Minnesota, and Wisconsin. Dan Fitch, who toured with his Merry Minstrels throughout the country, including the rural Midwest, would not have been surprised about the genre's popularity in the land of Lincoln. As he reported to *Billboard*, just prior to the launching of WLS, "Minstrelsy is an American institution and every effort should be made to keep it at the high pinnacle which it enjoys in our field of amusement and entertainment."[22]

At approximately the same time that Fitch made his declaration of minstrel devotion, a veteran blackface performer named "By-Gosh" was engaged in a forty-week tour of the area around Chicago. In his fifteenth year on the road, he generally played "towns ranging in population from 2,000 up to 500,000, and average[d] a town a week." By-Gosh belonged to the "Seldom-Fed" minstrel troupe, and he specialized in integrating younger members of the audience into his act. This involved putting local kids into character. By-Gosh supervised and managed "all makeup details," *Billboard* reported, and "he corks up an average of 3,000 characters every season or about thirty at every performance." After his departure, if any of the newly minted "colored" celebrities wanted to blacken up again, they had only to travel to the Windy City, where one of the largest manufacturers and retailers of minstrel paraphernalia, Chicago Costume Works, advertised that it had in stock a greaseless and "smooth as silk" brand of blackface makeup. While there, they might browse through a large selection of minstrel songsters, folios, and joke books, many of them published locally. They definitely would pick up a manual that demonstrated "How to Put on a Minstrel Show," a prolific genre of instruction books produced in places like Chicago, Minneapolis, and Des Moines during the 1920s and 1930s.[23]

Obviously, midwestern rural radio listeners who tuned in to the National Barn Dance were familiar with blackface minstrelsy. Many probably grew up looking forward to the seasonal appearances of minstrel companies whose colorful monikers, such as Georgia Jubilee, Alabama Stompers, Showboat, Levee Loungers, Sunny Southland, and Dixie Strutters, evoked exotic images of land and leisure in the Old South. Surely Carl Wittke, an Ohio native, was not alone when he wrote in 1930 of his "happy memories of the burnt cork semicircle" or of his "real love for the old-time minstrel show." A renowned historian, Wittke was able to distinguish between the "stage Negro" and individuals of "genuine" African descent. (From a later perspective, however, his distinctions seem a bit hazy. The minstrel or stage type, he argued, was characterized by "an unusually large mouth and peculiar kind of broad grin"; such a performer fancied dressing "in gaudy colors and in a flashy style" and had a huge appetite for watermelons and chickens and using long words he could not understand or accurately pronounce. This was in contrast, he maintained, to the "genuine darky" upon whom the minstrel was based, a "folk-figure of a simple, somewhat rustic character, instinctively humorous, irrationally credulous, gifted in song and dance, interesting in spontaneous frolic, [and] endowed with artless philosophy.") While Wittke may have recognized the various distortions, one wonders if other minstrel enthusiasts appreciated the subtleties of such distinctions. Or did they engage in their own subtle yet complicated mental and racial transactions? In other words, when listeners heard dialect transmitted through their radio speakers, what exactly did they "see"?[24]

It could be argued that on several levels they saw or felt reassurance. As a remnant of the nineteenth century (in the antebellum era, such "Ethiopian delineations" represented the country's first popular music craze), blackface minstrelsy served as a reminder of a bygone era. It reminded rural inhabitants living in a modern world of an older "mentality and morality" that no longer seemed operative. "How to Cork Up" manuals often reflected or exploited the tendency of minstrelsy to evoke such nostalgia. As one instruction booklet from 1938 informed its users, "the real minstrel is a blend of old and new. The songs of yesteryear blend with the songs of today. The comedy, though new, carries with it some of the aroma of the pleasant past. Thus does the minstrel live up to its name as entertainment both for old and young."[25]

On another level, the minstrel show enhanced stereotypical perceptions of African Americans as "loveable, easy-going, [and] irresponsible colored people." Consequently, rural radio listeners, when they heard a disembodied dialect, unconsciously referenced an innocuous (at least to them), debased, and ultimately illusory image of "blackness" and "black" people. Such a representation worked as a "safe" counter to realistic portrayals of African Americans, a particularly significant development as blacks became more publicly prominent during the Jazz Age, Harlem Renaissance, and New Deal era. And no matter how harmless the WLS Hayloft Gang member and bone player Joe Smith may have seemed (upon joining the barn dance cast, *Billboard* observed of the Uncle Remus–like Smith, "Pretty good for a 78-year-old youngster"), his caricatured presence conveyed a serious message. Implicitly endorsing the inferiority of blacks, the minstrel image reiterated the superiority of whites. And as the flip side of the ancestral European ruralite, it functioned to inform listeners as to who they were, and especially who they were not. Yet blackface also served as an escape hatch, a means for whites to discard, temporarily, the societal "rules" that made them "superior." It allowed them to engage in unrestrained frivolity without social repercussion. As the former Hayloft regular Red Foley later explained in lyrics that could be interpreted as homage both to the radio barn dance and its minstrel affiliation, "Civilized people live there all right, but they all go native on a Saturday night."[26]

Foley's "explanation," of course, hinted at the peculiar merging of blackface and white rural culture. The story of Malcolm Claire, the featured blackface or dialect performer on the National Barn Dance, likewise highlighted this paradox. Claire, who appeared as "Spareribs," was a vaudeville veteran born in Alabama (figure 36). He followed "Old Pappy," otherwise known as Clifford Soubier, a minstrel performer who had "long fascinated WLS radio audiences with his old darky sketches." Claire had created his Spareribs on-air persona as a "composite character of a score of old southern darkies who had told him stories in his youth." In addition to his barn dance duties, he also hosted (in blackface) a very popular children's morning show on WLS. Interestingly, he served as "a veteran guide in the misty realms of make-believe. His fairy stories for children, related in the soft dialect of the 'deep south' negro [*sic*], have won their place among the finest children programs in radio." Claire, telling his stories in "the manner of a southern colored character," had also won the hearts and trust of parents, who generally feared that the content of Jazz Age radio would have a negative impact on their children. One mother, writing in to *Stand By!* expressed her gratitude for the "nice stories" told by Spareribs. Ironically, she also related how a recent issue of the radio magazine containing a picture of the thirty-something Claire on the cover, sans makeup, had confounded her daughter, a fan of the show. Apparently for many, the dialect he utilized blurred the racial and the rural. "Who's dat?" the child asked, pointing at the picture. When her mother explained that it was Spareribs, the girl balked. "No," she exclaimed, perhaps ignoring the one feature, or lack thereof, that would have seemed obvious. "Spare Ribs [*sic*] is an old man. He talks just like my grandpa."[27]

Notwithstanding the distorted (although apparently complicated) blackface representations of black life, the National Barn Dance generally excluded allusions to African

Figure 36. "Spareribs" (Malcolm Claire), pictured here in 1934, was eventually transformed into Uncle Mal, sometime in the later 1930s. Collection of Debby Gray.

Americans. Even its constant references to the past, a past that seemingly came to life from school textbooks that exalted the nation's founding and sustaining mothers and fathers, refused to acknowledge the black presence in America. An example of such myopic vision can be found in a *Rural Radio* article that connected the music of the barn dance to the nation's origins. "This carryin' on—old-time fiddlin' and banjo pluckin' and good humored singin'," it declared, ironically failing to mention spirituals, the blues, or even blackface minstrelsy, "is really the true folk music of America, the songs sung and whistled by the earliest pioneers who made it possible for America to become the great nation it is today." Such expunging walked a fine line between an overemphasis on a European heritage and simply an erasure of the African. Yet it followed a national trend of the post–World War I period to rewrite history according to popularized current academic theories of inherent racial differences. "Hillbilly is the only folk music America has," another *Rural Radio* article argued along racial lines. "The Indians didn't give us any music. They seemed to be as lacking in that respect as they were deficient in a sense of humor. . . . What about the Negro spiritual? It was written by a people imported to the New World. Its main value is its faithful reflection of instincts and superstitions born on another continent."[28]

Many white rural residents within the radius of the WLS signal, like whites in other portions of the country, likely viewed African Americans as permanent outsiders, a people from a "dark" continent whose "instincts and superstitions" separated them from the descendants of Europeans. Their habits and experiences, past and present, were perceived as alien. They certainly had not been part of what the *Family Album* called the "greatest of all the forces that changed this Middle West from a wind-swept wilderness to its present beauty and prosperity, the fellowship of neighborliness." Yet while the past, as it was recounted, appeared to be safe, the present was a constant cause for concern. And the present, at the moment, was jazz, a blight on the plains that those of pioneer stock "called 'nigger music' and 'whorehouse music' and 'nice' people turned up their noses at it." Many undoubtedly associated the music with the African American brothel or the African jungles. As one generally erudite yet panicked observer noted, "Jazz originally was the accompaniment of the voodoo dancer, stimulating the half-crazed barbarian to the vilest deeds." Another opined, "Jazz, the impulse for wildness that has undoubtedly come over many things besides the music of this country, is traceable to the negro [*sic*] influence."[29]

The possibility that jazz might permanently alter traditional values seemed real, at least to those who were paying attention. A medical examiner warned that the influence of jazz "is as harmful and degrading to civilized races as it always has been among savages from whom we borrowed it," and "may tear to pieces our whole social fabric." The president of the Christian Endeavor Society considered the dancing associated with jazz to be "an offence against womanly purity, the very fountainhead of our family and civil life." And of course, Henry Ford, who also worried about the immorality of modern dancing (or the "syncopated embrace," as it was frequently called), was left to explain why he and others felt compelled to protect American culture from the lower, inferior, and degenerative orders that were threatening to topple all that was held dear:

> We are not actuated by any kind of prejudice, except it may be a prejudice in favor of the principles which have made our civilization. There had been observed in this country certain streams of influence which were causing a marked deterioration in our literature, amusements, and social conduct; a general letting down of standards we felt everywhere . . . As a young man I liked to dance, but the only dances we knew were what are now called the "old-fashioned dances"—the Schottische, the polka, the chorus jug, quadrilles, gavottes, and the like. The younger people nowadays, so we found, did not know these dances.[30]

There can be little doubt that the National Barn Dance and its contemporary country cousins elsewhere (WHO Iowa Barn Dance Frolic, WSM Grand Ole Opry, WWVA Wheeling Jamboree, WHAS Renfro Valley Barn Dance, among others) hoped to acquaint younger people with an older style of music and dancing. They obviously wanted to sway their children away from jazz. "It is an accepted axiom that big cities are wicked, but small towns and rural districts are clean. This view is not well founded," one concerned observer noted. "Our Middle West is supposed to be a citadel of Americanism and righteousness. Probably it is. Yet a survey of its length and breadth shows that it is badly spotted with the moral smallpox known as jazz." Older styles of music could serve as a much needed antidote. A *Family Album* emphasized, "The old square dances of pioneer days had something about them that has endured through all the years. The National Barn Dance programs on WLS have brought back and popularized many of these old dances, in order that the younger generation might see what the old square dances really look like." And one writer advised, "So far as the younger generation is concerned, they should like old-time music best." Yet one young listener confided, "My brother and I always have an argument on Saturday night. He wants jazz and I want the barn dance. Will someone please tell me what to do?"[31]

Such a question was significant. In fall 1935, generational concerns coalesced into a full-fledged debate and divide, one that revealed much about the WLS audience. The "debate" began when correspondents to the "Listener's Mike" column of *Stand By!* complained that WLS "isn't what it was a few years back. There's too much up-to-date music and songs. We want good old cowboy songs, hillbilly numbers, and novelties." Despite the fact that the radio lineup had changed very little, if at all, over the preceding months, others wrote in and agreed that they wanted to hear only old-time music. "We want all the programs to be of this nature. We all grow tired of this modern stuff. . . . The good old songs are best."[32]

In response, a group of letter writers self-identified as the "Sophs and Juniors of Carmel, Indiana" countered that they disagreed with those who had bashed "up-to-date music. Older people may like old music but how about us young people. Here's to more popular music." The editors realized a good story when they saw it (and they also knew which side they would favor), as *their* response indicated: "This looks like good material for a debate. The Carmel Sophs and Juniors seem concerned that young folks prefer music in the modern manner. Perhaps there are others of the younger generation who would tell a different story."[33]

Sure enough, as the editors expected, the floodgates opened. Not surprisingly (after all, the editors virtually had set the terms and tone of the debate), "Listener's Mike" epistolists sided against the pop-minded pupils. Numerous missives began, "We heartily disagree" (alternately: "We disagree emphatically . . .") "with the Sophs and Juniors of Carmel, Indiana." Specifically, "I am a young girl and I prefer the good old-time music. So do my brothers and sisters. . . . Modern music can't compare with the good old mountain, hill country and country songs." Similarly, a Marion, Wisconsin, teenager proclaimed, "I prefer old-time music and I think there are many other young people who do." Relative oldsters also chimed in: "I am twenty-eight, and I much prefer old-time music. You can hear popular songs all along the dial. Give us the old songs and music we like best." Others followed a similar argument, one that insinuated the besieged status of WLS and its audience: "There are so many stations featuring popular music. We find a grand relief to hear more of the old favorites" or "The more old-time music the better. Those people who like popular music can get it on almost any other station, so why not let good enough alone." Finally, as one apparently agitated writer pronounced, "Do the Sophs and Juniors of Carmel Indiana all have broken arms, or is the dial on their radio immovable? I heartily disagree with them. Please keep WLS as it is."[34]

As it was, WLS provided an alternative to the "hundreds of stations on the air." In the words of one listener, its distinctiveness derived from making available "music as our fathers, mothers, uncles, and aunts used to sing and dance to. Songs that were written from life and could be sung by people who didn't have time or money to take lessons and study notes. Popular music? It's about the silliest jumbled-up mess I ever listened to." And as another perceptive observer asked, if popular music "is put on over WLS, what will the older folks do for amusement? They like the good old-time music and drama and they depend on radio to bring it to them. So let's let them have it, with lots of luck to the Sophs and Juniors for their choice of entertainment." Without much support, the Sophs and Juniors had no choice but to concede. "My goodness!" they concluded in their final entry to *Stand By!* "Are we supposed to be properly subdued? All we want is a little popular music every now and then."[35]

WLS, of course, had never completely excluded popular music from its airwaves. The National Barn Dance itself featured many acts that clearly incorporated jazz instrumentation and pop sounds in their performance styles. Groups like the Prairie Ramblers certainly adapted modern techniques that souped up the string band tradition. Such innovations, however, did not transform them into a jazz orchestra. They remained a highly energetic string band bound by country convention. Even ensembles such as the Novelodeons and Four Hired Hands, highly skilled bands that included instruments associated with jazz, like clarinets, trumpets, and trombones, were apt more to "mix rollicking comedy with melody" than they were to encourage a "syncopated embrace." The Hoosier Hot Shots perhaps were the most popular group of this type. Producing "the most uproarious and astounding musical efforts ever heard," the four Indiana farm boys comprising this musical assemblage certainly were entertaining. Few at the time, however, would have confused them with Jimmie Lunceford, Count Basie, or Louis Armstrong.[36]

At best, much of the "popular music" on the WLS National Barn Dance, and many of the musicians who performed it, treated "jazz" as a funny and harmless novelty. This is not surprising. To parody jazz, in many ways, was to negate its larger social impact and implications. After all, the barn dance phenomenon owed its birth to a mission meant to censure the ill effects of modern life. With jazz serving as the proxy for all that seemed wrong about modernity (urban decadence, sexual permissiveness, drinking, crime, and individualism run amok), rural natives were anxious to support a version of popular culture that soothed their apprehension. As a concerned correspondent argued, "We can retrieve our high purpose in radio." Making fun of jazz while adhering to old-fashioned musical styles and material confirmed their values, values that they had always assumed had sustained the national culture, but which had somehow been abandoned. "Surely, if Americans can claim any music of its own it must be the folk music of our Common people," one listener complained. "Thousands of people cannot be wrong and there are ten people to one who prefer the good old-time music and songs."[37]

In the National Barn Dance, such "right-thinking" people had won a victory in their battle against changing times. They had harnessed the power of technology to spread traditional standards and morals on a weekly basis, and had proven that their way of life, though beleaguered, was not yet extinct. Accentuating an agenda that emphasized wholesomeness, harmony, and community in a world where the majority seemed to have lost its way, the National Barn Dance provided a means of cultural resistance. "WLS has built itself up to one of the most widely recognized stations today," a Milwaukee resident declared, "and not through popular music."[38]

For at least a few hours on Saturday night, WLS devotees could gather around their radios to make a statement not only about what they liked, but who they were. And, again, who they were not: One correspondent wrote, "We wish to add our voice concerning the popular music and especially that termed jazz. We think jazz is characteristic of the reckless—heedless—delirious attitude of some of our population." Another person said, "Your artists seem like home folks and their music has a place which jazz can never fill," while a third opined, "If they want popular music, there are all kinds of stations that play such tommyrot."[39]

Celebrating the five-hundredth performance of the program on a national network some twenty years after its inauguration, *Newsweek* declared that the WLS National Barn Dance was "probably the best that radio will ever get to authentic Americana." Perhaps. It certainly "strove to recreate the homey atmosphere of the American family at play." However, the barn dance did more than merely present a collection of cultural artifacts frozen in time. Through a very modern medium, it offered a dynamic critique of the present. Its avowal of traditional values represented a means to combat forces that were antagonistic to the agrarian way of life. It successfully equated concepts such as home, motherhood, morality, and community with the experiences of white rural people. As one Wisconsin woman explained, "When I listen to the Barn Dance, I feel as though I have friends there, even if I have never seen any of them. They seem near and dear to me, week after week." In embracing their on-air family as they had constructed it, WLS listeners implicitly rejected the values associated with African Americans, if not African Americans themselves.[40]

The denunciation of urban jazz culture likewise reiterated a white rural identity, as another Wisconsin neighbor alluded: "We can hear the modern music on nearly every other station on the dial and I hope that WLS will always stick to the good old sweet songs." Like Henry Ford, who "sentimentalized and pillaged the past" in order to make the present more palatable, barn dance enthusiasts demonstrated that innovation and tradition could happily coexist. WLS radio listeners utilized popular culture to create an imagined yet very real community, one that soothed their anxieties about the various changes rocking the world around them. In the end, they safely steered their way into an uncertain future accompanied by familiar sights and sounds, listening to the folks that were most nearly like themselves.[41]

NOTES

1. "Over the Cracker Barrel," *Rural Radio*, September 1938, 12; ibid., October 1938, 29. See also "They Call Us Home Folks," *Behind the Scenes Souvenir Booklet* (Chicago: Prairie Farmer Publishing Company, 1932), 8–9.

2. Michele Hilmes, *Radio Voices: American Broadcasting, 1922–1952* (Minneapolis: University of Minnesota Press, 1997), chapter 3 ("who we are"); "We Face the Future," *WLS Family Album, 1939*

(Chicago: Prairie Farmer, 1939), 3 ("to me"); "The Ridge Runners," *WLS Family Album, 1933* (Chicago: Prairie Farmer, 1933), 20 ("cut loose," "set their feet").

3. George Biggar, "WLS Accomplishments in Education and Entertainment," 16, WLS National Barn Dance folder, clipping files, Country Music Hall of Fame, Nashville, Tennessee.

4. D. K. Wilgus, "An Introduction to the Study of Hillbilly Music," *Journal of American Folklore* 78 (1965): 196 (Wilgus quotes); George Biggar, "How the WLS Barn Dance Began," *Stand By! Prairie Farmer's Radio Weekly*, October 19, 1935, 2 ("It was but natural"); Harold Halpern, "'Lum 'n' Abner' Promoters of Better Understanding between Rural and City Folk," *Rural Radio*, June 1938, 2 ("different picture"). For a discussion of WLS and "southern" fans living in Chicago, see Bernard Abel, "The National Barn Dance," *Chicago*, October 1954, 20–25. For country music historians and the National Barn Dance, see Timothy A. Patterson, "Hillbilly Music Among the Flatlanders: Early Midwestern Radio Barn Dances," *Journal of Country Music* 6 (Spring 1975): 12–18. For a more recent work that addresses the significance of southern migrants to the popularity of WLS, see James N. Gregory, *The Southern Diaspora: How the Great Migrations of Black and White Southerners Transformed America* (Chapel Hill: University of North Carolina Press, 2005).

5. For statistical information, see "No. 653 Population, Farms, and Farm Property—Summary: 1850 to 1940," in *Statistical Abstract of the United States, 1944–1945* (Washington, D.C.: U.S. Department of Commerce, 1945), 597. For general historical information on agriculture of the period, see David M. Kennedy, *Freedom from Fear: The American People in Depression and War, 1929–1945* (New York: Oxford University Press, 1999), esp. 16–22.

6. Francis Scott Fitzgerald, *The Great Gatsby* (New York: Wordsworth, 1993), 115.

7. Bill C. Malone, *Country Music U.S.A.*, rev. ed. (Austin: University of Texas Press, 1985), 68 ("designed to create"); Charles Wolfe, "The Triumph of the Hills: Country Radio, 1920–50," in *Country: The Music and the Musicians*, rev. and updated, ed. Paul Kingsbury (New York: Abbeville Press, 1994), 51 ("spreading like kudzu"). The discussion on WBAP as producing the first barn dance program can be found in the preceding Malone and Wolfe works. For an early discussion of rural radio's response to a changing agricultural landscape, see William M. Randle, "History of Radio Broadcasting and Its Social and Economic Effect on the Entertainment Industry, 1920–1930" (Ph.D. diss., Western Reserve University, 1966).

8. David L. Lewis, *The Image of Henry Ford: An American Folk Hero and His Company* (Detroit: Fort Wayne State University Press, 1976), 223–24. Much of the biographical information on Ford is based on Steven Watts, *The People's Tycoon: Henry Ford and the American Century* (New York: Knopf, 2005).

9. The appellation "people's tycoon" is from Watts's book title. "Henry Ford Shakes a Wicked Hoof," *Literary Digest*, August 15, 1925, 40. Henry Ford, with Samuel Crowther, *Today and Tomorrow* (1926; repr., Cambridge, Mass.: Productivity Press, 1988), 226 ("dances that originated").

10. Henry Ford, *Today and Tomorrow*, 227. For more on the Ford fiddle contests and their relationship to the emergence of modern country music, see Richard A. Peterson, *Creating Country Music: Fabricating Authenticity* (Chicago: University of Chicago Press, 1997), esp. 59–62.

11. George C. Biggar, "The National Barn Dance," in *The Country Music's Who's Who, 1965*, ed. Thurston Moore (Denver: Heather Publications, 1964), 17.

12. Bill Irvin, "Barn Dance Set for 40th Birthday Show," *Chicago's Sunday American Magazine*, April 26, 1964, 4; John Lair, "Bunk House and Cabin Songs" typescript, March 7, 1936, collection of Kristine McCusker, Department of History, Middle Tennessee State University; "An Open Letter to the Publisher," *Rural Radio*, February 1939, 12.

13. George Biggar, "Those Good Old Days: Program Director Recalls Old Time and Old Timers," *Stand By!* April 13, 1935, 8 ("backbone," "dedicated"); Boris Emmett and John Jeuck, *Catalogues and Counters: A History of Sears, Roebuck and Company* (Chicago: University of Chicago Press, 1950), 624 (remaining quotations). For the population figures of the Midwest, see "Series A 172–194, Population

of Regions by Sex, Race, Residence, Age, and Nativity," *Historical Statistics of the United States, Colonial Times to 1970, vol. 1* (Washington, D.C.: U.S. Department of Commerce and Bureau of the Census, 1975), 22. For farm family radio ownership, see Herman S. Hettinger, *A Decade of Radio Advertising* (repr., New York: Arno Press, 1971), chapter 3; J. Fred MacDonald, *Don't Touch That Dial: Radio Programming in American Life, 1920–1960* (Chicago: Nelson-Hall, 1979), chapter 1.

14. *Prairie Farmer* petition, reprinted in James F. Evans, *Prairie Farmer and WLS: The Burridge D. Butler Years* (Urbana: University of Illinois Press, 1967), 181. My account of the sale, as well as much of the information on WLS during the years when Sears, Roebuck owned the station, is dependent upon Emmett and Jeuck, *Catalogues and Counters*, esp. 624–27.

15. Evans, *Prairie Farmer and WLS*, 186, 193. References to WLS sponsors were located in Douglas B. Craig, *Fireside Politics: Radio and Political Culture in the United States, 1920–1940* (Baltimore: Johns Hopkins University Press, 2000), 241. All of the information regarding WLS programming and off-the-air goodwill activities can be found in Evans, *Prairie Farmer and WLS*, 183–204.

16. George Biggar, "Foreword," *WLS Family Album, 1930* (Chicago: Prairie Farmer, 1930), 2; Biggar, "Those Good Old Days," 16 (quoting "We feel"); "Listener's Mike," *Prairie Farmer's New WLS Weekly*, February 16, 1935, 18 ("I must tell you"), 2 ("I have laughed").

17. "Listener's Mike," *Stand By!* October 5, 1935, 2 ("Don't get too much"); "Listener's Mike," *Prairie Farmer's New WLS Weekly*, March 16, 1935, 2 ("Let's have more"); "Listener's Mike," *Stand By!* December 21, 1935, 2.

18. Biggar, "Those Good Old Days," 9 ("only natural"); Biggar, "Foreword," 2 ("book of pictures"); "What They Like to Eat," *Behind the Scenes Souvenir Booklet*, 27 ("we thought").

19. "Listener's Mike," *Prairie Farmer's New WLS Weekly*, February 23, 1935, 2 ("I feel I know"); "They Call Us Home Folks," 8–9 ("You seem just like"); George Biggar, "When the Cowbells Ring Out on Saturday Night: It's National Barn Dance," undated ms., file folder on WLS–National Barn Dance, Country Music Hall of Fame and Archives, Nashville, Tennessee ("To the average" and "But if the listener").

20. George Biggar, "Mountain Music Plus," *Stand By!* June 8, 1935, 5 ("We northerners"); George Biggar, "Minstrels in the Hayloft," *Prairie Farmer's New WLS Weekly*, March 23, 1935, 5 ("certain members"); Dolly Sullivan, "When One Man Is a Family," *Rural Radio*, August 1938, 6 (quoting "if properly produced"). Nothing in the weekly radio magazines indicates that sponsors or the station considered African Americans in creating their programming. Not surprisingly, histories that address African Americans in Chicago, when they do discuss their relationship to radio, pay very little attention, if any, to WLS, which suggests that black radio audiences were not tuning in to the Prairie Farm station. See, for example, Nicholas Lemann, *The Promised Land: The Great Black Migration and How It Changed America* (New York: Knopf, 1991); Barbara Dianne Savage, *Broadcasting Freedom: Radio, War, and the Politics of Race, 1938–1948* (Chapel Hill: University of North Carolina Press, 1999); Lizabeth Cohen, *Making a New Deal: Industrial Workers in Chicago, 1919–1939* (New York: Cambridge University Press, 1990); Derek W. Vaillant, "The Sounds of Whiteness: Local Radio, Racial Formation, and Public Culture in Chicago, 1921–1935," *American Quarterly* 54 (March 2002): 25–66.

21. For the itinerary and attendance reports of the WLS Minstrels, see the numerous advertising announcements that appeared in *Stand By!* during fall 1935. For example: "Don't Fail to Remind Your Local Theater Manager to Get Early Bookings on the WLS Minstrels—There are Thirty Great Entertainers Included in its Cast—A Real Revival of an Old-Time Minstrel With its First Part—Olio—and a Grand Finale by the Entire Company," *Stand By!* September 28, 1935, 15. For descriptions of the standard "Old-Time Minstrel" format and cast of characters, see the following contemporary guidebooks on putting together a minstrel show, all located in the Blackface Minstrel Collection at the Center for Popular Music at Middle Tennessee State University: William DeVere, *Devere's Negro Recitations and End Men's Gags: Adapted to the Use of Amateurs and Professionals* (Chicago: Charles T. Powner, 1946), 5–9; *That Corking Good Minstrel Book* (Syracuse, N.Y.: Willis N. Bugbee, 1949), 7–8;

J. C. McMullen, *The Lazy Moon Minstrels: A Complete Minstrel Show* (Boston: Fitzgerald, 1934), 7. For "cork-opry," see Bob Emmett, "Minstrelsy," *Billboard*, August 24, 1935, 25.

22. "Minstrels," *Billboard*, July 7, 1923, 46. Minstrel appearance information can be corroborated in another recurring feature of *Billboard*, "The Route Department," which provided entertainment tour schedules.

23. For the account of By-Gosh, see "Minstrelsy," *Billboard*, September 29, 1923, 46. On the Chicago Costume Works, see advertisement headed "Introducing the Best Yet! Jack Weber's Blackface Make-Up," *Billboard*, May 5, 1923, 57. For a sampling of the various guidebooks not mentioned above, see the following, all in the collection of the Center for Popular Music: LeRoy Stahl, *The Five Star Minstrel Book: Suggestions and Material for Staging a Complete Minstrel Show* (Minneapolis: Northwestern Press, 1938); LeRoy Stahl, *The Varsity Minstrels* (Minneapolis: Northwestern Press, 1941); *Kaser's Complete Minstrel Guide* (Chicago: Dramatic Publishing Company, 1934); Catherine Marshall, *Kiddie-Kutups Minstrels: A Complete Minstrel Show for Children* (Chicago: Dramatic Publishing Company, 1934); Harold Rossiter, *How to Put on a Minstrel Show* (Chicago: Max Stein, 1921). For the most comprehensive history of the Amos and Andy phenomenon, see Melvin Patrick Ely, *The Adventures of Amos 'n' Andy: A Social History of an American Phenomenon* (New York: Free Press, 1991).

24. Carl Wittke, *Tambo and Bones: A History of the American Minstrel Stage* (reprt., Westport, Conn.: Greenwood, 1971), vii ("happy memories"); Wittke's characterization of "folk figure" was adapted from Francis Pendleton Gaines, *The Southern Plantation: A Study in the Development and Accuracy of a Tradition* (New York: Columbia University Press, 1924), 3, quoted in Wittke, *Tambo and Bones*, 7–8. For the various monikers, see Stahl, *Five Star Minstrel Book*, 88.

25. Charles Hamm, "The Last Minstrel Show," in *Putting Popular Music in its Place* (Cambridge: Cambridge University Press, 1995), 363 ("mentality and morality"); Stahl, *Five Star Minstrel Book*, 5 ("real minstrel"). For examinations of blackface minstrelsy that have influenced my perceptions, see Dale Cockrell, *Demons of Disorder: Early Blackface Minstrels and their World* (New York: Cambridge University Press, 1997); Robert C. Toll, *Blacking Up: The Minstrel Show in Nineteenth-Century America* (New York: Oxford University Press, 1974); Eric Lott, *Love and Theft: Blackface Minstrelsy and the American Working Class* (New York: Oxford University Press, 1993).

26. Bob Emmett, "Minstrelsy," *Billboard*, May 11, 1935, 26. Red Foley's lyrics are to the 1947 recording of "Tennessee Saturday Night."

27. "Old Pappy," *WLS Family Album, 1932* (Chicago: Prairie Farmer, 1932), 41 ("long fascinated"); "Man on the Cover," *Prairie Farmer's New WLS Weekly*, March 2, 1935, 15 ("composite character"); "Pa Smithers at WLS," ibid., March 9, 1935, 7 ("veteran guide" and "manner of a southern colored character"); "Listener's Mike," *Stand By!* April 6, 1935, 11 ("'Who's dat?'"). An instruction manual from the mid-1920s may have recognized the blurring between black and white rural culture. Under "Corn-Fed Cutups: A Novelty White-Face Minstrel Show," the author suggested how to put on a country program. The standard characters were present but were not black. They were what observers from later in the century may have recognized as a *Hee Haw* ensemble. According to the booklet, the material "may be used as a First Part or as an Afterpiece." It was set up to provide "Fifty Minutes of Side-Splitting Fun in a Country General Store." See Walter Ben Hare, *The Minstrel Encyclopedia* (Boston: Walter H. Baker, 1926), 66.

28. Jack Harris, "From the Hills of Tennessee," *Rural Radio*, July 1938, 7 ("carryin' on"); Lambdin Kay, "Stay the Way," ibid., April 1938, 19 ("Hillbilly").

29. "Dedication," *WLS Family Album, 1942* (Chicago: Prairie Farmer, 1942), 2 ("greatest of all forces"); Milton Mezzrow and Bernard Wolfe, *Really the Blues* (New York: Random House, 1946), 61 ("called 'nigger music,'"); Ann Shaw Faulkner, "Does Jazz Put the Sin into Syncopation?" *Ladies Home Journal*, August 1921, 34 ("Jazz originally"); "Too Much Jazz Basis for New Role of Laurette Taylor," reprinted in Neil Leonard, *Jazz and the White American: The Acceptance of a New Art Form* (Chicago: University of Chicago Press, 1962), 38 "(impulse for wildness").

30. Paul Whiteman and Mary Margaret McBride, *Jazz* (New York: J. H. Sears, 1926), 5–6 ("harmful and degrading"); Frederick Lewis Allen, *Only Yesterday: An Informal History of the Nineteen Twenties*, 32nd ed. (New York: Blue Ribbon Books, 1931), 92 ("womanly purity"), 90 ("syncopated embrace"); Henry Ford, with Samuel Crowther, *My Life and Work* (Garden City, N.Y.: Doubleday, Page, 1922), 250 ("We are not actuated"); Ford, *Today and Tomorrow*, 226.

31. John R. McMahon, "Our Jazz-Spotted Middle West," *Ladies Home Journal*, February 1927, 38 ("accepted axion"); "Allemand Right!" *WLS Family Album, 1934* (Chicago: Prairie Farmer, 1934), 38 ("old square dances"); "Listener's Mike," *Stand By! Prairie Farmer's Radio Weekly*, November 9, 1935, 2 ("younger generation"); ibid., December 12, 1935, 2 ("My brother"). Also see Morroe Berger, "Jazz: Resistance to the Diffusion of a Culture-Pattern," *Journal of Negro History* 32 (October 1947): 461–94.

32. "Listener's Mike," *Stand By! Prairie Farmer's Radio Weekly*, August 31, 1935, 13 ("isn't what it was"); ibid., October 5, 1935, 2 ("grow tired").

33. "Listener's Mike," *Stand By!* October 19, 1935, 2 (letter from "Sophs and Juniors" and editorial response).

34. "Listener's Mike," *Stand By!* November 16, 1935, 2 (first quotation); ibid., November 9, 1935, 2 (next four quotations); ibid., November 23, 1935, 2 (last quotation).

35. "Listener's Mike," *Stand By!* December 14, 1935, 2 ("hundreds of stations" and "music of our fathers"); ibid., November 9, 1935, 2 ("what will older folks do"); ibid., November 23, 1935, 2 ("My goodness").

36. "The Novelodeons," *WLS Family Album, 1938* (Chicago: Prairie Farmer, 1938), 27 ("rollicking comedy"); "The Hoosier Hot Shots," *WLS Family Album, 1934* (Chicago: Prairie Farmer, 1934), 30 ("uproarious").

37. "Listener's Mike," *Stand By!* November 2, 1935, 2 ("retrieve our high purpose"); "Radio Farm Digest," *Rural Radio*, May 1939, 25 ("Surely").

38. "Listener's Mike," November 9, 1935, 2.

39. "Listener's Mike," November 23, 1935, 2 ("wish to add"); George Biggar, "Saturday Night Treasure Chest," *Stand By!* August 31, 1935, 13 ("artists seem like home folks"); "Listener's Mike," ibid., November 23, 1935, 2 ("tommyrot").

40. "And That Is Hay," *Newsweek*, May 3, 1943, 64 ("authentic Americana"); "All Veteran News," December 1938, in Chuck Hurt Scrapbooks, file folder on WLS–National Barn Dance, Country Music Hall of Fame and Archives, Nashville, Tennessee ("homey atmosphere"); Biggar, "Saturday Night Treasure Chest," 13 (quoting "When I listen").

41. "Listener's Mike," *Prairie Farmer's New WLS Weekly*, February 23 1935, 15 ("We can hear"); William Leuchtenburg, *The Perils of Prosperity, 1914–1932* (Chicago: University of Chicago Press, 1958), 175 ("sentimentalized").

6 PATRIARCHY AND THE GREAT DEPRESSION

Kristine M. McCusker

Chicagoans suffered mightily during the Great Depression, as the many factories that made up its economy shuttered their doors, throwing hundreds of thousands of residents out of work. In the worst years of the depression (1931–33), the historian David Kennedy writes, 50 percent were unemployed in the city and "lost wages from unemployment were estimated at $2 million per day in late 1931; relief expenditures totaled $100,000 per day." Ironically, men lost their jobs in greater numbers than women because men were concentrated in heavy industries (car, tractor, and steel production) that were particularly hard hit, whereas job segregation had relegated women to "light" industry jobs (wiring light bulbs, for example), waitressing, secretarial work, or teaching, all of which experienced less unemployment. Chicagoans noticed the effect on families as breadwinners sat idle while their wives and children supported the family, and as men's status and respect diminished within the family. One woman (who remained employed while her husband was not) remarked, "You know, who make the money he [*sic*] is the boss."[1]

Chicago residents—as well as those in the surrounding four states who made up the National Barn Dance's main audience—looked out their windows (or around their living rooms) and saw utter chaos. But when they listened to the National Barn Dance, they heard something different, comfortable, and warm. They heard the soothing sounds of lullabies, sung softly and sweetly by pioneer fathers and virtuous mothers who promised, as George C. Biggar, the WLS promotional director, wrote, to "radiate simplicity, informality, friendliness, understanding and good clean fun." At the precise moment when the Great Depression threatened patriarchal families through an attack on the family economy, the National Barn Dance tried to reaffirm their potency, arguing that past families were wholesome and traditional and that the current economic situation could not dislodge such families from American homes. Performers were "staunch men and women" whose behavior was part of a traditional past, a stable set of relationships that were sincere and natural, reinforced by old-time music.[2] If listeners simply tuned in, their belief in this kind of family would be preserved.

The gendered images barn dance performers portrayed reinforced the male-breadwinner ethic just as it was under substantial attack by the Great Depression. By gender, I mean the ways that Americans defined the roles for men and women and the various assumptions associated with being either male or female. Rather than fixed entities as the label "traditional" seems to imply, "gender" implies that those roles are fluid and change over time. In this particular case, the National Barn Dance used two primary means to counter these new challenges and changes to gendered relationships within the family, to make solid that which seemed remarkably fragile. First, it presented stage characters who implied all was well within the family even when it seemed otherwise. A gendered stage—where men played the patriarch and women the sacrificing mother—was critical to this task. Fan ephemera, especially the annual *Family Album* WLS produced throughout the 1930s, were another potent means of preserving the breadwinner ethic since fans received them and enjoyed them in their homes, reinforcing what fans heard on stage. Barn dance radio, broadcasters proclaimed loud and clear, would save the family in desperate economic times. But those images had the attendant effect of making the National Barn Dance the most popular program nationally during the 1930s, expanding its popularity beyond the upper Midwest and making it one of the most popular radio programs in general that listeners tuned into whether they were in Chicago, Los Angeles, or Atlanta.[3] The National Barn Dance was the cutting edge for barn dance programs nationwide, and its influence was felt on multiple levels, including and especially in its views of gender relationships within the patriarchal family.

Historians are limited by what evidence remains from a given era, meaning the assertions we make have to be proven by extant primary source material. In the case of the National Barn Dance, the script material that does survive, though limited, suggests that radio men began to change how the Barn Dance was presented sometime in the late 1920s. It would be a remarkable shift, one that was accompanied by equally important shifts in business practices, hidden (sort of) from the listener. The effect would be to make a regional radio program, heard by just a few, into a nationally important event.

The new image performers promoted suggested male musicians and singers were like the pioneer men who wrenched the mountain South from "savages" (in their words) to build an independent nation and to make a home for women who would raise patriotic children. At least, that is what Bradley Kincaid told WLS listeners in some scripts that remain from either 1928 or 1929. Kincaid, who had migrated from Kentucky to Chicago to attend the YMCA College there, believed that the working-class music (which he referred to as "hillbilly") then popular on the National Barn Dance was immoral, and he used his mountain people to proclaim old-time music's importance in solving contemporary problems. Limited evidence hampers us in examining how extensively he used this new image, at least on stage, since Kincaid saved only four scripts from his time at WLS, all of them speeches that seem to be fundraisers for his alma mater, Berea College; none of them seems to be a script from a National Barn Dance program. Most likely, there were no National Barn Dance scripts to save, since most were not written until the early 1930s when sponsoring companies demanded they see and "clear" (or approve) a script. But other material—namely, the songbooks the entrepreneurial Kincaid sold from WLS's stage—suggest the ideas he laid out in those speeches were then applied wholesale to his character on the air (figure 37).

As Kincaid held his fundraiser, the Great Depression had yet to hit Chicago and audiences were still tuning in to radio as a novelty during the late 1920s, the Jazz Age. The Jazz Age and jazz babies with their fancy gin flasks and Charleston dancing were in full rage, but it was a lifestyle that Kincaid abhorred. He proffered, instead, a lifestyle nurtured by Berea College, where students were taught to be Christian citizens. Its students (represented on stage by the Berea College Girls' Glee Club when he held fundraisers) were mountaineers whose lives

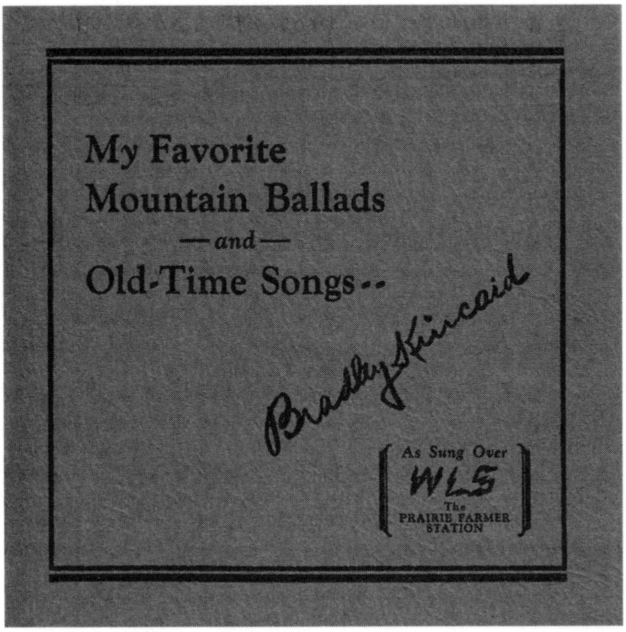

Figure 37. Ephemera such as this Bradley Kincaid songbook linked listeners to performers and became effective marketing tools for both the stars and WLS. Bradley Kincaid Collection, Southern Appalachian Archives, Berea College.

spent in isolation had allowed "an atmosphere of reverence and simplicity and the spirit of pioneer freedom" to remain intact from the past to the present. It was an atmosphere forged by the colonization of the rugged mountain South, by the mountaineers' "aggressive qualities," Kincaid told audiences, which had "subdued an unbroken wilderness," "founded Commonwealths, [*sic*] and made possible the building of a great nation west of the Alleghenies." It was a world where patriotism still existed, where mutual respect and cooperation were common rather than being rapidly disappearing values, as they seemed to be in modern Chicago.[4]

Necessary—no, essential—to taming the modern world of jazz babies were the traditional and timeless southern patriarchal families anchored by "dauntless old warrior-farmers." The venerable mountain man had stayed "the hand of hostile savages and open[ed] up vast areas of virgin land to the home-loving white settler who longed for a place where he could rear his children in peace," and in doing so he had been "patriotic in a very marked degree," according to Kincaid. In his scripts, he assumed midwestern men were nearly as visionary as southern men (important for a program broadcast to the heartland from Chicago), but it was not an intrinsic midwestern value that supported that pioneering spirit. Rather, it was the mountain man who had ventured out from the mountain South to "civilize" the Old Northwest that made that latter region and those men worthy of mention.[5]

By the warrior-farmer's side was the southern mother, who sacrificed herself to the good of her children and, by extension, the nation. Kincaid told listeners that she was "willing to serve that her children may be happy; she is willing to grow weak if only they will grow strong." It was her sacrifices that made the mountain South the moral region it was, and it was her children (like Kincaid) who would tame the flappers and jazz babies who cared more about dancing and drinking than patriotism and sacrifice for the good of the nation.[6]

Jazz Age gender roles represented by the gin-swigging, free-wheeling flapper with bobbed hair, so contradictory to his traditional mountain family, caused Kincaid the most angst and elicited his most vehement disapproval. A mountain man did not "bother his brains," Kincaid sniffed, "about 'Trial Marriages,' or 'Companionate Marriage,' or 'Birth Control,' or certain other social questions which seem to be driving some minds towards the brink of the social precipice." Nor did his wife worry about "'family budgeting,'" "careers outside the home," "diets for people who are reducing," or "professional advice about child-bearing and child-rearing." Mountain men and women stayed focused: the man completed his duties as a father and patriarch, keeping his family noble and honorable while his wife completed her duties within the home. For Kincaid, mothers were especially dutiful since they subordinated their "own personal ambition to the welfare of [their] offspring."[7]

How did music play a part in this vision? According to Kincaid, music was an almost physical link to the mountaineer past. When mountaineers played fiddle tunes like "Buck Creek Girls," "Forked Deer," and others, those songs, Kincaid claimed, were ones that the "Master of Mount Vernon [George Washington] used to dance to on the merry-making occasions which broke the monotony of duties on his great Virginia farm." Listeners could almost feel the presence of Washington and that noble past, or so it seemed. Ballads like "Pretty Fair Miss" (which the Girls' Glee Club sang one evening) were relics from that same colonial past that had fostered the patriotic values mountaineers possessed. As Kincaid told his listeners, "The young women of the more remote parts of the Mountains [*sic*] love to sing these old ballads and songs while they are doing the housework. It drives away lonesomeness. They sing as naturally as the wood thrush sings, and for very much the same reason."[8]

Kincaid's popularity eventually led him to greener pastures, and broadcasters searched for a new mountain man to replace him. They found him in John Lair, a former insurance executive and Kentuckian, who produced many of the National Barn Dance's regional programs and who discovered some of the program's most popular entertainers, including Lulu Belle Wiseman, Red Foley, and Lily May Ledford (figures 38, 39). It was during his tenure that the National Barn Dance and WLS itself became more professional, following many of the tricks of the radio trade touted by the most successful radio stations across the nation. Probably the most important strategy was the selling of air time to sponsors. While there were earlier partnerships, the most successful one was between Miles Laboratories' Alka-Seltzer and the National Barn Dance, broadcast over NBC. Miles Laboratories endorsed a one-hour portion of the National Barn Dance, beginning in January 1933, and quickly extended its contract when the sales of Alka-Seltzer increased by $1.2 million in that year alone.[9] The National Barn Dance, Miles accountants stated in their 1936 annual report, "was primarily responsible for the wonderful increase in Alka-Seltzer sales."[10] Because its sponsorship produced the desired results (increased sales), Miles expanded the amount of money it paid to the National Barn Dance from approximately $120,000 in 1933 to $329,000 in 1934, almost $567,000 in 1935, and $766,000 in 1936.[11] Other sponsors, including Aladdin Lamps, Pinex Cough Syrup, and Hamlin Wizard Oil (a muscle relaxant), followed suit, sponsoring the regional portions of the Barn Dance (figure 40).

Sponsors required written scripts and, later, transcriptions (from the recorded broadcasts of shows) so they could approve performers' material. If they were going to pay for the program, the program had better be to their liking and sell the product in appropriate ways. Because of this practice, more script material exists from the 1930s than before. John Lair was especially diligent in writing and then preserving his scripts, music, and other documents. His collection of script material—a remarkably rich and substantial set of documents—seems to begin with his earliest days on WLS (some of his early scripts are undated, but are most likely from 1930 and 1931),[12] stretching from his time on WLS to his days at Cincinnati's WLW, and on to when he ventured out on his own to start the Renfro Valley Barn Dance.

Sponsors were one new reality, but so too was an economic downturn that proved remarkably long lived and stubborn. Although most historians put the start date of the Great Depression as October 19, 1929, the day of the stock market crash, most Americans did not feel its effects until 1930 and 1931, when banks across the nation began to fail and unemployment rose to 25 percent. Those who remained employed worked at reduced hours

Figure 38. Born Myrtle Eleanor Cooper in 1913 in North Carolina, "Lulu Belle" became white hot in 1933 and 1934 and was elected Radio Queen in 1936. In the early years, her comedy was as well known as her music. Southern Music and Radio Photographic Collection, Southern Appalachian Archives, Berea College.

and for reduced pay, especially in heavy industries such as automobile manufacturing and steel production. Ironically, radio's burgeoning popularity made it one industry that did not feel the effects of the Depression, and the women who wired radios continued to work throughout the 1930s. Alka-Seltzer's success during the 1930s also kept workers (two-thirds of them women) stuffing pill bottles with the elixir that promised to relieve stress.

President Herbert Hoover, a popular Republican president elected in 1928, seemed

Figure 39. Lily May Ledford was discovered by John Lair and brought to Chicago from her native Kentucky. She later followed Lair to Renfro Valley. John Lair Collection, Southern Appalachian Archives, Berea College.

unable to counter the crisis. Hoover believed individuals would help out their friends and neighbors in the spirit of the pioneering days, an image remarkably similar to Kincaid's vision of rugged mountain people. But the president failed to account for some harsh new realities: in this era, few were left untouched by the Depression and few had extra resources to donate. Large numbers of families were left destitute from job losses and bank failures. It is unclear how this affected family dynamics specifically, but many men abandoned their families and took to the rails as hobos in search of work (including my own grandfather). At the same time, a substantial number of women kept their jobs or entered the workforce

Figure 40. One measure of Lily May Ledford's fame was reflected in a commercial comic strip, which paired her with barefoot, gun-toting, pipe-smoking stereotypical mountain characters. John Lair Collection, Southern Appalachian Archives, Berea College.

when their husbands were laid off. The comment by the woman quoted in the opening of this chapter suggests that stressed families were reimagining who was in charge, something that historians of the Depression era, such as Lizabeth Cohen, have examined but have not been able to nail down definitively in terms of absolute numbers.[13] As one California woman wrote to Eleanor Roosevelt in 1934, "My work has continued and my salary alone has just been sufficient to make our monthly payments on the house and keep our bills paid. But with the exception of two and one-half months work with the U.S. Coast and Geodetic Survey under the C.W.A., my husband has not worked since August, 1932."[14] Even as Franklin Roosevelt promised a new deal for Americans, people were stressed and scared, wondering what their future held for them and for their families.

Radio tended to avoid mentioning the Great Depression and its attendant problems because producers thought their job was to enliven the audience, not demoralize them. John Lair was not as circumspect in his early days on the barn dance, in 1930 and 1931.[15] On one show in September 1931, for example, he told audiences, "Lot of you folks is bin astin fer blues—that's easy understood, tho, —lots of folks is got the blues this year that never had em before."[16] But even as he acknowledged the problems, he found ways to make light of them, to whisk them away with a song and a giggle using a unique group of musicians and comedians called the Cumberland Ridge Runners. That original group included Red Foley, Karl and Harty, Slim Miller, and Hugh Cross. No women performed on Lair's regional shows (typically broadcast before or after the national *Alka-Seltzer Hour*) until he hired Jeanne Muenich to play Linda Parker, the Sunbonnet Girl, in January 1932.

Like Bradley Kincaid, Lair set his shows in the mountain South until western imagery became popular in the mid-1930s, and then he mingled the two in his *Bunk House* and *Log Cabin* shows. And also like Kincaid, he cast his male characters as descendants of mountain South pioneering stock, but with a twist: his pioneers had migrated to the big city (Chicago, in this instance) and set about recreating their home communities, only this time they invited Chicagoans to join in from their living rooms. At their head was John Lair, the avid song collector, benign patriarch, and master of ceremonies who managed his performers (like any good father) on stage and off. He typically showed up with his "trusty" notebook, ready to regale the audience with a song and a story about it, music that had reportedly existed for many years in the "isolated" southern mountains.

The community the benevolent patriarch Lair headed initially focused on the core of a mountain home—the front porch—and from that front porch the Cumberland Ridge Runners played lively music, featuring a fiddle, banjo, and guitar and mountain voices singing together in ways reminiscent of their upbringing. Male performers were good ol' boys, willing to tickle the listener's funny bone, play some good music, and generally have a good time. Hugh Cross was one of those good ol' boys, having fun on stage even when the moment might be a sad one. After Cross sang "Messing the Blues," one night, Lair told his audience, "Good thing we aint got this here television up here. Ole Hugh woulda spoiled things with that big grin of hisn. He kaint leave it off long enough to sing the blues, even."[17]

While they might have been funny, the Ridge Runners were also "natural" musicians, meaning their talent was organic, learned in the home, not nurtured by outside sources. They could not read music and in fact eschewed external influences that might change the authenticity of their music. Lair featured that natural musicianship on a show from 1934, whereby a fictitious music teacher attempted to teach fine music and musicianship to an equally fictitious Kentucky community. As the fake teacher told the audience, "They [the Ridge Runners] insist that they don't know one note from another, yet they sit here with an air of unconcern and play the most stirring music I've ever heard."[18]

But while they were willing to "cut up" and act natural, male performers were also noble men who acted like their pioneering forebears. The pioneering past the Ridge Runners staged was a Kentucky one, filled with "a breed of . . . men an wimmin fit to carry on their heritage of hard work an tribulation," Lair told listeners.[19] In some ways, Lair's shows were not as romanticized as Kincaid's. "Wimmin," Lair said on one show, "are walkin' 20 miles with a baby in their arms to git a head of cabbage to feed their starvin' brood on."[20] But he echoed Kincaid's assertion that those hardships produced strong, capable, hardworking "wimmin" and men who could save the nation. Lair told his listeners, for example, "The wolves howled along their trail [and] the indun always had a fire ready to torture their flesh er destroy their home. New-made graves dotted the clearins around the cabins, but the survivors kept grimly on."[21] By emphasizing the hardships and fortitude of early mountaineers who built a nation by staving off wolves and "savages," Lair announced to his audience that those values still existed, represented on the National Barn Dance by the Ridge Runners.

Lair made that historical link more explicit and concrete in shows and music ("songs with a past," he called them) focused on historical events. In his Civil War commemorative show, for example, Lair attempted to recreate the devastating battlefields of the 1860s, interspersing his comments with music to bolster the image of the honorable man in listeners' imaginations.[22] His intent was to make all male participants, whether northern or southern, noble warriors who had common, wholesome upbringings and who had brought those good solid American values from their farms and pastures to the battlefield. He told audiences about "thousands of dyin boys cryin out in their last precious minnits fer Mother, like this boy [Mac and Bob sing 'Break the News to Mother']. An Mother heard. Don't think she didn't. No matter how fer apart they were. Here's a song about one Mother who knew her boy would never come whistlin up the lane agin[,] never smell the honeysuckle coverin the old palin' fence around the yard, never see another sunset acrost the pasture field ner sing around the farm with the joy of livin."[23]

As this particular script suggests, women were metaphors in these early programs, sanctified images to fight over, not real women who sang to audiences on stage. But radio's common implication that it was "real life"—that it was not a special kind of fiction that was artificial and tainted—required Lair to put women on stage. Even more remarkable, he proved to have a special talent for discovering outstanding female performers, including Lulu Belle Wiseman, Lily May Ledford, and Cousin Emmy. That first outstanding female star he found was Muenich, who performed as Linda Parker (figure 41). The Sunbonnet Girl was a female image he built based on a common musical icon named the "sentimental mother" by ethnomusicologists. The sentimental mother had roots in a Victorian idol, the deified mother who was the mistress of the home and the moral guide for men.[24] Lair combined the sentimental mother with a musical tradition called the "elegiac tradition" to dramatize children's separation from mothers. He also provided her a home place, the southern mountains, and gave her some of

Figure 41. The Cumberland Ridge Runners. Homer "Slim" Miller, in the foreground, holds up the stereotype of the hillbilly fiddler (albeit with socks on); left to right, rear: Karl Davis, John Lair, Linda Parker, Harty Taylor, Red Foley, and Hugh Cross. John Lair Collection, Southern Appalachian Archives, Berea College.

the same tasks that Kincaid had used regarding her role in southern life specifically and American life in general, for example, to preserve old ballads and other songs from the colonial era. But Lair modernized her for radio stages, which required young, attractive women. The old, careworn mother became a young woman, pretty, perky, peppy, and ready to sing mountain ballads and tunes from the past.[25] This image would form the basis for all female characters on barn dance radio stages and in country music after the earlier genre's demise.

What did such a woman sing and perform on the National Barn Dance? As Lair told listeners, she was a living example of the past, a remnant of a bygone time and a better place that was calm and filled with noble women. One night on a Hamlin Wizard Oil show, Lair told listeners that a young man had found "a purty young girl, singin a song he had often heard his mother sing frum the time he wuz jest a baby. She wuz a mighty purty girl, standin' there in the door with her head throwed back an the monin sun runnin it's [*sic*] fingers through her hair." Then, Linda Parker stepped up to the mike to reenact that old-timey moment by singing "Barbara Allen," an old English folk tune considered a remnant of the colonial era. The script then described the marriage of the two, the commitment they shared, and her sacrifices to make him a better man. Lair said, "He wuz seein agin the rosy-cheeked laffin-eyed girl that she wuz then—the girl that had proved a greater treasure to him than the gold he had started out to seek for. The girl that stood there by his side, slippin her hand into his . . ." [Linda Parker then sang the song "Maggie"].[26]

The *Family Album* and fan magazines, both tools of a modern radio business (after all, broadcasters had to keep in touch with the listener/customer once the radio was turned off), reinforced the images projected from the stage by touting the dynamic nature of the patriarchal family, rather than its potential demise. But the *Family Album* was far more explicit in that goal since its appearance once a year, rather than weekly (as with *Stand By!*), allowed editors to shape a substantial message to listeners in a careful and concerted manner. Indeed, the whole idea behind the *Family Album* was to tout WLS as a family station and, simultaneously, to reinforce traditional economic roles for men and women on and off the air. That latter intention was only hinted at, however, in the first *Family Album*, published in 1930 (see figure 3), but the hint was a strong one. Featured on the front cover was a family settled around the radio, Father with his newspaper and his pipe, Mother with her sewing, Daughter feeding her doll a bottle, and Son playing with a model airplane, each representing the magazine's caption, "The Happy Radio Home." This first edition was more disorganized than later editions, simply displaying pictures of various studio broadcasters and performers (including studio musicians) and including a long list of stations that interested rural listeners across the region could tune in to. Group photos introduced various writers and broadcasters, but there were no pictures of individual performers who were popular (such as Kincaid).[27]

By 1933, however, the *Family Album* had evolved into a more professionally produced magazine that not only featured WLS's performers but also highlighted the gender-segregated labor force at the station, alive, well, and quite contrary to the experience of many

Chicagoans during the Great Depression. It was also a more consciously packaged product, indicative of the barn dance's (as well as the station's) evolution from a local broadcasting agent to a national phenomena that anchored NBC's Saturday-night schedule by the mid-1930s. Pictures highlighted popular groups who were all part of the family of entertainers, for example, the Cumberland Ridge Runners, the square dancers and square dance bands, and Martha Crane and her *Home Maker's Hour* staff, the latter probably one of many attempts to build a daytime audience among women who remained home with their children. Indeed, editors told viewers that "thousands of homes have come to look forward to Martha Crane's daily visit as if she were a member of the family."[28]

Besides stars, the publication portrayed staff employees listeners never heard on the air, the people who dealt with more mundane details than a polka or square dance, but whose work was important to keeping the station up and running. Those off-air staff people replicated on-air gendered images. WLS men were managers, power brokers, or bosses. They announced programs, managed the station, or engineered programs in ways that kept technicalities from getting in the way of fans' listening pleasure. Men like Floyd Keepers, managing editor of the *Prairie Farmer* magazine, were patriarchs still firmly in charge of the station's business and family. Next to the "market men" and engineers were the "office girls," an "important part of our family circle," who answered the thousands of letters that arrived at the station daily from fans.[29] Secretarial work—a kind of office housekeeping—was their contribution to the radio family, keeping the basic, mundane elements of the station going just like mothers who worked hard with little notice at similar boring duties.

If the earliest issues of *Family Album* were a mishmash of pictures and the mid-1930s versions were more professional documents touting the radio family, by 1938 the *Family Album* reached out more broadly, proclaiming radio's mission in preserving American culture in general, not just the family. "We face the future," that album said in its opening pages that year, lauding the WLS Creed that described radio as a "God-given instrument which makes possible vital economic, educational and inspirational service to the home-loving men, women and children of America."[30] Employees, already placed in their proper occupational roles in the radio family in earlier albums, now appeared with their families in the pages in a way that reinforced the idea of radio's ability to serve the public through "home-loving" citizens. One of those home-loving citizens was the station's continuity director, Frank Baker, whose "fine family," as album pages described his wife and two children, appeared in a photo with him.[31] Of course, it was barn dance performers and, in essence, the barn dance family who anchored these pages. Lulu Belle Wiseman, 1936's "Radio Queen," cuddled in a photo with her husband, Scotty, but their daughter Linda Lou's attendant picture told audiences that "Linda Lou is really the boss in the family. Linda may take her mother's place as Radio Queen some day."[32] Where there were no pictures of performers with their spouses, an image of the husband or wife was superimposed over other family pictures. Patsy Montana was a popular subject for the photographer's lens and she sometimes appeared with fans (figure 42), but other pictures showed Montana and her daughters, with a picture of her husband, Paul Rose, superimposed.[33] The intent, of course, was to maintain the image of the patriarchal family even though it might be awkward to do so.

Even when the chaos of the outside world was at its worst, the National Barn Dance tried to reassure its listeners that family life, under significant attack beyond its radio studios, was just fine and dandy on stage. Fathers were the benevolent patriarchs in charge (and employed), mothers sacrificed to make a good home for their families, and children still respected their elders. That was the message for the Great Depression. But as a new crisis loomed on the horizon—a world war that would require the energies and commitment of a nation and a new way of presenting the *Family Album*—the program's intention shifted in order to fulfill its responsibilities in that new task. At least the scant evidence makes us think so. Few National Barn Dance show scripts or sound recordings exist after 1937, most of them recorded for the Armed Forces Radio Network during the war, and we know only in limited ways exactly what happened on stage. Fan documents gradually diminished in quantity, perhaps due to wartime rationing or need. We do not know what happened when

Figure 42. Patsy Montana signs autographs. Courtesy of Michael Montana.

other shows, especially the Grand Ole Opry, began eating away at the audiences and sponsors of the National Barn Dance. But we do know that the image of a traditional, stable, constant family was an important one in the 1930s, and it was that image that made the National Barn Dance so popular to listeners nationwide.

NOTES

1. David Kennedy, *Freedom from Fear: The American People in Depression and War, 1929–1945* (New York: Oxford University Press, 1999), 88; Lizabeth Cohen, *Making a New Deal: Industrial Workers in Chicago, 1919–1939* (New York: Cambridge University Press, 1990), 246–48 (quote, 248).

2. George C. Biggar, "When the Cowbells Ring Out on Saturday Night: It's National Barn Dance Time," preface, in Lair, *100 Barn Dance Favorites*, n.p.

3. Ibid.

4. Bradley Kincaid, "A Close-Up of the Mountaineers," n.d. [ca. 1928–29], Bradley Kincaid Papers, Southern Appalachian Collection, Berea College (hereafter, Kincaid Papers).

5. Bradley Kincaid, "America's Debt to the Mountains," n.d. [ca. 1928–29], Kincaid Papers.

6. Ibid.

7. Ibid.

8. Ibid.

9. Miles Laboratories, Annual Report, 1934, Bayer Corporate Archives (hereafter, BCA).

10. Miles Laboratories, Annual Report, 1936, BCA.

11. Ibid.

12. I referred to names of personnel to learn a general date for this undated material.

13. Cohen, *Making a New Deal*, 246–48.

14. Quoted in Robert S. McElvaine, ed., *Down and Out in the Great Depression: Letters from the "Forgotten Man"* (Chapel Hill: University of North Carolina Press, 1983), 54.

15. Ann Lair Henderson, telephone interview by Kristine M. McCusker, January 4, 1999.

16. Untitled radio script, September 26, 1931, John Lair Papers, Southern Appalachian Collection, Berea College (hereafter, Lair Papers).

17. Ibid.

18. Hamlin Wizard Oil radio script, February 24, 1934, Lair Papers.

19. Untitled radio script [ca. 1930–31], Lair Papers.

20. Ibid.

21. Ibid.

22. Hamlin Wizard Oil radio script, February 24, 1034.

23. Untitled radio script, [ca. early 1930s], Lair Papers.

24. William Ellis, "The Sentimental Mother Song in American Country Music, 1923–1945," Ph.D. diss., Ohio State University, 1978, 23.

25. I first presented information that appears in this paragraph in my article "'Bury Me beneath the Willow': Linda Parker and Definitions of Tradition on the National Barn Dance, 1932–1935," *Southern Folklore* 56 (1999): 223–44.

26. Hamlin Wizard Oil radio script, February 24, 1934.

27. *Family Album, 1930* (Chicago: Agricultural Broadcasting Company, 1930).

28. *Family Album, 1934* (Chicago: Agricultural Broadcasting Company, 1933).

29. Ibid., 46, 52.

30. *WLS Family Album* (Chicago: Prairie Farmer Publishing Company, 1938), 3.

31. Ibid., 9.

32. Ibid., 15.

33. Ibid., 20.

7 COWBOYS IN CHICAGO

Don Cusic

If you see a picture of a cowboy hat propped on a guitar you think "country music." If you see a singer walk on stage wearing cowboy boots and a cowboy hat, you think "country singer." If you see a real cowboy on a horse, you probably assume the cowboy loves country music. Or if you see someone wearing a cowboy hat and driving a pickup truck, you probably assume there's a country music station playing on the radio. So just how did country music become connected to cowboys and the West? And how did the cowboy become so closely identified with country music? After all, it didn't start out that way. Country music was first identified with the rural South, particularly mountaineers.

So what is the connection between cowboys and the great urban city of Chicago? There were cowboys in Chicago before the image of cowboys dominated country music; in fact, country singers dressed as cowboys in Chicago pioneered the popular singing cowboy movies in Hollywood and prompted country performers to wear western clothes for their performances. One of the most popular entertainers who came out of Chicago during the period 1932–35 was an entertainer who sang country songs dressed as a westerner.[1] Gene Autry became one of the most famous men in American entertainment during the first half of the twentieth century. He was one of the most influential country acts in the history of the genre, changing the "look" of country artists and introducing the "singing cowboys" to Hollywood. The singing cowboy movies became commercially successful and gave country music its first national exposure as well as a positive image. Ironically, the roots of the singing cowboys go back to WLS and the National Barn Dance in Chicago in the early 1930s. Autry established himself as a "star" while he was in Chicago and popularized the cowboy look for country entertainers. Because of the success of Gene Autry, WLS and the National Barn Dance were never without a cowboy star during the entire time the Barn Dance was on the air. When Autry moved to Hollywood and became a singing cowboy star in the movies in the mid-1930s, he brought a number of WLS acts to California to appear in his pictures with him. And the movie industry, trying to find singing cowboys to replicate Autry's success, often looked to Chicago and WLS, where it found a wealth of talent.

The cowboy as a romantic hero was rooted in American culture by the beginning of the twentieth century. The cowboy who drove cattle up the trails in the nineteenth century was a low-paid, hired worker who had a mostly boring though sometimes dangerous job. For the cowboy to become a romantic hero, the cattle had to be taken out of the picture, and this was done by show business.

First came the dime novels, which often used the West as a setting for adventure stories. Buffalo Bill Cody was one of the early western heroes of these dime novels; later, Cody organized a traveling wild west show. Cody's show reached the height of its fame in Chicago in 1893 at the World's Columbian Exposition. (The western show was held in a lot across from the main entrance to the fair.) Buffalo Bill Cody may have been America's first show business superstar; at the time of his death in 1917 he was certainly one of the most well known Americans.[2]

Intellectuals also helped. The historian Frederick Jackson Turner, whose "frontier thesis" was also presented in 1893 in Chicago during the world's fair, asserted that "the existence of an area of free land, its continuous recession, and the advance of American settlement westward, explain American development."[3] Turner's essay has been considered "the single most influential piece of writing in the history of American history."[4] This thesis makes the cowboy an essential figure, standing symbolically between the past and present of American history. The cowboy—or westerner—was a product of the savagery of the American frontier who "tamed" the West and became a mediator between civilization and that unruly region. The cowboy was a pioneer hero whose presence was a comfort to those facing a new frontier in a world filled with tomorrows that would not be like the past. The cowboy, therefore, was a comforting figure, assuring all who feared the future that it, too, could be tamed. Thus the nation looked to those who embraced the image of the cowboy to calm fears about the present and lead it into the future.

Politicians and highbrow writers were also important. In 1901, Theodore Roosevelt became president after William McKinley was assassinated. Roosevelt had lived in the West in the 1880s and written about it; he was widely known as "the cowboy president," and his connection with the West (and the Rough Riders) brought attention to cowboys and the West. Owen Wister, a Harvard classmate of Roosevelt, wrote *The Virginian*, which became a popular, best-selling novel when it was published in 1902 and established his central character as the prototype of the western hero.[5] Another novelist, Zane Grey, became the first great western novelist; his novels influenced countless other writers and his success proved there was a huge public demand for realistic westerns. A number of Grey's books were made into movies, including *Riders of the Purple Sage* and *The U.P. Trail.*

The movies have a long history with westerns. The first "feature" movie was a western, *The Great Train Robbery*, filmed in 1903 by Edwin S. Porter. The first person to create a series of western films was Broncho Billy Anderson, who also created the first western hero/character, Broncho Billy. Anderson and his partner, George K. Spoor, formed Essanay Film Manufacturing Company in Chicago before moving west to become the first film company headquartered in California. The Broncho Billy films began in 1908 and by 1920 were finished. Hollywood, California, was established as a center for movie making with the tremendous success of *The Squaw Man*, directed by Cecil B. DeMille, a western released in 1913.[6] During the silent film era, westerns became popular with audiences who loved action, drama, and western scenery. William S. Hart, who dominated western movies between 1915 and 1925, starred in films that were sentimental and romantic. The next major cowboy star after Hart was Tom Mix, who introduced flashy clothes to the silver screen cowboy's image. While Hart insisted on realism, Mix introduced escapism and the elements of the mythic cowboy: the loner who was clean living, fun loving, and who always did the right thing.[7]

After movies came music. In 1925 Carl T. Sprague, who worked at Texas A&M University, went to New York and recorded "When the Work's All Done This Fall," which sold 900,000 copies. This was the first "hit" recording of a cowboy song. Country music's biggest star, Jimmie Rodgers, recorded seven cowboy songs during the 1930s and even dressed like a cowboy during his later years. So the "cowboy" was well established as an American hero by the beginning of the 1930s.

The cowboy had a positive, national appeal, and the National Barn Dance also sought a positive, national appeal. The initial WLS owner, Sears, Roebuck, was a national organization that wanted to reach a national audience. By having "prairie" in its name, the *Prairie Farmer* magazine tended to look toward the West; under its eventual ownership the National Barn Dance stressed that "prairie ballads" were the essence of its musical selections. Thus the cowboy image fit WLS and the National Barn Dance as well as its owners and sponsors, especially during the Great Depression, when Americans had doubts about their country and their future and needed heroes. Moreover, Chicago was almost like a wild west town during the 1920s and 1930s with its gangsters led by Al Capone and corrupt city officials, as Lisa Boehm explains in this volume; for Chicago, the cowboy represented basic law and order.

By 1930, what became known as "country music" was well established and had become an important part of American music.[8] Although this "country" music was generally labeled "old familiar tunes" or "folk" music, the general term used in the music trade was "hillbilly" music. By 1930, however, the hillbilly was not a revered figure.

The "rube," or hillbilly, had been part of vaudeville, caricatured as an unlettered, uncultured, unsophisticated, moonshine-swigging mountaineer who was far removed from civilization. As J. W. Williamson points out in his book *Hillbillyland*, the hillbilly "drinks hard liquor—and not at cocktail parties. He's theatrically lazy but remains virile. He nearly always possesses the wherewithal for physical violence—especially involving dogs and guns. He's gullible when skepticism would be wiser and he's stupid when smart would be safer. He reminds us symbolically of filth."[9] Eventually, the cowboy would replace the hillbilly as a more positive image for listeners.

Rural life, like the hillbilly, was also looked down upon. The gap between the lifestyles of "city" and "country" people widened during the 1920s due to a number of technological advances: radio became part of American homes, the invention of the microphone improved phonograph records, and electricity became common in cities. In *Electrifying America: Social Meanings of a New Technology, 1880–1940*, David E. Nye notes that by 1930, about 70 percent of all homes in the United States had electricity and that by 1934, 96 percent of homes in towns and cities had lights. The homes that did not have electricity were primarily in rural areas, which increasingly separated the rural population from city dwellers; having electricity took on social and cultural significance: having electricity meant "progress" and moving up in the world.[10] Life in the city became increasingly different and distinct from life in the country, primarily because of electricity, so the "image" of the city dweller became someone who was cultured, sophisticated, worldly, savvy, and "hip," while the rural counterpart was increasingly seen as the opposite. During the late 1920s and 1930s, the music of the city was jazz, pop, classical, and big band, while the music linked to the rural areas was often known as "hillbilly."

Still, almost half the U.S. population resided in rural areas or small towns, and many city residents had a rural background. Americans romanticized their rural past while at the same time rejecting it. They also embraced their image and life as city dwellers yet were dismayed by the "evils" of the city: crime, corruption, loose morals, and the fact that the city was not as "neighborly" as the idealized country life. The Scopes trial, in Dayton, Tennessee, during twelve hot days in July 1925, pitted the "progressive" thinking of those who believed in evolution against the small-town values and thinking that were represented by William Jennings Bryan and his belief in the Bible. By the end of the trial, the rural townfolk of Dayton (as well as other small towns) were held up to ridicule because of their religious beliefs, while those who sided with the rational arguments of Clarence Darrow saw themselves as progressive—moving forward in a nation governed by scientific thought and secular reasoning despite rural America's pulling them backward into a religious fundamentalist past.[11]

The one figure in America's rural past who did not suffer a negative stereotype was the cowboy. Here was a pioneer who helped tame the wild west, a lone figure of honesty, integrity, and "neighborliness" who presented an image that rural or formerly rural Americans could embrace. Even city dwellers could embrace the cowboy and the image of a frontier that was confronted with courage and strength, because they too were facing a frontier of an America that was changing through technology, culture, and scientific thought.[12] The cowboy was a member of the working class but with a distinct difference: he did his work on a horse, looking down on the world while the world looked up to him. Also, western clothing was worn by the rancher as well as his hired hands, the working cowboy. The rancher represented wealth, success, ownership, and a worldliness beyond the everyday realm of the cowboy. Americans increasingly melded those two disparate images when they thought of westerners.[13]

Perhaps it is not surprising that the cowboy would become a central figure for country music in Chicago. The cowboy was distinctly Anglo-American, a "true" American at a time when many Americans were looking for the authentic. Perhaps it is also not surprising that it was a "singing cowboy" or a "cowboy singer" who would emerge as a star in Chicago. Chicago was, after all, a major entertainment center, the "toddlin' town" whose attractions were legion. In fact, it was second only to New York in terms of entertainment, its downtown area filled with ballrooms where big bands performed, clubs where jazz was played, and radio stations with network links. Los Angeles had a movie industry, but it would not be an entertainment center until World War II; Nashville would not emerge as a center for country music until after the war. In terms of country music prior to World War II, Chicago was the big "it." The city had the biggest and best country radio show, the National Barn Dance, on one of the nation's most powerful radio stations, WLS, and the audience who loved country music could easily hear the Chicago station. Also, Chicago's population included a number of people with rural roots, and "Chicagoland" encompassed a rural Midwest where performers could travel from the Barn Dance in Chicago to perform live for their fans. The stage was set in Chicago for a cowboy singer; all it needed was its star.

Gene Autry was born in Tioga, Texas, but spent many of his growing-up years in southeastern Oklahoma. After high school, he became a telegrapher with the Frisco Railroad and then, while working as a telegrapher, began his career as a recording artist, going to New York in 1929 to record with both Victor and the American Record Company (ARC). While in New York, Autry befriended Frankie and Johnny Marvin, who had established themselves as entertainers in the city. Through the Marvins, Autry obtained auditions with record labels as well as musical partners; Frankie Marvin would remain with Gene Autry until Autry retired from show business in 1960 and began his career as a baseball team owner. At ARC Autry worked with Art Satherley, who supervised his recordings. The label produced recordings for discount stores and Sears. Most of these stores issued the recordings under their own imprint; Sears leased recordings from ARC and sold them in their Sears catalog under the Conqueror label. Gene Autry began his career as a Jimmie Rodgers imitator, recording Rodgers's songs as well as tunes that sounded like they were Jimmie Rodgers songs.

In fall 1931, Jeff Shea, music buyer for Sears, approached Art Satherley about Autry's appearing on a show on WLS in Chicago sponsored by Conqueror Records. Shea told Satherley that Sears could not pay Autry—and neither could WLS—but thought it would be a good business venture because the exposure on WLS would boost sales of his records. Satherley offered Autry thirty dollars a week from the petty-cash account at ARC, and Autry accepted. Satherley also encouraged Autry to capitalize on his Texas and Oklahoma background and present a "western" image.[14] During that time Gene Autry recorded "That Silver-Haired Daddy of Mine," which was released about the same time he began at WLS.

Autry debuted on WLS on December 1, 1931, on *Tower Topics Time*, an early-morning radio show hosted by Anne Williams and Sue Roberts. Heard Monday through Friday, the show was sponsored by Sears and featured news about Sears and its products. Autry's segment was "Conqueror Records Time," which featured Autry singing a song he had recorded and released on that label.[15] Anne Williams gave Gene Autry a big buildup each morning, introducing the twenty-four-year-old singer with phrases such as "I see a cowboy riding—here he comes—he's fence riding—he's repairing a fence right now. Now he's got that done, and he's very fast on his horse and just as a fresh as a daisy early in the morning. It's our own Gene Autry!" These introductions were an important step in establishing the "western" image of Autry, who was billed as "Oklahoma Yodeler."[16]

Since Autry was touted as a "cowboy," he began to dress like one, getting his first cowboy outfits from Sears; before this time, Autry had worn street clothes when he sang. "That Silver-Haired Daddy of Mine" was advertised in the Sears, Roebuck catalog and sold a reported thirty thousand copies during its first month out. Autry performed the song regularly, and it soon became a favorite with listeners. The song, which paints the picture of "a vine-covered shack in the mountains," fit the image that WLS wanted to present to its audience: a family-oriented, family-friendly station that reached a rural-based audience who enjoyed hearing wholesome stories and songs evoking sweet memories of an idyllic past. Dressed in western garb, Autry presented the visual image of a cowboy while singing songs that were in reality about mountaineers.[17]

Although Autry appeared on WLS shows during the week and often appeared on the National Barn Dance, he was not a member of WLS because he was not on its payroll. Autry was an independent singer, aligned with Sears, which sponsored him on shows on WLS. Because Sears was interested in selling merchandise—specifically records—Autry invested a lot of time and interest in his work, recording more than any WLS act. Sears also introduced a "Roundup Guitar" endorsed by Autry that it advertised in its catalog, and with the help of Anne Williams, Autry compiled a songbook, *Cowboy Songs and Mountain Ballads*, published by M. M. Cole, sold through the Sears catalog (figures 43, 44).[18]

Autry quickly became popular in Chicago. In June the *Prairie Farmer* announced, "Two full houses each Saturday night continue to be the rule at the two National Barn Dance shows at the Eighth Street Theatre. . . . There's just as much fun at either performance—6:30

Figure 43. Gene Autry knew he had achieved success once he saw his image in the 1933 Sears catalog. As the copy implies, buy this famous reproduction "Roundup" guitar and the next big star just might be born. From the Sears Archives; used with permission.

or 9:30 P.M. The antics of Bessie and Prof Dunck, Slim Miller, Spareribs, Wilbur and Ezra, Maple City Four, Old Timers and others never fail to amuse the audience highly. And the house is 'as still as a mouse' when Linda Parker, Gene Autry, Hugh Cross or 'Aunt Sally' sings and Bill Vickland reads his closing poem."[19] In the *WLS Family Album, 1933* (released at the end of 1932), there is a picture of Gene Autry in a hat that looks like a combination cowboy hat and fedora, dressed in a suit and tie, with the message that "no program with Gene Autry is quite complete until he sings 'Silver-Haired Daddy.'"[20] The popularity of Gene Autry as a "cowboy singer" during 1932 on WLS led him to record his first cowboy songs in January 1933 in Chicago, including "Cowboy's Heaven," "Little Ranch House on the Old Circle B," and "The Yellow Rose of Texas." Increasingly, Autry sang western songs, which enhanced his image as a cowboy singer.[21]

Every cowboy needs a companion, though, and Smiley Burnette, who starred as Gene Autry's sidekick "Frog Millhouse" in Autry's movies, joined Autry when the singer was performing on WLS. The first time the duo performed together on stage was on Christmas

Figure 44. The Gene Autry songbook, marketed and sold by Sears, brought the star's music closer to fans. Collection of Debby Gray.

Eve 1933 at the Eighth Street Theatre in Chicago. This performance began a partnership that would prove momentous for twenty-six-year-old Gene Autry's life.

Lester Alvin Burnette was born in Summum, Illinois; when he was ten, young Burnette lived next door to two part-time orchestra leaders, Bill and Maude Baird, in Concord, Illinois, who lent him musical instruments to learn to play. Burnette was a fast learner and extremely talented. Jonathan Guyot Smith notes, "By the time he entered high school, Burnette had mastered several dozen instruments."[22] Burnette started work for WDZ in

Tuscola, Illinois, as a staff announcer and entertainer in spring 1930. The name "Smiley" came from a children's show he hosted. Gene Autry needed an accordion player at the end of 1933, and Burnette was recommended to him. On December 19, 1933, Autry phoned Smiley and offered him a job; they first met three days later in Smiley's home. After hiring Smiley, Autry then ordered two suits and a stage outfit for Smiley from Sears.

In summer 1934, Gene Autry went to Hollywood, where he had a featured role in the film *In Old Santa Fe*, starring Ken Maynard. Burnette also appeared in the movie, performing his own number, "Mama Don't 'Low." After this appearance, Autry starred in a twelve-chapter serial, *The Phantom Empire*, which finished filming in December 1934. Autry returned to Chicago and during the first two months of 1935 was on *Sears Junior Roundup* on Saturday mornings on WLS. At the end of March, Autry moved to Louisville, where his booking agent, J. L. Frank, had moved with the Log Cabin Boys. Autry appeared on WHAS before he returned to Hollywood to star in his first feature, *Tumbling Tumbleweeds.* He remained in Hollywood after this time, starring in a series of singing cowboy movies. He became "America's Favorite Cowboy" and "Public Cowboy Number One," and his success as a singing cowboy inspired other studios to film singing cowboy pictures. It also motivated radio performers to dress like cowboys on barn dances in Nashville, New York, Atlanta, Los Angeles, Chicago, and other cities.

Autry's success in Chicago during 1932 inspired WLS and the Barn Dance to add western acts to their roster. The Girls of the Golden West joined WLS in 1933. Dolly and Millie Goad were born in Mount Carmel, Illinois, and grew up in East St. Louis. The name "Girls of the Golden West" was suggested by a family friend; it came originally from an opera by Puccini in 1910 as well as a story by Bret Harte. The two young women adapted that name for their act and changed their own surname from "Goad" to "Good" because it sounded better. Mother Goad, who loved old songs and sang them around the home, sewed the costumes for her daughters and made them ornate, western-styled outfits with fringe and yokes. From 1936 to 1938 the Girls of the Golden West were on a program sponsored by Pinex Cough Syrup with Red Foley and Lily May Ledford.[23]

In summer 1933 Patsy Montana (see figure 42) visited the World's Fair in Chicago and met the Girls of the Golden West because her mother had corresponded with them (figure 45). Montana also made it a point to meet the announcer Hal O'Halloran because her mother loved his voice. During one of those visits Patsy discovered that the Prairie Ramblers were looking for a girl singer and had auditions scheduled that afternoon. For her audition Patsy sang a Stuart Hamblen song, "Texas Plains," and got the job; the group played the *Wake Up and Smile* show on WLS each morning at 6:30 and 8:30.[24]

In a hotel room alone during a road trip in 1934 she decided to clean out her purse and came across a scrap of paper with "cowboy's sweetheart" on it. J. L. Frank, who was booking and managing several acts at WLS, including Fibber McGee and Molly and Gene Autry, had jotted down that phrase, thinking it would be a good idea for a song. As Montana sat in her

Figure 45. Cast members from the NBD on tour at the Paramount Theater in Aurora, Illinois, early 1930s. Front row: Chick Hurt is seated at extreme right and Salty Holmes is second from right. Back row: Gene Autry wears a large white cowboy hat; Millie and Dolly Good (The Girls of the Golden West) are identified by their belts; Patsy Montana, fourth from the right, is flanked by Tex Atchison (with the loosened bandana) and Jack Taylor (with the tied bandana); Mac and Bob are on the far right. Courtesy of Michael Montana.

room, the words came quickly, and she sang them to the tune of Stuart Hamblen's "Texas Plains." That song—"I Want to Be a Cowboy's Sweetheart"—became the first country or western record by a woman to sell a million copies. It was originally recorded in a New York studio on August 16, 1935, by Patsy Montana for the American Recording Company.[25] The "sweetheart" she was thinking of as she wrote the song was Paul Rose, whom she married on July 3, 1934.

"Little Georgie Goebel" toured as "The Littlest Cowboy" during his time on the WLS Barn Dance (figure 46). Goebel began on the Barn Dance in 1933; he sang cowboy ballads,

Figure 46. The power of youth on the National Barn Dance: Carolyn DeZurik, "Little Georgie" Goebel, and Mary Jane DeZurik. Courtesy of Don Gill.

wore a five-gallon hat, and strummed a ukelele.[26] During his time on WLS, Goebel played a character named "Jimmy" on the *Tom Mix Straight Shooters Show*. After World War II he went to Hollywood, changed the spelling of his surname, and in the 1950s starred in *The George Gobel Show* on television.

In October 1933, the Westerners joined WLS and the National Barn Dance. The *Prairie Farmer* promoted the group heavily and broadcast regular programs of their western music. The Westerners started on the National Barn Dance about a month after the show went full time on the NBC network.[27] Comprised primarily of the Massey family from the K-Bar Ranch near Roswell, New Mexico, the group consisted of Allen, Curt, and Louise Massey; Louise's husband, Milton Mabie; and Larry Wellington, an accordionist. The group began as amateurs led by their father, the old-time fiddler and rancher Henry Massey.

In 1928 an agent with the Redpath Lyceum Bureau, a booking agency for the Chautauqua circuit, had discovered the Masseys and convinced them to become professional entertainers. They first joined WIBW in Topeka, Kansas, where they were known as the Musical Masseys, then moved to KMBC in Kansas City, where they hired Wellington, who became the only nonfamily member of the group. The ensemble spent five years at KMBC before a WLS talent scout in the Midwest heard them and hired them for WLS, where they were given a two-year contract. They began broadcasting in September 1933 and the following month began recording for the American Recording Corporation, which also recorded Gene Autry and Patsy Montana. In 1938 the group went to Hollywood where they appeared in the Monogram feature *Where the Buffalo Roam*, starring Tex Ritter; they also starred in several movie shorts for Paramount. In 1939 the group moved back to Chicago and WLS, where they appeared on the daytime *Plantation Party* show, broadcast on NBC.

Dressed in full western attire, the Westerners were the real deal; they knew the western lifestyle firsthand (figure 47). They quickly became one of the most popular acts, during one month drawing over 200,000 letters—a record for WLS acts. The Masseys were fluent

Figure 47. The Westerners (left to right): Milt Mabie, Larry Wellington, and siblings Louise Massey, Curt "Dott" Massey, and Allen Massey. The group bounced between Chicago, New York, and Hollywood through the years. Collection of Debby Gray.

in Spanish, and many of their songs had a Spanish tinge. Their most famous song was "My Adobe Hacienda," written by Louise Massey Mabie and Lee Penny. The group disbanded in 1947 when Louise and Milt decided to retire and move back to New Mexico.[28]

Western music became so popular that WLS featured an hour of cowboy songs on its broadcast on Saturday night, September 26, 1936. According to *Stand By!* the publication of WLS,

> The opening tune will be "Pony Boy" by the entire ensemble followed by "Leather Britches" by the Hayloft Band. Lulu Belle and Scotty will then sing "Old Chisholm Trail," the Hoosier Hot Shots will perform "Horse with the Lavender Eyes," Sally Foster will sing "Home in Wyoming" and the Maple City Four with the Novelodeons will perform "I'm an Old Cowhand." "All Day on the Prairie" will be performed by Henry Burr while Uncle Ezra, the Octette and Verne, Lee & Mary will sing "I'm a Wild and Woolly Cowboy from the West Side of Town." The concluding number will be "Cowboy's Lament," performed by the Ranch Boys, accompanied by the ensemble.[29]

WLS did surveys of the "favorite songs" of listeners, and on November 14, 1936, *Stand By!* reported that two of the eight favorites were western songs. The "Eight Favorite Hayloft Songs" were "Take Me Back to Renfro Valley," "Old Shep," "Bury Me beneath the Willow," "My Pretty Quadroon," "Montana Plains," "That Little Boy of Mine," "Little Black Moustache," and "Yellow Rose of Texas."[30]

After World War II, the music of the West continued to appeal to the nation. Rex Allen (see figure 26) was the biggest star on WLS from 1945 to 1949, before he went west to Hollywood and became the last singing cowboy star. Allen grew up on a ranch about four miles outside Willcox, Arizona, eighty-five miles east of Tucson. His father, Horace Allen, was a fiddler who played for dances in and around Willcox. He bought Rex a guitar from Sears when the youngster was eleven years old; the idea was for Rex to accompany his father's fiddling but soon the boy began to sing.[31]

In 1939 Rex Allen won a talent contest and began a career on radio with WTTM in Trenton, New Jersey, and later joined WCAU in Philadelphia, where he played fiddle and sang harmony with the Sleepy Hollow Gang. In summer 1946 he did shows at country music parks, where he met stars such as Lulu Belle and Scotty from the National Barn Dance and Roy Acuff from the Grand Ole Opry. Allen auditioned for the Barn Dance and performed on that show for the next four and a half years. While in Chicago he married Bonnie Linder, one of the Linder Twins (Connie and Bonnie), who had joined WLS in 1943.

In 1949, Allen left Chicago for Hollywood, where he signed as a contract player with Republic. His first film, *The Arizona Cowboy*, was released in 1950, and Allen had written the theme song for the movie, "I'm an Arizona Cowboy." Over the next four years, Allen starred in nineteen singing cowboy movies with Republic. Rex Allen's career at Republic ended with *The Phantom Stallion*, released in 1954 and generally acknowledged to be the last singing cowboy movie.

Bob Atcher was the last star performer on WLS and the National Barn Dance to use the cowboy image. Born in Hardin County, Kentucky, Atcher first appeared on radio in Louisville and then moved to Chicago in 1932. In 1943 he had a hit with Bonnie Blue Eyes (Loeta Applegate), "Pins and Needles (In My Heart)." In the mid-1940s he recorded for Columbia; in 1946 he was on the country chart with "I Must Have Been Wrong"; in 1948 he had "Signed, Sealed and Delivered"; and in 1949 he had two chart hits, "Tennessee Border" and "Why Don't You Haul Off and Love Me?"[32] In 1942 Atcher was on CBS's *Wrigley Spearmint Show* with big-band leader Ben Bernie; he also hosted three daily Chicago-based radio shows on WBBM in 1948 before he joined the National Barn Dance in 1949, replacing Rex Allen (figure 48).

In an interview, Atcher said he was invited to come to WLS to talk about the Barn Dance and "didn't know the other people in the room at the time," but he learned later they "included a representative of Phillips Petroleum." After that meeting, WLS executives called and asked him how much money it would take for him to become a member of the Barn Dance. Atcher talked it over with his manager, then named a price that was three times what he was making at CBS; the WLS executives agreed to the figure. "I found out later that they already had guaranteed I'd be on the Phillips 66 sponsored segment of the NBC network Barn Dance show," said Atcher. "So I sold out pretty cheap."[33] Atcher stayed with the Barn Dance through its move from WLS to WGN in 1960 and was still on the show when it ended its run on WGN television in 1971.

Why did cowboys in Chicago fade away? The essential reason is because the National Barn Dance ended. But there are several related reasons. The competition from rock 'n' roll was intense; WLS and other stations preferred it to country music after the station was sold to ABC. The end of the singing cowboy era in Hollywood came in 1954, and the shift away from cowboys on television came during the 1960s. The cowboy shows starring Gene Autry and Roy Rogers, which aimed for a young audience, and whose audience of young males sought to emulate their heroes, gave way to adult westerns with more gritty realism and no heroes. As scholars delved into studies of the West, a rewriting of the western myth took place whereby the cowboy (and more specifically white settlers) were seen more as villains and interlopers who exploited and nearly destroyed the Native Americans (who were on the land first) and wreaked havoc on the environment.[34] Simply put, the country changed, entertainment changed, and the cowboy simply was not as appealing to the generation that came of age during the 1960s as it had been to preceding generations.

There were other factors as well. First, Chicago wanted to be a "city," and the city person is perceived as cultured, sophisticated, and worldly, the exact opposite of the image of rural or country people. As Chicago sought to place itself on the national stage as a great city, it naturally preferred to play down its roots as a center for agriculture. The five-hundred-acre stockyards were wiped out, and the Sears catalog was no longer essential to rural Americans; thus Chicago increasingly lost its connection to farmers and agriculture when it ceased to

Figure 48. Bob Atcher appeared before an enthusiastic crowd at Riverview Park in Chicago. Courtesy of Maggie Atcher.

be the essential link between western beef and eastern dinner tables. The influx of African Americans from the South and white flight made it a town noted for blues, jazz, and rhythm and blues, and the city promoted itself that way. In his book *The Promised Land*, Nicholas Lemann notes that "by the 1940s Chicago had supplanted Harlem as the center of black nationalism in the United States."[35]

Other forces were also at work. Country artists, for example, have noted that Chicago was filled with "northerners" who did not care for country or country people. The town was not as "friendly" as the South, and "country people" simply did not feel comfortable there. Lulu Belle observed that the effect of network involvement on the Chicago show was to make it more sophisticated, so "the country people started listening to Nashville because it had more of the country stuff." Also, she said, more stringent musicians' union rules in Chicago made it necessary to have a sixteen-piece orchestra on the show just to get it on the network; this rule not only gave the Barn Dance an increasingly uptown flair, it created a budgetary millstone. With a cast of as many as a hundred performers during its heyday, it neither needed nor could survive such unnecessary luxuries as an orchestra—whose members, Lulu Belle says, did little but "sit around reading their racing forms."[36]

The move toward a "pop" type of sound—away from traditional country music—and the desire to be more "sophisticated" and to shed the rural image were mentioned in an article published in the October 1954 issue of *Chicago Magazine*, where Bernard Asbel notes that the word "hillbilly" was strictly forbidden at WLS and that the station manager, Glenn Snyder, wanted none of the "hungry hillbilly" sound. The article states, "The WLS 'family' dissociates itself from the twang of 'hungry hillbilly'—meaning the South—and directs itself to lovers of 'better music.'" Homer and Jethro star Jethro Burns noted, "It's educated hillbilly. You can educate this Northern audience to anything, and popular music is getting in the saddle. You can't change the Southern audience." The article singles out Bob Atcher, stating he "first sang songs publicly on the . . . University of Kentucky radio station," and calls Scotty Wiseman "an 'educated hillbilly,'" noting "he just earned his master's degree." The article calls attention to the fact that cast member Woody Mercer had a law degree from the University of Arizona and that John Dolce, a square dance caller, "was born in Palermo, Italy." Slim Briggs, who appeared as a guest on WLS, "just returned from a successful engagement in Paris," and Betty Ross "has a master's degree in biology from New York University."[37] This was a complete turnaround from the earlier emphasis on the ideas that common sense was better than book learning and that uneducated country folk were more down-to-earth and practical than college intellectuals who had their heads stuck in a cloud.

In an interview with Jack Hurst, Bob Atcher, who was the last star (and the last cowboy) on the WLS National Barn Dance, expressed regret that he left CBS, stating, "I thought they were going to really perk it up and start bringing in fine new acts. Instead, they let their best acts go, I think, and what they replaced them with was pseudo-country, made up principally of Chicago people who weren't country and weren't pop; they weren't even what you would call old time."[38]

In his book *Prairie Farmer and WLS: The Burridge D. Butler Years*, James F. Evans, writing about the early years of the National Barn Dance, notes, "The Barn Dance was ideal for its times, not only because it brought a song and joke but also because its genuine rural flavor was in lock-step with a fast-urbanizing America's longing glance backward at an agrarian heritage. A lack of polish and refinement probably was its greatest strength, not for the sake of those traits but for the genuineness which they signaled."[39]

Since the National Barn Dance was essentially a vaudeville or variety show aimed at a rural audience, part of that variety included cowboy entertainers. The program presented a "wholesome" image, and cowboys were considered quintessentially American and wholesome. But reading that synopsis of the early appeal of WLS and the National Barn Dance, it becomes painfully obvious that by 1960 when WLS was sold—or 1971 when the National

Barn Dance went off the air completely—times had changed, music had changed, and Chicago had changed. The only thing that hadn't changed was the cowboy. The cowboy never really left Chicago; instead, Chicago left the cowboy.

NOTES

In researching my biography of Gene Autry (McFarland, 2007), I did a lot of research in Chicago on WLS and the National Barn Dance; especially helpful was the Chicago Historical Society (now called the Chicago History Museum), where I found back issues of the *Prairie Farmer.* My position as editor of the *Western Way*, the quarterly publication of the Western Music Association, led me to interview a number of people connected to the singing cowboys and WLS.

1. Jim and Wynette Edwards, *Chicago Entertainment between the Wars, 1919–1939* (Chicago: Arcadia, 2003), 45–58.

2. There are a number of books on Buffalo Bill Cody. I recommend Larry McMurtry, *The Colonel and Little Missie: Buffalo Bill, Annie Oakley and the Beginnings of Superstardom in America* (New York: Simon and Schuster, 2005), and R. L Wilson, *Buffalo Bill's Wild West: An American Legend* (New York: Random House, 1998).

3. Frederick Jackson Turner, *The Frontier in American History*, foreword by Ray Allen Billington (New York: Henry Holt, 1974), 1.

4. John Mack Faragher, *Rereading Frederick Jackson Turner* (New York: Henry Holt, 1994), 1.

5. For more information see Philip R. Loy, *Westerns and American Culture, 1930–1955* (Jefferson, N.C.: McFarland, 2001).

6. For more information on the history of western movies see George N. Fenin and William K. Everson, *The Western: From Silents to the Seventies* (New York: Penguin, 1977).

7. For more about Hart and Mix, see ibid.

8. For a history of country music see Bill Malone, *Country Music, U.S.A.: A Fifty Year History* (Austin: University of Texas Press, 1968).

9. J. W. Williamson, *Hillbillyland: What the Movies Did to the Mountains and What the Mountains Did to the Movies* (Chapel Hill: University of North Carolina Press, 1995), 2–3; see also Anthony Harkins, *Hillbilly: A Cultural History of an American Icon* (New York: Oxford University Press, 2005).

10. David E. Nye, *Electrifying America: Social Meanings of a New Technology, 1880–1940* (Cambridge, Mass.: MIT Press, 1991), 22.

11. For an extensive discussion of the Scopes trial, see Edward J. Larson, *Summer for the Gods: The Scopes Trial and America's Continuing Debate Over Science and Religion* (Cambridge, Mass.: Harvard University Press, 1998).

12. There are a number of books that deal with the idea of the frontier in America; see, for example, Richard White and Patricia Nelson Limerick, *The Frontier in American Culture* (Berkeley: University of California Press, 1994); Robert V. Hine and John Mack Faragher, *The American West: A New Interpretative History* (New Haven: Yale University Press, 2000); Patricia Nelson Limerick, *The Legacy of Conquest: The Unbroken Past of the American West* (New York: Norton, 1987); Jane Tompkins, *West of Everything: The Inner Life of Westerns* (New York: Oxford University Press, 1992); Michael Wallis, *The Real Wild West: The 101 Ranch and the Creation of the American West* (New York: St. Martin's, 2000); and Geoffrey C. Ward, *The West: An Illustrated History* (Boston: Little, Brown, 1996).

13. Some of these ideas have been presented in Bill Malone's *Singing Cowboys and Musical Mountaineers: Southern Culture and the Roots of Country Music* (Athens: University of Georgia Press, 1993), and Richard Peterson's *Creating Country Music: Fabricating Authenticity* (Chicago: University of Chicago Press, 1997).

14. Arthur "Uncle Art" Satherley, interviews by Douglas B. Green, June 27, 1974, and April 27, 1975, as part of the Oral History Project at the Frist Library and Archive, Country Music Hall of Fame, Nashville.

15. Gene Autry, as quoted in Morris Gelman, "Gene Autry Recalls 53 Mostly Golden Years," *Daily Variety*, October 28, 1980, 202.

16. Ibid.

17. For more information on this topic see Richard Peterson's *Creating Country Music* and Bill Malone's *Singing Cowboys and Musical Mountaineers*.

18. For the songbook, see Gene Autry, *Cowboy Songs and Mountain Ballads* (Chicago: M. M. Cole, 1932) (copies of which are in the Country Music Foundation library.) Jonathan Guyot Smith kindly provided information via e-mail, March 9, 10, 2005.

19. "List'ning in with Prairie Farmer: WLS, The Voice of Agriculture," *Prairie Farmer*, June 11, 1932, 22.

20. *WLS Family Album, 1933* (Chicago: Prairie Farmer, 1932), 38.

21. Tony Russell, *Country Music Records: A Discography, 1921–1942* (New York: Oxford University Press, 2004), 71–87.

22. Jonathan Guyot Smith, "Smiley Burnette: It's Nice to Be Important, But More Important to Be Nice," *DISCoveries* 71 (April 1994): 26–30.

23. See Don Cusic, "Girls of the Golden West," *Western Way* 16 (Spring 2006): 12–13; Don Cusic, *Cowboys and the Wild West: An A-Z Guide, from the Chisholm Trail to the Silver Screen* (New York: Facts on File, 1994). Other sources include Paul Kingsbury, ed., *The Encyclopedia of Country Music* (New York: Oxford University Press, 1998), 204; and Douglas B. Green, *Singing in the Saddle: The History of the Singing Cowboy* (Nashville: Vanderbilt University Press, 2002), 61–62.

24. Patsy Montana, with Jane Frost, *Patsy Montana: The Cowboy's Sweetheart* (Jefferson, N.C.: McFarland, 2002), 51–53.

25. Russell, *Country Music Records*, 634.

26. Jack Hurst, "Barn Dance Days: Chicago's National Barn Dance," *Bluegrass Unlimited* (April 1986): 56, 58–64. Basic information on Georgie Goebel also came from entries about him on several Web sites: www.imdb.com; www.classicsquares.com; http://en.wikipedia.org; and www.nndb.com (all accessed November 8, 2007).

27. See Don Cusic, "Louise Massey and the Westerners," *Western Way* 16 (Spring 2006): 10–11; Wayne W. Daniel, "The Ranch Romance of Louise Massey and the Westerners," *Journal of Country Music* 20, no. 3 (1999), 37–41; and Wayne W. Daniel, "They Put the West in Country-Western Music: Louise Massey and the Westerners," *Nostalgia Digest* 28 (April/May 2002): 26–33.

28. See Daniel, "Ranch Romance."

29. "Cowboy Barn Dance," *Stand By!* September 26, 1936, 9.

30. "Favorites," *Stand By!* November 14, 1936, 11.

31. Cusic, *Cowboys and the Wild West*, 6. Other sources include Kingsbury, *Encyclopedia of Country Music*, 10; Green, *Singing in the Saddle*, 266–68, 302; and an interview I did with Rex Allen Jr. on May 31, 2006, which is included in the article "Rex Allen, Jr.: A New Generation on the Range," *Western Way* 16 (Summer 2006): 6–9.

32. Green, *Singing in the Saddle*, 217–18; Kingsbury, *Encyclopedia of Country Music*, 19–20. See also the Web sites at www.richsamuels.com, www.wlshistory.com, and www.wgngold.com (all accessed November 8, 2007).

33. Quoted, Hurst, "Barn Dance Days," 60.

34. Works in which scholars have reinterpreted the West include Richard White, *It's Your Misfortune and None of My Own: A New History of the American West* (Norman: University of Oklahoma Press, 1993); Richard Slotkin, *Gunfighter Nation: The Myth of the Frontier in Twentieth-Century America* (Nor-

man: University of Oklahoma Press, 1998); and Limerick, *The Legacy of Conquest.* The film *Little Big Man* is also an excellent example of reinterpreting the West.

35. Nicholas Lemann, *The Promised Land: The Great Black Migration and How It Changed America* (New York: Vintage, 1991), 64.

36. There is an excellent two-part article on Lulu Belle Wiseman by William E. Lightfoot. See Lightfoot, "From Radio Queen to Raleigh: Conversations with Lulu Belle: Part I," *Old Time Country* 6 (Summer 1989): 4–10; and "From Radio Queen to Raleigh: Conversations with Lulu Belle: Part II," *Old Time Country* 6 (Fall 1989): 3–11. Additionally, see Lightfoot, "Belle of the Barn Dance: Reminiscing with Lulu Belle Wiseman Stamey," *Journal of Country Music* 12, no. 1 (1987): 2–15.

37. Bernard L. Asbel, "The National Barn Dance," *Chicago Magazine*, October 1954, 23.

38. Hurst, "Barn Dance Days," 62.

39. James F. Evans, *Prairie Farmer and WLS: The Burridge D. Butler Years* (Urbana: University of Illinois Press, 1969), 231.

8 THE NATIONAL FOLK FESTIVAL

Michael Ann Williams

In May 1937, George Biggar, promotional director of Chicago radio station WLS, made arrangements for the station to provide musical acts and promotion for the Fourth Annual National Folk Festival. Biggar assured the station's program manager, Harold Safford, that he felt that the folk festival's director, Sarah Gertrude Knott, would provide adequate credit to the radio station, but he added a word of caution to his memo. While the station should work as much as possible with Knott, the festival itself was "often rather disappointing to the public from a showmanship standpoint."[1]

The uneasy alliance between the National Folk Festival and WLS provides a platform for examining the similarities and differences between two forms of theatrical presentation of traditional culture, the radio barn dance and the folk festival, through the specific institutions that had the temerity to label themselves as "National." At the time of its sojourn in Chicago, the National Folk Festival had been in existence for only three years and its glory years at Constitution Hall, funded by the *Washington Post*, lay immediately ahead. The National Barn Dance, created in the mid-1920s, had already reached its heyday as one of the most popular barn dance shows on the airwaves.

The flourishing of barn dances and folk festivals in the mid-1930s seems an apt part of the zeitgeist of the decade that celebrated the "art of the common man." However, both emerged in the previous decade in an undercurrent of nostalgia that flowed against the tide of the Jazz Age. Rural Americans, as well as those newly urbanized, sought solace in the representations of an older, more traditional America. For many, America's past came to be personified by a single region, Appalachia. The growing popularity of "hillbilly" music at midwestern stations such as WLS fed not only on the homesickness of urban migrants from the South, but also on its appeal to midwesterners who longed to believe that, somewhere, old-time life and values still existed. The romance of the cowboy would soon overtake the allure of Appalachia on the radio airwaves, but during much of the thirties, the past still resided in the American South.

Similarly, the first modern folk festival emerged in 1928 as part of a tourist event sponsored by the chamber of commerce in Asheville, North Carolina, long a favorite mountain destination for summer visitors. The following year, Bascom Lamar Lunsford, a musician and country lawyer, broke away from the Rhododendron Festival to establish the Mountain Dance and Folk Festival. Within three years, two more folk festivals emerged in Appalachia: Jean Thomas's American Folk Song Festival, held near Ashland, Kentucky, and Annabel Morris Buchanan's White Top Festival in southwest Virginia.

Some scholars have argued that the folk festival as a form began in opposition to the commercialization of traditional music promoted by the recording industry and radio.[2] However, if the festival appealed to a slightly more well-heeled audience, both the radio barn dance and the Appalachian festivals peddled the same romanticized nostalgia about the region. The dapper festival promoter Lunsford eschewed the hillbilly trappings, but, starting in 1937, he began a series of lifelong collaborations with a radio entrepreneur, John Lair, who launched his career at WLS. Although Jean Thomas promoted images of the authentic Elizabethan character of Appalachia, for years she featured the former WLS star Bradley Kincaid as emcee of her festival. He was one of many performers who could easily perform at either venue. Thomas herself eagerly sought radio gigs for her featured performer, J. W. Day, who performed as "Jilson Setters." In 1934 Thomas sent a registered letter to WLS in which she complained that a song Day had written had ended up in the repertoire of John Lair's group, the Cumberland Ridge Runners. However, she implied that if financial arrangements could be made for her to bring Day to Chicago to perform a "program of ancient Elizabethan music," she might overlook this transgression.[3] Of the three early festival promoters, Annabel Morris Buchanan perhaps clung to her notion of authentic tradition most tightly, but even the White Top festival in its early days featured performers who could easily move between the festival stage and the radio microphone.

In 1934 the folk festival broke free of Appalachia with the emergence of the National Folk Festival, first staged in St. Louis at the Keil Opera House. While Sarah Gertrude Knott, the organizer, sought the advice of her predecessors in the festival world, especially Lunsford, her inspiration came from the "folk drama" of Frederick Koch, a former pageant master who had established the Carolina Playmakers. Furthermore, she drew guidance from the liberal beliefs of Paul Green, the Pulitzer Prize–winning playwright, who served as the president of the National Folk Festival Association for two decades. The National Folk Festival was adamantly multicultural in makeup. However, with the Ozarks at her back door, Knott could not neglect the traditions of the upper South, and she staged a series of mini-festivals in rural Arkansas and Missouri to identify performers for the big festival. She and her judges struggled with the radio influence on these musicians, and the question of the relationship of folk music to "hillbilly" and country music "pestered" Knott for all of her active career.[4]

Although Knott proved adept at attracting the attention of the media, as well as academic folklorists, her festivals failed to be commercially successful. From St. Louis, Knott moved her festival to Chattanooga in 1935 (one of the few times she situated her festival in the Appalachian region) and then to Dallas, the best funded and largest festival of the early years, thanks to its affiliation with the Texas centennial. Following the huge Texas undertaking, Knott and her business manager shopped around for another city willing to support the festival. With time running short, the Adult Education Council of Chicago agreed to sponsor the next festival as part of the Chicago Charter Jubilee celebration. Knott did not have adequate time to stage mini-festivals to locate participants, as she had for the previous festivals; instead she stepped up her efforts to enlist the help of folklorists, collectors, and the media. Chicago's WLS, home of the National Barn Dance, soon found itself receiving her appeals for help locating fiddlers, dancers, and harmonica players to represent the state of Illinois.

Knott possessed few reservations about soliciting the help of the media. Throughout most of her career, newspapers provided unpaid publicity, and the *Washington Post*, *Philadelphia Bulletin*, and *St. Louis Globe-Democrat* at various times sponsored the festival. She occasionally paid lip service to the academic folklorists who believed that radio and other forms of mass entertainment had a detrimental effect of folk tradition. In 1939 Knott wrote in an article in the *Southern Folklore Quarterly*, "With the picture show, radio and other forms of newer entertainment now within the easy reach of most, many of the forms that served an older, simpler America will pass unnoticed unless stimulus is given to those who carry in their hearts these fine traditions."[5] In reality, however, Knott and her business manager, M. J. Pickering, eagerly sought the support of radio. Only months before moving their operations to Chicago, Pickering and Knott met with NBC officials, made a contact at CBS, and pursued commercial sponsorship for a "National Folk Festival of the Air."[6] When Pickering settled on Chicago as the site for the Fourth Annual National Folk Festival, Knott did not let purist beliefs keep her from pursuing the support of the radio station with one of the most popular barn dances in the country.

For its part, the management at WLS had long kept its eye on the burgeoning folk festival movement. Keen to appeal to a more middle-class audience than that represented by commercial "hillbilly" music, WLS attempted to position itself as a purveyor of "authentic" folk music. In the early 1930s, the station relied to a large extent on John Lair, a Kentuckian, to provide this stamp of authenticity. Lair, a southern migrant of a different ilk than the many who sought factory jobs in the northern cities, came to Chicago in the mid-1920s to work for Liberty Mutual Insurance. Surprised to hear familiar music coming over the airwaves of Chicago radio, Lair initially approached the WLS performer Bradley Kincaid, a fellow Kentuckian, with the idea that he could provide the balladeer with new old songs to add to his repertoire.[7] Rebuffed by the popular performer, Lair resolved to bring his own musicians to Chicago, and he soon wormed himself into the WLS establishment (figure 49). The newly created genre of the radio barn dance suited Lair's passions well as it combined the vernacular musical traditions he loved from his childhood with the entertainment traditions of vaudeville stage, which Lair had been introduced to during his involvement in the theatrical revue *Atta Boy* during his stint in the army. With a keen sense of the creative possibilities of the media and an ability to satisfy both his sponsor and his own intellectual curiosity, Lair discovered his life's work.

Figure 49. A rare glimpse of Lair live on stage in the 1930s in Chicago. John Lair Collection, Southern Appalachian Archives, Berea College.

Although John Lair held a genuine fascination for folk music and a respect for academic folklorists, he never let concerns for authenticity stand in the way of entertainment. While the original core of his first group, the Cumberland Ridge Runners, consisted of two "boys from back home," Karl Davis and Hartford Connecticut Taylor, Lair soon branched out, recruiting the Indiana fiddler Slim Miller for his comic appearance and the nightclub singer Linda Parker for her good looks and voice. Despite his willingness to manipulate reality, however, Lair spent a lifetime researching music and constantly pitched programs to WLS that featured himself in the role of genial professor, sharing his knowledge of song histories. Lair's first radio show at WLS, the *Aladdin Barn Dance Frolic*, premiered in December 1930. The following April, Lair began producing a program explicitly billed as a folk music show, sponsored by Olson Rugs.

In his early days hanging around the station, Lair found at least one soul mate in his passion for folk music. Steve Cisler left WLS just as Lair became established at the station, but in January 1931, Cisler wrote to Lair encouraging him to join in his schemes. He proposed a series of programs recorded in New York that would feature Lair's "Renfro Band" and leading performers of "old time music," including Bradley Kincaid, Jimmie Rodgers, and the Carter Family. Cisler then suggested an even more ambitious scheme: a network radio program that would feature "genuine folk music" from across the United States, including dances from Kentucky, sacred harp singing from Alabama, Texas cowboy singing and dancing, a Swedish American barn dance, a jug band from Memphis, and a plantation frolic from Louisiana.[8] Although the plan never came to fruition, it is noteworthy that more than three years before Knott launched the first multicultural folk festival, Cisler proposed a similarly diverse radio show.

While WLS mostly limited its folk offerings to Appalachian and cowboy fare, early on it had a fairly broad vision of its own role. The 1931 *WLS Family Album* included a passage that sounds much like something Sarah Gertrude Knott could have written a few years later: "In building the musical programs at WLS, we have followed many trails and made many interesting discoveries. These mountain songs, the plaintive and humorous cowboy ballads of the West, the Negro spirituals and work songs as sung by the Metropolitan Church Choir of 100 Negro voices, native Indian music—these are all part of WLS. They are a basic part of American life and culture."[9] When George Biggar reviewed the Second Annual National Folk Festival in Chattanooga for WLS's weekly magazine, *Stand By!* he seemed genuinely pleased by the broad spectrum covered by the festival: "If I had had any idea that American 'folk' music and songs originated only in the cabins of our southern mountains and around the 'bunkhouses' of our western ranges, I learned differently while attending the National Folk Festival in Chattanooga, Tennessee, in May."[10] Whatever his later reservations about the festival's "showmanship," Biggar wrote glowing articles on both the Second and Third National Folk Festivals.

Both Lair and Biggar also paid attention to the ongoing Appalachian folk festivals. A series of photographs in the Lair Collection at the Southern Appalachian Archives, Berea College, picture both men attending the American Folk Song Festival in Kentucky sometime during the mid-1930s. In 1935 Lair visited the White Top Folk Festival, which he characterized as a "folk festival by the folk and for the folk," in an article he wrote for *Stand By!* While Lair derided other festivals as overemphasizing "dry, scholarly discourse," he praised the two academic folklorists, John Lomax and George Pullen Jackson, he met at White Top. Still, he could not resist suggesting that the local population found the radio barn dance better entertainment. As he was leaving the area, Lair wrote, he encountered a local man at the train station who exclaimed, "I'd a-walked ever step of the way up ole White Top jest to shake hands with somebody frum ole WLS."[11]

By the time he attended the White Top festival, Lair had left his day job in insurance and had joined WLS full time as the music librarian. Lair immediately attempted to appeal to WLS's aspirations for reaching a more middle-class audience. Referring to the popularity of a "certain kind of music" on the station, Lair wrote, "'Hillbilly' music, as a fad, is subject to decline in due course, but the basic folk music on which it is founded improves with age and we can consider that we are building for the future when we do anything to increase it's [*sic*] importance in the minds of our listeners." Lair proposed to the management that he produce a series of shows focusing on the origin and history of certain folksongs. He added, "I would use a variety of talent on these programs, attempting to bring in all types and classifications of folk music, as well as such better class music as our artists are capable of delivering. I would try, in so far as possible, to devote most time and attention to that type of music which is sincere and friendly without being flippant or trashy, working on the basis that 'hillbilly' does not have to be poorly done to be appreciated."[12] In turn, WLS referred to Lair as an "outstanding authority" on American folk music in its next *Family Album.*[13]

John Lair stood ready to make his next great career step when Sarah Gertrude Knott came calling in 1937. Although George Biggar as promotional director may have handled the negotiations with the station, Lair seems to have served as the immediate liaison with Knott. Obligingly, the radio station featured the National Folk Festival's program daily on its *Dinnerbell* show during the week of the festival. One day's broadcast featured Knott, Lair, and Elsie Mae McGill, who presented old songs from the Kentucky mountains. Other days featured the diverse scope of the National Folk Festival, including lumberjacks, anthracite miners, and a Spanish quartet from the Southwest.[14] WLS also lent some of its staff, including Floyd "Salty" Holmes and Check Stafford, both harmonica players, to represent Illinois at the festival itself.

A variety of performers felt comfortable on either the folk festival or barn dance stage. The cowboy performer Romaine Lowdermilk, long a Knott favorite, became a regular on WLS, possibly after Biggar discovered him at the Chattanooga National Folk Festival. At the Chicago festival, however, another radio station, KOY Phoenix, sponsored Lowdermilk. Bascom Lamar Lunsford, who served as a close advisor to Knott, performed on stage at the

Chicago National Folk Festival with the popular WLS duo Lulu Belle and Scotty (figure 50). Lair had managed the young Myrtle Cooper's career and crafted her image as Lulu Belle until the radio station paired her with Scott Wiseman, whom she subsequently married. During the festival Lair, Lunsford, and Scott Wiseman got together to play music and reminisce, during which time Lunsford agreed to sell the rights to his song "Mountain Dew"

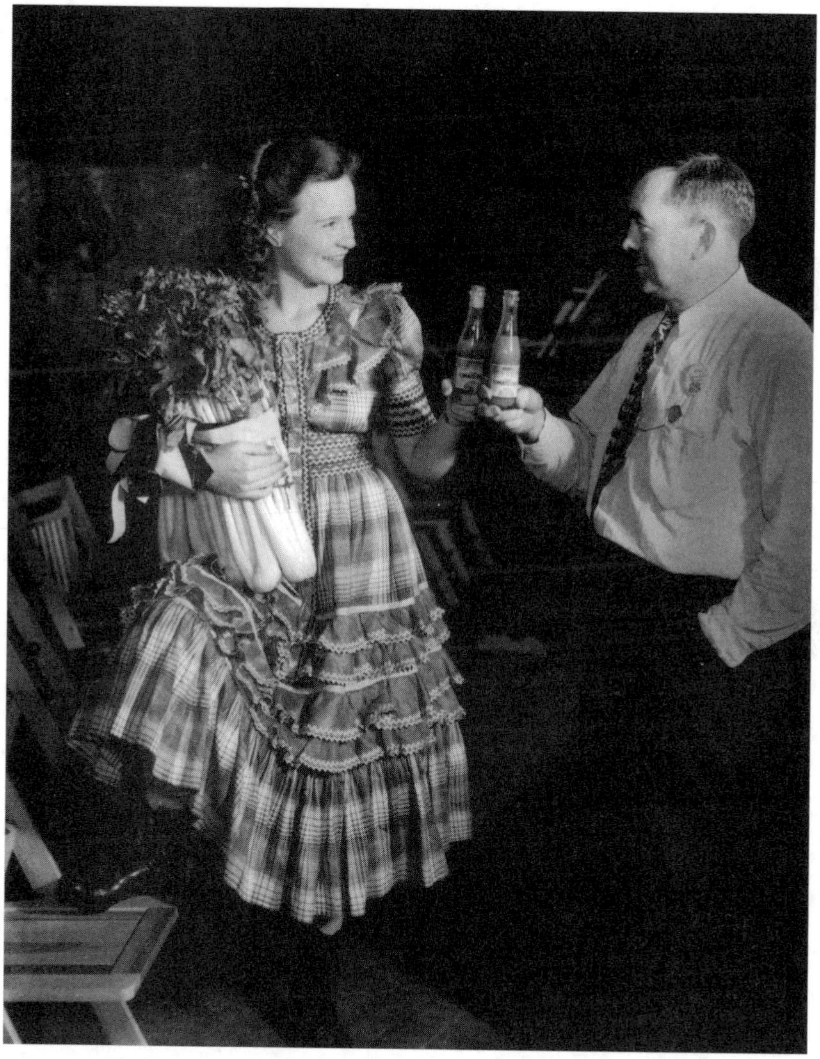

Figure 50. State Fairs across the Midwest were lucrative public relations venues for NBD stars. Lulu Belle appeared with Roscoe Fraser pitching tomato juice—and celery, perhaps—at what is believed to be the Indiana State Fair in 1938. Courtesy of Indiana State Archives.

to Wiseman in order to raise money for his trip home (as Knott seldom paid her performers or advisors). With added lyrics by Wiseman, the song became a hit for Lulu Belle and Scotty, even though WLS management did not believe that it was proper fare for its radio station.[15] The 1937 festival also seems to have precipitated a closer relationship between Lair and Lunsford, who soon afterward began a series of collaborations.

Just months after the Chicago National Folk Festival, John Lair, eager to be his own boss, left Chicago and WLS behind. He and a number of his acts relocated to Cincinnati, where he produced shows for WLW, with the strongest signal in the country, and began to build his Renfro Valley complex in Rockcastle County, Kentucky, where he would stage his barn dance in a "real barn." For a brief time, Lair and Knott continued to see that future collaborations would be mutually beneficial. Knott always kept an eye out for individuals who could identify and present performers on stage for her festival, and Lair was keen to promote his reputation. After the Chicago festival, Knott appointed Lair to the festival's board, and the following February her business manager, Pickering, wrote to Lair, pointing out the "very high-brow way in which we have included you on our National Committee," as "Student of the Origins of American Folk Music."[16] Lunsford also served on the National Folk Festival's board, as well as "Folk Dance Director" for Lair's Renfro Valley Barn Dance.

In March 1938, Knott recruited Lair and Lunsford to put on an Ohio River Folk Festival in order to identify performers for the next National Folk Festival, scheduled for Constitution Hall in Washington, D.C. Alan Lomax, then a young folklorist working for the Library of Congress, characterized the offerings as "largely hill-billy and very little folk," although a few years later his attitude toward the "stuff that comes over the air from Nashville, Covington, Cincinnati and the other radio stations that feature mountain music" softened considerably.[17] For her part, Knott seemed to have relatively few reservations about the festival, and Lair's Coon Creek Girls not surprisingly won a spot to perform at the festivities in Washington. Lair apparently relished his role advising Knott on the authenticity of folk traditions and how to present them on stage. Possibly because of their participation in the National Folk Festival, Lair and the Coon Creeks found themselves invited to the White House the following year to perform as part of a program of music for the king and queen of England.

Ultimately Lair became disillusioned with the National Folk Festival, which seldom paid its performers. Later in life he recalled, "We were invited [to the National Folk Festival] every year, but I don't like their method. They want you to pay all your own expenses and come up and they keep the gate, you know."[18] Lair would be dropped from the board a few years later for his lack of interest.[19] Another two decades would pass before Lair and Knott would again cross paths. When the National Folk Festival sojourned for two years in Kentucky in the mid-1960s, Knott called on John Lair to help find talent for her stage. She also envisioned that country music radio could be used to promote interest in folk music. The year before the National Folk Festival moved to Covington, Kentucky, she wrote Lair,

"And John, for several years I have had in mind the idea of having noted country singers on tv and radio cross the country—feature the genuine folk music they know—giving a shot in the arm—just show how many still know these traditional songs, and play the instruments in the traditional way. What about starting this at Renfro Valley?"[20]

In the years of the folk revival that followed the 1953 release of Harry Smith's *Anthology of American Folk Songs*, a number of "hillbilly" musicians found new careers on the folk music circuit. Among these performers was Lily May Ledford, who first received national exposure on the stage of the National Barn Dance. Although as a young woman she often chafed at the old-fashioned mountain image Lair projected on her and the other Coon Creek Girls, she hit the folk festival circuit with the same old-time dresses that Lair had once prescribed. Given the opportunity finally to craft her own image, Ledford stuck to a representation that reflected her Kentucky mountain roots, rather than the sophisticated look she longed for as a young performer.

If uncritical folk revival audiences tended to accept as authentic the early barn dance performers such as Ledford, the people who crafted these performers' images and helped promote them more often have been dismissed as artificers. Similarly, in recent decades the early creators of folk festivals have fallen under the scrutiny of scholars for their intervention in and construction of tradition. Both groups undoubtedly had notions of what constituted folk tradition and how it could be transformed to a staged event, and they clearly shared as much in their goals as they disagreed on format.

In 1937, as the worlds of the National Folk Festival and the National Barn Dance intersected, neither form had hardened into the cultural phenomena that would later emerge as the folk revival and country music radio. While the performers who entertained on the National Barn Dance were typically presented as mountain folk or cowboys, the management at WLS seemed open to a broader cultural mix. The station's own representations of Native American and African American culture seldom moved beyond the stereotypical, yet staff members wrote enthusiastically about the range of expression displayed at the National Folk Festival and willingly represented a small part of it on their airwaves. WLS's small embrace of multiculturalism, in fact, seemed stronger than that of the monocultural Appalachian folk festivals of the same era.

Issues of class, of course, informed the phenomenon. Knott's folk festival, which opened first in an opera hall, targeted a relatively well educated, urban, theater-going public. This was less the case for those who made up the generally more rural and small-town radio audience for the National Barn Dance, although certainly there might have been some overlap between the live audiences for both shows. In embracing the concept of folk music, WLS aspired to capture the middle-class audience attracted to Knott's festival. Lair catered to their predilections by offering a populist version of "folk," which avoided the lower-class taint of "hillbilly." However, he knew that he had to pitch his shows broadly, and he did so by infusing his programs with a large dose of vaudeville-style entertainment and humor. At the same time, he sought to legitimatize his acts by offering them up as "authentic" tradition and by seeking the approval of scholarly folklorists. Although Lair did not have an academic background (or even a college degree), he crafted an on-air persona as a genial professor type who brought a certain air of distinction to a rather broadly drawn entertainment form.

Whatever the differences in intent of the organizers, the audiences for both the National Barn Dance and the National Folk Festival embraced entertainers as diverse as the cowboy Romaine Lowdermilk and the hillbilly comedienne Lulu Belle. Prior to the Chicago festival, Sarah Gertrude Knott sought to add to her roster new performers who could represent the Barn Dance's home state of Illinois and the Midwest in general. The Chicago National Folk Festival opened the door a crack to presentations of the culture of recent immigrants (who had previously been excluded from the National Folk Festival), such as the Lithuanian dance troupe led by a Chicagoan, Vyts Beliajus. The midwestern location allowed Knott to expand the offering of Native Americans and "older" ethnic groups such as Swedes and Germans. However, with no time to stage local preliminary festivals, as she had the previous three years, Knott felt hard pressed to represent adequately the Anglo-American traditions of Illinois. Instead she drafted WLS staff to fill this role, and they obligingly sent staff members who fit the bill.

George Biggar's reservations about the "entertainment value" of the folk festival go to the heart of the differences between the barn dance and the folk festival. With its roots in the folk drama movement and ultimately historical pageantry, the National Folk Festival aspired to a far more serious tone. Knott never lost sight of the didactic purpose of her festival. She aimed ultimately at education, not entertainment. Meanwhile Lair liberally sprinkled his entertainments with attempts at erudition. With enough vaudeville-inspired comedy, Lair's history lessons could be easily swallowed. However, whatever value Lair placed on educating his public about musical traditions, he never lost sight of the fact that he was in the entertainment business and that the purpose of a business was to make money. Knott sought underwriters and spent her own small inheritance but never saw money as more than a means to an end: perpetuating her festival.

Both Knott and Lair craved the approval of academics, but Knott had far more to lose from their displeasure. She needed enough commercial success to keep her enterprise afloat, but her cadre of academic advisors steered her clear of pandering too much to commercialism. From the outset, her mentor Paul Green warned Knott against including "local merchant commerce" in her plan.[21] Although sponsors frequently rejected many of Lair's pitches for more educational programs, his passion for research remained undaunted. With a relatively generous budget from WLS, Lair pursued his research into vernacular music, and his daughters reported that it was frequently the center of family vacations.[22] However, while Lair had a passion for researching folk tradition that outweighed Knott's, his research and writing became more a hobby than a career.

While the ultimate goals of the National Folk Festival and the National Barn Dance were quite different, both presentations were forms of theater. John Lair and Sarah Gertrude Knott possessed a passion for the limelight that equaled, or perhaps exceeded, their passion for folk tradition. Each recontextualized folk tradition, adapting it to the theatrical forms they knew from personal experience. Although both used the rhetoric of authenticity in their presentations, the relative authenticity of the barn dance and folk festival is perhaps a moot point. Both acceded more to the conventions of the theatrical forms from which they derived inspiration than to the demands of tradition. Perhaps the more interesting issue is not what differentiates the two modes of cultural productions, but ultimately what connects them.

NOTES

The material for this essay was drawn from my larger study, *Staging Tradition: John Lair and Sarah Gertrude Knott* (University of Illinois Press, 2006). Research was conducted primarily in the Sarah Gertrude Knott Collection, Special Collections, Folkife Archives, Western Kentucky University (SGKC), and the John Lair Collection, Southern Appalachian Archives, Berea College (JLC).

1. George C. Biggar, memo to Harold Safford, May 12, 1937, box 1, JLC.
2. David Whisnant, *All That Is Native and Fine* (Chapel Hill: University of North Carolina Press, 1983), 184–85.
3. Jean Thomas, registered letter to Manager, Station W.L.S., January 17, 1934, General Business Correspondence 1930–36, JLC.
4. Sarah Gertrude Knott, "Some Questions Which Pester Me," ms., National Folk Festival Files, Archive of Folk Song, Library of Congress.
5. Sarah Gertrude Knott, "The National Folk Festival—Its Problems and Reasons," *Southern Folklore Quarterly* 3 (June 1939): 121.
6. M. J. Pickering, letter to Messrs. Hatfield and Weil, January 1, 1937, KFC3/D2, SGKC.
7. John Lair, tape-recorded interview by Loyal Jones, Renfro Valley, Kentucky, April 30, 1974, Special Collections, Berea College.
8. Steve Cisler, letter to John Lair, January 16, 1931, box 1, JLC.
9. *WLS Family Album, 1931* (Chicago: Prairie Farmer, 1931), 44.
10. George C. Biggar, "Mountain Music Plus: Capers at Folk Festival Show Nation Has Rich Heritage of Song, Story and Dances," *Stand By!* June 8, 1935, 4–5, 11
11. John Lair, "High Jinks on White Top," *Stand By!* September 14, 1935, 5, 11.
12. John Lair, "A Plan for Extending the Activities of the WLS Music Department" [undated, probably 1936], JLC.
13. *WLS Family Album, 1936* (Chicago: Prairie Farmer, 1936), 30.
14. WLS program sheet for May 23, 1937, box 1, JLC.
15. Loyal Jones, *Minstrel of the Appalachians: The Story of Bascom Lamar Lunsford* (Boone, N.C.: Appalachian Consortium Press, 1984), 36, 70.
16. M. J. Pickering, letter to John Lair, February 4, 1938, box 1, General Business Correspondence 1937, JLC.
17. Alan and Elizabeth Lomax, Journal of the Indiana Field Trip, entry for March 27, 1938, Library of Congress.
18. John Lair interview, April 30, 1974.

19. M. J. Pickering, letter to Paul Green, November 24, 1943, Paul Green Collection, Southern Historical Collection, Wilson Library, University of North Carolina at Chapel Hill.

20. Knott, letter to Lair and Edith James, October 10 [1962], box 9, JLC.

21. Laurence G. Avery, ed., *A Southern Life: Letters of Paul Green, 1916–1981* (Chapel Hill: University of North Carolina Press, 1994), 219.

22. Barbara Lair Smith, tape-recorded interview by David Baxter, Hopkinsville, Kentucky, March 3, 1995; Ann Lair Henderson, tape-recorded interview by David Baxter, Renfro Valley, Kentucky, May 16, 1995, both in collection of the author.

AFTERWORD

Stephen Parry

In May 2005, I conducted an interview with Chad Berry at his home in Maryville, Tennessee, for my documentary film *The Hayloft Gang: The Story of the National Barn Dance.* I mentioned that it would be a significant addition to have a companion book of essays and photographs to complement the film, but I was not sure how to go about achieving this. Berry was immediately enthusiastic about the idea and agreed to help coordinate the book. I offered some suggestions for contributors, scholars that I had worked with as advisors for the film project. It was through Chad Berry's efforts, encouragement, and editing skills that this book became a reality.

I was born in 1960, the year that the National Barn Dance signed off the air, so I have no personal recollection of the program. My interest developed in 1993 after discovering live bluegrass music for the first time at Bill Monroe's festival in Beanblossom, Indiana. Captivated by the "the high, lonesome sound," I immediately bought a guitar, taught myself a few chords, and began attending bluegrass and folk festivals.

At festival jam sessions, I heard some of the old-timers talk about listening to the WLS National Barn Dance broadcast out of Chicago back in the 1930s and 1940s. Names like Arkie the Arkansas Woodchopper, the Girls of the Golden West, and the Hoosier Hot Shots intrigued me. I have always been interested in 1930s culture, having heard my grandmother's heartbreaking stories of the Great Depression; yet, at the same time, she also told of the "good old days" she enjoyed. I grew up in a small town in northern Indiana and still hold a natural sentimentality and affinity toward small-town, rural life, which is the very essence of the National Barn Dance.

In 2002, I started some research about the program and was amazed to discover that this great American cultural institution was such a well kept secret. Most works on both broadcasting and country music history gave the National Barn Dance only a passing mention. From 1924 to 1960, the National Barn Dance was heard by millions of Americans. The program's immense popularity and unique format inspired hundreds of small barn-dance radio shows that blanketed the country, particularly when the Great Depression put a major dent in the record industry.

It was not until the late 1940s that the Grand Ole Opry in Nashville challenged the National Barn Dance as the premiere country music radio program. The Grand Ole Opry and Nashville's Ryman Auditorium are household names today because the city was able to write its own version of the history of country music, and as a result, the story of the National Barn Dance was neatly swept under the rug.

Yet, as a documentary filmmaker, I felt that the history of the National Barn Dance had the makings for a compelling and engaging film. It was a story that needed to be told. The National Barn Dance intersects with key elements of the American experience: migration, urbanization, ethnic and racial negotiations, the rise of commercial country music, and regional and national tensions in radio. I wanted to create a film that would use this social, cultural, and historical context as a vehicle to tell the story, thereby giving our audience a greater understanding of the significance and impact of the National Barn Dance and its role in shaping American music and popular culture.

Being a nonacademic, I turned to the experts to gain a diverse and balanced perspective on our subject and time period. The project members teamed with a group of award-winning scholars with solid records of academic achievement. Our advisors represent the fields of American history, migration studies, folklore, sociology, American studies, and media studies. In addition to offering advice and direction, many of them appear in on-camera interviews in the film.

Kristine McCusker's work immediately stood out: her articles "'Bury Me beneath the Willow': Linda Parker and Definitions of Tradition on the National Barn Dance, 1932–1935" and "Dear Radio Friend: Listener Mail and the National Barn Dance, 1931–1941," offered fresh insight on the National Barn Dance and 1930s culture. McCusker came on board early as an advisor for the film. Bill C. Malone, Richard Peterson, and Charles Wolfe provided their collective knowledge of country music history.

Hal Barron gave us his perspective on the role that radio played in the rise of rural consumer culture in the 1920s. Sears, Roebuck and Company ventured into broadcasting in 1924 with the start of radio station WLS in Chicago, and even its call letters touted the World's Largest Store. Sears effectively related its new radio station to the products sold in its catalogs. This enticed customers to purchase "Silvertone" radio receivers, which enabled them to tune in every Saturday night to the National Barn Dance and order phonograph records and sheet music of their favorite WLS performers.

I began the documentary with my own preconceived notion that the National Barn Dance primarily showcased Appalachian string-band music, a version of the Grand Ole Opry that originated in Chicago. As Paul Tyler, with the Old Town School of Folk Music in Chicago, pointed out to me early in the project, the Barn Dance was a unique mix of Americana music that was targeted toward a rural midwestern audience, featuring old familiar tunes, turn-of-the-century pop songs, and rural folk music, not necessarily southern music.

Michele Hilmes, Susan Douglas, and Susan Smulyan offered perspectives from broadcasting history and media studies. According to Susan Smulyan, "The National Barn Dance is the history of radio in miniature. It's a story that shows the intertwined nature of business, entertainment, listeners, the population shifts, race, and how they intertwine and get played out."[1]

Loyal Jones's writing on Bradley Kincaid, one of radio's first superstars, was a valuable asset to the film. WLS and Sears publicized Kincaid as the "Kentucky Mountain Boy with His Houn' Dog Guitar." He was receiving more than 100,000 fan letters a year and was the first performer to publish his own songbooks and sell them over the air and at personal appearances. "Bradley Kincaid," said Bill Malone, "did more than any other entertainer to export what was perceived as southern music to the North and exposed a new audience to traditional American folk tunes and ballads."[2]

Michael Ann Williams's research on the life and career of John Lair has been invaluable, along with Anthony Harkins's insight into how the National Barn Dance not only represented "folk" and "hillbilly" music, but misrepresented it as well. John Lair was a producer and promoter at WLS and served as the musical liaison between Chicago and his native eastern Kentucky. He was constantly searching for fresh talent with that "old-time" sound. John Lair and the National Barn Dance capitalized on America's fascination with the South and long-time interest in Appalachia, and he extended this romantic idea even further into the public's imagination.

The quintessential representation of this nostalgic rural image was the performance team of Lulu Belle and Scotty. Their music celebrated an ideal Appalachian Mountain past, expressing the themes of hard work, a sense of place, and old-fashioned ruralism. Lulu Belle and Scotty would spend over a quarter century in front of National Barn Dance audiences at WLS. William Lightfoot offered his personal observations on Lulu Belle and Scotty Wiseman and served as a gracious tour guide of the region surrounding the Wisemans' home near Spruce Pine, North Carolina.

I continue to be amazed at the immense popularity that the National Barn Dance enjoyed during its heyday of the 1930s and 1940s. The loyalty of the fans bordered on fanaticism. Listeners from small towns in Ohio and Wisconsin or isolated farms in North Dakota and Tennessee as well as urban dwellers in Chicago and Detroit tuned in religiously every Saturday night. The Barn Dance also appealed to second-generation ethnic immigrants throughout the upper Midwest and struck a familiar chord with displaced southern migrants who came north in search of better opportunities.

Chad Berry helped to illuminate the southern migration experience. "The music changed," he told me, "because of these numbers of people who were living in the North and had migrated from the South. The themes became more anti-urban as they celebrated Mom and Dad back home. They talked about the guilt that some southern migrants had about leaving the home place, leaving the way of life that was known to them, leaving their parents behind."[3]

As a filmmaker, I wanted to explore the interaction that the National Barn Dance created among sponsors, musicians, and listeners and how this dynamic profoundly altered country music and radio programming. WLS effectively staked its claim on the rural market and the rural consumer. From 1929 to 1957, the station published an annual *WLS Family Album* featuring photos and embellished biographies of the stars portraying homey and wholesome images. From 1935 to 1937, WLS printed a weekly fan magazine, *Stand By!* that featured the latest happenings of the Hayloft Gang and offered a chance for listeners to write in to the station.

Letters and fan magazines conveyed a sense of how the meanings of the show were constructed by the listeners themselves, and how those meanings evolved over time as the historical setting of the show changed.[4] We have located many of these letters, along with surviving scripts in the John Lair and Bradley Kincaid collections housed in the Southern Appalachian Archives in the Hutchins Library at Berea College in Kentucky. Harry Rice, the library's sound archivist, was instrumental in helping us to access and navigate these collections.

Alka-Seltzer saw the commercial potential of this down-home, folksy programming, and in 1933 NBC was broadcasting one hour of the sponsored program in cities coast to coast, making the National Barn Dance the first nationally broadcast country-music radio program. The network broadcast helped to make Lulu Belle the most popular woman on radio in 1936 and launched performers like Patsy Montana to national stardom.

By the late 1930s, the National Barn Dance had fully embraced the western phenomenon that celebrated the legend of the cowboy as a working-class hero and a romantic symbol of the American dream. Douglas B. Green discussed with me this western culture and the contribution of the cowboy singer Gene Autry and his early career on the Barn Dance. Autry, of course, was the first of many National Barn Dance performers who would go on to Hollywood.

I am deeply indebted to David Wylie and his encyclopedic knowledge of the National Barn Dance. I could go to Wylie with almost any question and he would have the answer. Debby Gray was very generous in giving us access to her extensive collection of Barn Dance memorabilia and sharing her personal stories and remembrances. In addition, Wayne W. Daniel was a wonderful resource for published materials and for his knowledge of the National Barn Dance in the post–World War II era.

One of the first questions I asked was, How can we visualize a film about a radio show, a sound medium? I uncovered a wealth of archival film footage and photographs to illustrate the story. A rare find was a thirty-minute film with sound of a live broadcast of the National Barn Dance from the Eighth Street Theatre from the mid-1950s featuring Bob Atcher, Arkie the Arkansas Woodchopper, Colleen and Donna Wilson, and Dolph Hewitt. I was delighted to find silent footage of a 1946 appearance of the Barn Dance cast at the Illinois State Fair with a special guest, Roy Rogers, performing with the Prairie Ramblers. Silent film footage of the Hayloft Gang at a 1936 benefit for victims of the Great Depression showed us the Hoosier Hot Shots, Uncle Ezra, and Lulu Belle, who was obviously expecting her first child.

The performers and fans of the National Barn Dance are two of the few primary sources available to us. Since many of these folks are now in their eighties and nineties, I realized the importance of interviewing them, if only for the significance of having their oral histories preserved and archived for future generations.

Captain Stubby and the Buccaneers were famous on the Barn Dance in the 1950s for their unique brand of midwestern country music and humor. Sadly, Tom Fouts, "Captain Stubby," passed away in May 2004, at the age of eighty-five. I was fortunate to shoot a delightful on-camera interview with him the previous October that captured his natural wit and humor.

I had the pleasure of talking with Thomas Hoyt "Slim" Bryant (now aged ninety-nine), the guitar player with Clayton McMichen and the Georgia Wildcats, a progressive string band that performed on the Barn Dance in 1933. Bryant described playing a live broadcast from an airplane high above Chicago's Century of Progress World's Fair as the program was relayed back to the National Barn Dance audience at the Eighth Street Theatre. He offered a first-hand account of life on the barn dance radio circuit: "You'd play on the radio for five or six days, and then you would be making personal appearances. In five or six days, you created an audience that would commit to the theaters or the school houses to see what you looked like."[5]

As a way to further brand the WLS–Prairie Farmer enterprise, touring road units were sent out to small towns throughout the Midwest. James Buchanan, who turned one hundred in 2007, shared with me his amusing stories of working the road shows in 1936. He entertained with his band, the Kentuckians, and sold subscriptions to *Prairie Farmer* magazine, *Stand By!* and the *WLS Family Album.* Buchanan had the foresight to keep a detailed scrapbook of his experiences.

John Lair discovered nineteen-year-old Lily May Ledford, a talented mountain fiddler and banjo player from the Red River Gorge of eastern Kentucky. He brought her to Chicago in 1936 to join the Hayloft Gang. Ledford's granddaughter, Cari Norris, inherited her grandmother's Vega White Lady banjo along with her love for traditional folksongs. Norris performed a few of her grandmother's tunes for us and recounted Ledford's adjustment to life in the big city as a performer on the most popular country music show on the airwaves.

Our film crew traveled to Arizona and interviewed sisters Colleen Allen and Donna Asklund, who performed on the Barn Dance in the 1950s as the Beaver Valley Sweethearts. They described how the fans lined up waiting for autographs and deluged them with baby gifts when their children were born. Patsy Montana's daughter, Beverly Losey, shared her memories of life backstage at theaters and fairgrounds while touring and performing with her mother.

Attempting to tell the rich story of the National Barn Dance in a sixty-minute documentary film was a challenge. We have just scratched the surface. The essays in this book give additional definition, shape, and meaning to the National Barn Dance. I anticipate that this volume will create a renewed interest and appreciation for the once great radio program that left its indelible mark on broadcasting history and forever changed the face of country and popular music. I hope this work will encourage new research and scholarship surrounding the National Barn Dance and its place in American culture.

NOTES

1. Susan Smulyan, tape-recorded telephone interview by Stephen Parry, Chicago, January 17, 2004.
2. Bill C. Malone, videotaped interview by Stephen Parry, Madison, Wisconsin, March 29, 2004.
3. Chad Berry, videotaped interview by Stephen Parry, Maryville, Tennessee, May 13, 2005.
4. Susan J. Douglas, tape-recorded telephone interview by Stephen Parry, Chicago, January 19, 2004.
5. Thomas H. Bryant, videotaped interview by Stephen Parry, Pittsburgh, Pennsylvania, October 13, 2003.

CONTRIBUTORS

CHAD BERRY is Goode Professor of Appalachian Studies, associate professor of history, and director of the Appalachian Center at Berea College. He is the author of *Southern Migrants, Northern Exiles* (University of Illinois Press, 2000). He was president of the Appalachian Studies Association for 2006–7 and is currently engaged in a research project exploring the development of Appalachian studies throughout the twentieth century.

MICHAEL T. BERTRAND is an assistant professor of history at Tennessee State University. His research interests focus on southern history, with an emphasis on comprehending the relationship between popular culture and social change. He is currently working on a manuscript about African American radio programming in the South between 1948 and 1963. In 2005 the University of Illinois Press released a paperback edition of his first book, *Race, Rock, and Elvis.* He is lead editor and moderator of H-Southern-Music.

LISA KRISSOFF BOEHM is an associate professor of urban studies and director of the Commonwealth Honors Program at Worcester State College. She is the author of *Popular Culture and the Enduring Myth of Chicago* (Routledge, 2004) and *Making a Way Out of No Way: African American Women, Domestic Work, and the Second Great Migration, 1940–1970* (forthcoming from the University Press of Mississippi). Krissoff Boehm is the past president of the North East Popular Culture Association.

DON CUSIC is the Music City Professor of Music Industry History at the Mike Curb College of Entertainment and Music Business at Belmont University and is the author of sixteen books, including *Cowboys and the Wild West* and *The Cowboy Way.* His biography of Gene Autry was published in 2007.

WAYNE W. DANIEL is a researcher and writer in the fields of country, gospel, and bluegrass music history. His works have appeared in both scholarly and general-readership publications. Daniel is the author of the book *Pickin' on Peachtree: A History of Country Music in Atlanta, Georgia* (University of Illinois Press, 1990).

LOYAL JONES is the former director of the Berea College Appalachian Center. He has written biographies of two Appalachian musicians, one being Bradley Kincaid, who began his career on WLS and the National Barn Dance. A forthcoming book (University of Illinois Press) explores country music humor, humorists, and comedians.

KRISTINE M. MCCUSKER is an associate professor of history at Middle Tennessee State University. She is the author of *Lonesome Cowgirls and Honky-Tonk Angels* (forthcoming from the University of Illinois Press) and the co-editor, with Diane Pecknold, of *A Boy Named Sue: Gender and Country Music.*

STEPHEN PARRY is a documentary filmmaker living in Chicago. His PBS documentary *The Hayloft Gang: The Story of the National Barn Dance* explores the seminal radio show and its unique place in American music and popular culture. The genesis of this project is Parry's passionate interest in early country and bluegrass music.

SUSAN SMULYAN, an associate professor in the Department of American Civilization at Brown University, is the author of *Selling Radio: The Commercialization of American Broadcasting 1920–1934* (Smithsonian Institution Press, 1994) and *Popular Ideologies: Mass Culture at Mid-Century* (University of Pennsylvania Press, 2007). Long interested in new media, Professor Smulyan has conceived and assembled three large websites: "Whole Cloth: Discovering Science and Technology through American History" (http://invention.smithsonian.org/centerpieces/whole_cloth); "Perry Visits Japan: A Visual History" (http://dl.lib.brown.edu/japan); and "Freedom Now" (http://www.brown.edu/freedomnow).

PAUL L. TYLER earned a Ph.D. in Folklore and American Studies from Indiana University and teaches as an adjunct in the social science and music departments of National-Louis University. After a long career as a working musician with the Volo Bogtrotters and other bands, he still teaches fiddle and early country music at the Old Town School of Folk Music in Chicago. He produced the CD *Folksongs of Illinois, Vol. 2* for the Illinois Humanities Council (available through the University of Illinois Press).

MICHAEL ANN WILLIAMS is head of the Department of Folk Studies and Anthropology at Western Kentucky University. She is the author of *Homeplace: The Social Use and Meaning of the Folk Dwelling in Southwestern North Carolina* and *Great Smoky Mountains Folklife.* Her most recent book is *Staging Tradition: John Lair and Sarah Gertrude Knott* (University of Illinois Press, 2006).

INDEX

Italicized page numbers indicate photographs.

ABC, 5, 114. *See also* American Broadcasting Company
ABC Barn Dance, 89–90
Acuff, Roy, 9, 180
Adamson, George, 33, 43
Adrian, Mich., 36
Adult Education Council of Chicago, 189
African American musical forms, and influence of, 11, 65–66
African Americans, and blackface, 139–44
Agricultural Foundation, Sears, Roebuck, 5, 21, 22, 120, 136
Alabama Stompers, 142
Aladdin Mantle Lamp Company, 23, 157
Aldrett, N. G., 43
Alka-Seltzer, 1, 6, 22, 27, 61, 74, 83, 85, 86, 89, 121, 157, 158, 202
Allen, Colleen, 203
Allen, Horace, 180
Allen, Rex, 77, *78*, 79, 180, 181
American Babel: Rogue Radio Broadcasters of the Jazz Age, 127
American Broadcasting Company, 86, 89. *See also* ABC; Blue Network
American Broadcasting–Paramount Theatres Inc. (AB–PT), 93, 94, 96
American Folk Song Festival, 188, 192
American Recording Company (ARC) 59, 172, 177
Amos and Andy, 141
AM radio, 88
Anderson, Andy, 77
Anderson, Benedict, 127
Anderson, Broncho Billy, 170
Anderson, William T. "Andy," *113*
Anthology of American Folk Songs, 195
Appalachia, 7–8, 188
Applegate, Loeta, 181
Arcadia, Ind., 60
Arkansas Woodchopper's Square Dance Band, 46. *See also* Arkie the Arkansas Woodchopper
Arkie the Arkansas Woodchopper, 27, 30, 33, 37, 41, 42, 49, 50, 53, 61, 62, 64, 73, 74, 80, 84, 85, 89, 91, 92, 93, 96, 106, 202. *See also* Arkansas Woodchopper's Square Dance Band
Armed Forces Radio Network, 84, 166
Arthur, George, 77
Asbel, Bernard, 32, 183
Asheville, N.C., 188
Ashland, Ky., 188
Askland, Donna, 203
Asparagus Joe, 60. *See also* Pie Plant Pete
Atcher, Bob, 15, 87, 88, 89, 90, 91, 92, 94, 96, 106, 181, *182*, 183, 202
Atcher, Maggie, 94
Atchison, David Shelby "Tex," 45, 54, *177*
Aunt Sally, 174
Autry, Gene, 9, 26, 28, 29, 30, 41, 42, 56, 57, 64, 65, 79, 94, 101, *105*, 168, 169, 172, 173, *174*, *175*, 176, *177*, 181, 202
Autry, Molly, 176

Bailey, Bill, 89
Baird, Bill, 175
Baird, Maude, 175
Baker, Frank, 165
Barrett, Pat, 60. *See also* Uncle Ezra
Barron, Hal, 200
Beaver Valley Sweethearts, The, 88, 91, 203
Beliajus, Vyts, 196
Benchley, Robert, 84, 85
Benny, Jack, 122
Berea College, 47, 155, 202
Berea College Girls' Glee Club, 155, 157
Bernie, Ben, 181
Berry, Chad, 116, 199, 201
Bertrand, Michael T., 11
Bessie and Prof Dunck, 174
Beverly Hill Billies, The, 12
Biggar, George C., 4, 13, 30, 32, 41, 43, 53, 55, 58, 62, 87, 89, 121, 132, 138, 139, 154, 187, 191, 192, 196
Big Maceo, 115
Big Yank, 23
Bill, Edgar, 20, 36, 48, 62
Black, Howard, 61
Black Hawk Valley Boys and Penny West, 77
Blanchard, Red, 87, 89, 91, 92, 93, 96
Blevins, Ruby, 14, 58. *See also* Montana, Patsy
Blue Grass Boys, The, 76, 77
Blue Network, 85–86

Blue Sky Boys, The, 50
Boehm, Lisa Krissoff, 4, 170
Bolick Brothers, The, 50
Bonn, Skeeter, 88
Bonner, Capt. Moses J., 20
Bonnie Blue Eyes, 181
Boone, N.C., 13, 53
Boone County Jamboree, 58
Boys from Virginia, The, 42. *See also* Smith, Blaine and Cal
Briggs, Slim, 183
British Archives of Country Music, 27
Brown, Georgia, 76
Brown, John, 36
Brown, Juanita (Mrs. John), 36
Brown, Phyllis, 91
Brusoe, Leizime, 44, 45
Bryan, William Jennings, 171
Bryant, Thomas Hoyt "Slim," 29, 35, 45, 61, *113*, 203. *See also* Clayton McMichen's Georgia Wildcats
Buchanan, Annabel Morris, 188
Buchanan, James, 203
Bufwack, Mary A., 13, 58
Burnette, Lester Alvin "Smiley," 63, 64, 174, 175, 176
Burnham, Daniel, 109
Burns, Kenneth C. "Jethro," 7, 88, 183. *See also* Homer and Jethro
Burns and Allen, 122
Burr, Henry, 30, 73
Butler, Burridge D., 5, 22, 32, 74, 79, 80, 85, 86, 96, 103, 104, 106, 131
Buttram, Pat, 61, 74, *76*, 84, 85, 106, 112
By-Gosh (blackface performer), 141

Cackle Sisters, The, 56. *See also* DeZurik Sisters, The
Callahan Brothers, The, 50
Campbell, Harry, Jr., 60
Canadian Broadcasting Corporation, 84
Cantor, Eddie, 122, 123
Capone, Alphonse "Al," 110, 112, 170
Captain Stubby, 15. *See also* Captain Stubby and his Buccaneers; Fouts, Tom
Captain Stubby and his Buccaneers, 87, 89, 90, 91, 203
Carlisle, Cliff, 56
Carolina Playmakers, The, 189
Carson, Jenny Lou, 82, 90, 112. *See also* Overstake, Lucille
Carter Family, The, 51, 64, 191
CBS, 121, 183
Century of Progress, the World's Fair of 1933 and 1934, 24, 107, 110, *111*, 112, 203. *See also* Chicago World's Fair
Chattanooga National Folk Festival, 192
Checkerboard Time, 56
Chicago, 101, 107, 120, 181; and dark reputation, 107–13; and midwestern culture, 102–7; and popular culture image, 108, 172
Chicago Charter Jubilee, 189
Chicago Civic Center, 79, 93
Chicago Civic Federation, 109
Chicago Costume Works, 142
Chicago Country Music Festival, 117
Chicago National Folk Festival, 193, 194, 196
Chicago Secret Six, 109
Chicago World's Fair, 14, 24, 59, 176. *See also* Century of Progress, the World's Fair of 1933 and 1934
Cisler, Steve, 191
Claire, Malcolm, 11, 143. *See also* Spareribs
Clark, Kenneth, 65
Clayton McMichen's Georgia Wildcats, 35, 42, 203. *See also* Georgia Wildcats, The; McMichen, Clayton
Cody, Buffalo Bill, 169
Cohen, Lizabeth, 160
Colvard, Jim, 76
Conqueror Records, 172, 173
Conqueror Record Time, 41
consumer culture, rise of, 200
Coon Creek Girls, The, 45, 122, 123, 194, 195
Cooper, John, 13
Cooper, Myrtle Eleanor, 13, 51, 52, 53, *158*, 193. *See also* Lulu Belle; Wiseman, Lulu Belle
Corn Crackers, The, 76, 86
Cornrow, Timothy, 43, 45
Corwine, Tom, 62
Cottrell, Jim, 76
Country Music Records: A Discography, 1921–42, 28, 42
Country Music Sources: A Biblio-Discography of Commercially Recorded Traditional Music, 42, 44
Country Music Story, The, 25
Country Music, U.S.A., 31
Cousin Emmy, 162
Cousin Tilford, 15, 89, 96
Cowbell Pete, 20, 43
cowboys, and Chicago, 168–84; and country music, 172–83; and romantic symbol, 169, 202; and working-class hero, 169, 172, 202
Craig, Douglas, 125
Crandill, Chester, 43
Crane, Martha, 165
Crockett, Alan, *28*, 45, 54
Crockett Family Mountaineers, The, 54
Cross, Hugh, *34*, 51, 52, 161, *163*, 174
Cross, Reggie, 60
Cumberland Ridge Runners, The, 29, 31, *34*, 37, 45, 51, 52, 65, 74, 106, 161, 162, *163*, 165, 188, 191
Cusic, Don, 7

Dalhart, Vernon, 28
Dandurand, Tommy, 20, 25, *35*, 39, 43, 44. *See also* Tommy Dandurand and His Gang of WLS

Daniel, Wayne W., 4, 26, 61, 115, 202
Daniels, Yvonne, 1
Darrow, Clarence, 171
Davis, Bill, *140*
Davis, Karl, *34*, *38*, 51, 90, *163*, 191. *See also* Karl and Harty
Dawn Busters, 86
Day, J. W., 188
Dean Brothers, The, 42, 56
Decca Record Company, 81, 82
Delmore Brothers, The, 50
DeMille, Cecil B., 170
Des Plaines Theater, 62
DeZurik, Carolyn, 55, *178*. *See also* DeZurik Sisters, The
DeZurik, Mary Jane, 55, *178*. *See also* DeZurik Sisters, The
DeZurik Sisters, The, 13, 55, 56, 63, 64, 80, 87, 89. *See also* Cackle Sisters, The; DeZurik, Carolyn; DeZurik, Mary Jane
Dingle, Charles, 85
Dinnerbell, 77, 192
Dinning Sisters, The, 81, 84, 85, 91
Dixie Strutters, 142
Doerksen, Clifford, 127
Dolce, John, 89, 91, 92, 183
Dolph Hewitt and the Sage Riders, 94
Doolittle, Jesse, *35*
Douglas, Susan, 127, 200
Dunigan, Jack, *29*
Du Sable, Jean Baptiste Point, 116
Dynamite Jim, 60

Edwards, Tommy, 1
Eighth Street Theatre, 2, 11, 22, 59, 61, 74, 79, 83, 92, 93
Electrifying America: Social Meanings of a New Technology, 1880–1940, 171
Elkhart, Ind., 22
Elkhart County, Ind., 1
Endeback, Christine, 64
Evans, James F., 120, 183
Evans, Sara, 117
Ezra Buzzington's Rustic Revelers, 44, 60

Fairmont State College, 53
fan ephemera, and means of preserving breadwinner ethic, 154, 164
Farm Week Festival, 107
Federal Radio Commission, 121, 136
Fell, Pete, 77
Finding Her Voice: Women in Country Music, 1800–2000, 13
Fireside Politics: Radio and Political Culture in the United States, 125
Fish, Bob, *140*
Fitch, Dan, 141
Fitzgerald, F. Scott, 132
Flannery Sisters, The, 37, 42, 63
Fleming, Sonny, 87
FM radio, 15
Foley, Clyde Julian "Red," 1, 26, 51, 52, 53, *57*, 58, 64, 73, 74, 80, *82*, 91, *113*, 143, 157, 161, *163*, 176
folk festival: and authentic music, 190–92; and didactic purpose of, 196; and form, 188; and issues of class, 195–96
Ford, Henry, 10, 134, 135, 145
Ford and Glenn, 36
Foster, Sally, 42, 52
Four Hired Hands, 60, 147
Four Hired Men, 36
Fouts, Tom, 87, 203. *See also* Captain Stubby
Frank, J. L., 176
Fraser, Roscoe, *193*
Fred Kirby and His Carolina Boys, 56
Fred Wagner's Hawaiian Five Hilo Orchestra, 20
Frill, Thomas, 43

Gallatin County, Ill., 60
Gardner, Robert, *39*, 50, 62. *See also* Mac and Bob
Garrard County, Ky., 47
Garrett, Alma, 15
Garrett, Roy, 15
Gary, Ind., 60
Gaylord Entertainment, 115
Geels, Francis, 62
gendered images, performer portrayals of, 58, 64, 154
Gentry Brothers, The, 51. *See also* McFarland, Lester
Georgia Jubilee, 142
Georgia Wildcats, The, 28, 36, 45. *See also* Clayton McMichen's Georgia Wildcats; McMichen, Clayton
Germanick, Sophia, 13
Gid Tanner and the Skillet Lickers, 28, 45
Gill, Rusty, 55, 61, 86
Girls of the Golden West, The, 34, 37, 42, 52, 57, 59, 63, 64, 106, 176, *177*, 199. *See also* Goad, Dorothy; Goad, Mildred; Good Sisters, The
Girls' Trio, 36
Gladstone, Mich., 63
Glosson, Lonnie, 42
Glosup, Eddie, 56. *See also* Dean Brothers, The
Glosup, Jimmie, 56. *See also* Dean Brothers, The
Goad, Dorothy "Dolly," *57*, 58, 176. *See also* Girls of the Golden West, The; Good Sisters, The
Goad, Mildred "Millie," *57*, 58, 176. *See also* Girls of the Golden West, The; Good, Millie; Good Sisters, The
Goatschel, W., 43
Goebel, George, 86, 177, *178*
Good, Millie, *105*. *See also* Goad, Mildred
Goodreau, Ed, *35*, 40, 44
Good Sisters, The, 58, 59, 106. *See also* Girls of the Golden West, The

Grand Ole Opry, 32, 93, 101, 103, 104, 114, 115, 167, 180, 199. *See also* WSM Barn Dance
Gray, Debby, 202
Great Chicago Fire, 108
Great Depression, 2, 5, 10, 72, 112, 153, 154, 157, 159, 161, 170
Great Ferris Wheel, 109
Green, Douglas, 7
Green, Douglas B., 202
Green, Nate, 85
Green, Paul, 189, 196
Gregory, James N., 11, 104
Grey, Zane, 170

Haley, Bill, 92
Hamblen, Stuart, 59, 176, 177
Hamlin Wizard Oil, 157
Hammond, Ind., 13
Haney, Eli, 76
Happiness Boys, The, 122
Happy Valley Family, 42
Hardin County, Ky., 181
Harkins, Anthony, 6, 11, 201
Harmony Girls, The, 36
Hart, Frank, 44
Hart, William S., 170
Harte, Bret, 176
Hawthorne, Pepper, 63
Hay, George D., 114
Hayloft Chorus, 37
Hayloft Trio, The, 62
Haymarket Square, 108
Haynes, Henry, 7. *See also* Homer and Jethro
Haynes, Henry D., 88
Hays, Will, 47
Heather, Jean, 85
Hewitt, Dolph, 87, 90, 92, 96, 202
Hewitt, Lisa, 117
Hillbilly: A Cultural History of an American Icon, 11
Hillbillyland: What the Movies Did to the Mountains and What the Mountains Did to the Movies, 171
hillbilly music, 7, 144, 171, 188
Hill Toppers, The, 42, 55, 65
Hilmes, Michele, 126, 131, 200
Holden, Jack, 77
Holmes, Christine, *105*
Holmes, Floyd "Salty," *28*, 54, 65, *105*, 177, 192
Holstein, Jim, 65
Homer and Jethro, 1, 6, 15, 88, 91, 92. *See also* Burns, Kenneth C. "Jethro"; Haynes, Henry
Hoosier Hot Shots, The, 28, 36, 42, 44, 60, 61, 66, 73, 74, 80, 81, 84, 85, 86, 94, *95*, 106, 147, 199, 202
Hoosier Sod Busters, The, 24, 60, 61, 106
Hoover, Herbert, 158, 159
Hope, Ark., 58
Hopkins, Colonel William, 19
Hopkins, Doc, 51, 52, 73, 74, 79, 80, 87
Hotel Sherman, 19, 25
Houchins, Kenneth, 65
Howe, Langdon, 77. *See also* Blue Grass Boys, The
Howlin' Wolf, 115
hungry hillbilly sound, 32, 183
Hurst, Jack, 183
Hurt, Charles "Chick," *28*, 44, 54, *177*
Hutchinson, Jimmy, 87

Illinois State Fair, 91, 93, 115
Ingram and Carpenter, 36
Insull, Samuel, 136
International Amphitheater (Chicago), 24
International Harvester, 137
International Square Dance Festival, 92
Iowa Farmers Union, 43
"Irish Washerwoman, The," 39, 40, 43, *43*
Isham Jones' College Inn Orchestra, 24
"I Want to Be a Cowboy's Sweetheart," 15, 58, 59, 62, 94, 177. See also Montana, Patsy

Jackson, Clayton, 46
Jackson, George Pullen, 192
James, Jimmie, 86, 91
Jane Addams's Hull-House, 109
Janes, Art, 106
Jazz Age, 6, 11, 133, 134; and denunciation of jazz culture, 144–48; and gender roles, 156; and influence of music, 117, 145, 147
Jim and Bob, 65
Jo and Alma, 37, 42, 64
Johnson, Frank, 52
Jones, Judie and Julie, 77, 91
Jones, Loyal, 6, 201
Jones Sisters, The, 77. *See also* Jones, Judie and Julie
Journal of Country Music, 26
Jungle, The, 102

Kankakee County, Ill., 44
Karl and Harty, 37, *38*, 51, 52, 64, 91, 161. *See also* Davis, Karl; Karl and Harty and the Cumberland Ridge Runners; Taylor, Hartford Connecticut "Harty"
Karl and Harty and the Cumberland Ridge Runners, 42
KDKA (Pittsburgh), 1, 77, 120
Keck, George Fred, 112
Keepers, Floyd, 165
Keil Opera House, 188
Kekuku, Joseph, 65
Kelly, Edward J., 107
Kelly, Joe, 61, 74, 84, 85, 106
Kendall, Dolores and Pauline 77
Kennedy, David, 153
Kentuckians, The, 203

Kentucky Girls, The, 42. *See also* Jo and Alma
Kentucky Ramblers, The, 14, 54. *See also* Prairie Ramblers, The
Kentucky School for the Blind, 50
Kentucky Wonder Bean, 40, 43, 59–60
Kettering, Frank, 60, 86
Kettering, Frank Delaney, *95*
Keystone Steel and Wire Company, 23
KFNF (Shenandoah), 20
Kincaid, Bradley, 1, 4, 11, 30, 32, 34, 37, 41, 42, 47, *48*, 49, 53, 125, 155, 156, 157, 161, 162, 164, 188, 190, 191, 201, 202
Kirby, Fred, 42, 56
Kirk, Rook, 77
Klatt, Lou, 92, 94
Klatts and Jammers, The, 94
Klein, Augie, 55, 86
Klein, Ray, 87
KMBC (Kansas City), 50, 55, 178
KMMJ (Grand Island, Nebr.), 76
KMOX (St. Louis), 58
KMPC (Los Angeles), 12
KMTR (Los Angeles), 59
Knob Noster, Mo., 49
Knott, Sarah Gertrude, 187, 188, 189, 191, 192, 194, 195, 196, 197
Koch, Frederick, 188
KOY (Phoenix), 192
Krause, Charles, 19
KVOO (Tulsa), 56
Kyriakoudes, Louis M., 114

Lair, John, 4, 6, 13, 16, 25, 30, 32, *34*, 43, 45, 46, 51, 52, 53, 62, *124*, 125, 135, 136, *140* (in blackface), 157, 161, 162, *163*, 164, 188, *190*, 192, 193, 194, 195, 196, 197, 201, 202, 203
Lange, Jeffrey, 31
LaPorte, Ind., 60
Larson, George A., 103
Layne, Bert, *29*
Ledford, Lily May, 13, 45, 157, *159*, 162, 176, 195, 203
Lee County, Va., 15
Lee Morgan and the Midwesterners, 94
Lemann, Nicholas, 182
Les Paul's trio, 65
Levee Loungers, 142
Lightfoot, William, 201
Linder, Bonnie, 75, 78, 180. *See also* Linder Sisters, The
Linder, Connie, 75. *See also* Linder Sisters, The
Linder Sisters, The, 75, 80. *See also* Linder, Bonnie; Linder, Connie; Sunbonnet Girls, The
Listening In: Radio in the American Imagination, 127
Little Brown Church of the Air, 24
Little Genevieve, 24, 80, 89. *See also* Morse, Ted "Otto"
Lizton, Ind., 51
Log Cabin Boys, 176
Lohman, Smokey, 90
Lomax, Alan, 194
Lomax, John, 192
Lombard, Ky., 45
Long, Huey, 47
Long, Jimmy, 56, 64
Losey, Beverly, 203
Loshe, Helen, 62
Louise Massey and the Westerners, 42, 55, 73, 74, 81, 94. *See also* Massey Family, The; Westerners, The
Loviglio, Jason, 127
Lowdermilk, Romaine, 42, 192, 196
Lujack, Larry, 1
Lullaby Time, 36
Lulu Belle, 11, 14, 53, 79, 182, 183, *193*, 196, 202. *See* Cooper, Myrtle Eleanor; Wiseman, Lulu Belle
Lulu Belle and Burrhead, 51, 53
Lulu Belle and Scotty, 1, 6, *8*, 27, 37, 42, 52, 61, 64, 73, 74, 81, 84, 85, 89, 90, 91, 92, 119, 180, 193, 194, 201. *See also* Wiseman, Lulu Belle; Wiseman, Scotty
Lunsford, Bascom Lamar, 53, 188, 192, 193, 194
Lunsford, Lee, 76, 86

Mabie, Louise Massey, 180. *See also* Massey, Louise
Mabie, Milt, 55, 178, *179*
Mac and Bob, 28, 37, *39*, 42, 50, 51, 59, 64, 65, 74, 86, 162, *177*
Maces Springs, Va., 51
Madison County, Ky., 51
Malin, Don, 47
Malone, Bill C., 10, 31, 40, 200, 201
Maphis, Joe, 77
Maple City Four, 24, 34, 42, 56, 60, 74, 86, 91, 174
Marshall County, Ill., 30
Martinez, Pete, 77
Marvin, Frankie, 28, 172
Marvin, Johnny, 172
Mason, Dixie, 42, 54
Massey, Allen, 55, 178, *179*
Massey, Curt "Dott," 45, 55, 178, *179*
Massey, Henry "Dad," 55, 178
Massey, Louise, 13, 55, 178, *179*. *See also* Louise Massey and the Westerners; Mabie, Louise Massey
Massey Family, The, 55, 65, 178, 179. *See also* Louise Massey and the Westerners; Musical Masseys, The; Westerners, The
Maxedon, Dean, 77
Maxedons, The, 77
Maynard, Ken, 176
McAdory, Pat, 52
McCormack, William, 44
McCormick, Cyrus, 102
McCusker, Kristine, 10, 11, 122, 124, 125, 200

McCutcheon, John T., 110, 112
McDowell, Buddy, 44, 45, 52
McFarland, Lester, *39*, 50, 51. *See also* Mac and Bob
McGee, Fibber, 176
McGill, Elsie May, 192
McKeesport, Pa., 77
McMichen, Clayton, 28, 29, 45, *113*. *See also* Clayton McMichen's Georgia Wildcats
Meade, Guthrie, 42, 44, 45, 46, 47, 49, 50, 51, 52, 53, 54, 55, 56, 58, 59, 60
Meissner, Fritz, 106
Memphis Minnie, 115
Mercer, Woody, 88, 183
Messina, Frank, 86
Midwestern Hayride, 77
migration, 11–15, 201
Miles Laboratories, 1, 22, 86, 89, 157
Milk Maids, The, 36
Miller, Bob, 28
Miller, Chuck, 77
Miller, Curley, 77
Miller, Harriet, 77
Miller, Homer "Slim," *34*, 45, 51, 52, 161, *163*, 174, 191
Mishawaka, Ind., 1
Mix, Tom, 170
Monroe, Bill, 62
Monroe, Harriet, 111
Monroe Brothers, The, 50, 51, 55
Montana, Patsy, 11, 14, 24, 27, 28, 41, 42, 54, 58, 59, 64, 74, 79, 81, 86, 90, 94, *105*, 106, 112, 165, *166*, 176, 177, 202, 203. *See also* "I Want to Be a Cowboy's Sweetheart"
Montana Cowgirls, The, 14
Moore, Wally, 87
Morgan, Craig, 117
Morgan, Lee, 94
Morse, Ted "Otto," 60, 80, 89, 91. *See also* Little Genevieve; Novelodeons, The
Mountain Dance and Folk Festival, 188
"Mountain Dew," 53, 193
Mount Carmel, Ill., 106, 176
Mount Vernon, Ky., 51
Moye, Claud, 60. *See also* Pie Plant Pete
Muddy Waters, 115
Muenich, Jeanne, 10, 51, 161, 162. *See also* Parker, Linda
Murdick, George, 43
Murphy's Feeds and Corn, 137
Musical Masseys, The, 178. *See also* Massey Family, The; Westerners, The
My Favorite Mountain Ballad and Old Time Songs, 48

Nashville, 115, 182; as premier setting for country music, 114–17
National Barn Dance: accidental beginnings of, 25; and appeal to hidden and ignored audiences, 125–27; and commercialization of country music, 88–93; and commercial recordings, 26–30; and contributions to country music styles, 64–66; and experiments in programming, 33–35; and focus on rural communities, 19–26; incompleteness of sonic record of, 27; international broadcast of, 84; last broadcast of, 93–94; and merger of radio and traditional music, 35–37; and music of postwar era, 72–97; and National Folk Festival, as theatrical forms, 187–97; performers as family, 125; performers as plain folks, 138; and radio history, 119–25; reasons for success of, 3–16; recedes from public view, 114–15; and recordings of rural musicians, 41–61; and vaudeville model, 122; and wartime patriotism, 74–81
National Barn Dance (film), 84, 85
National Barn Dance Orchestra, The, 44, 45
National Folk Festival, 6, 187, 188, 189, 192, 194, 195, 196, 197
NBC, 2, 33, 37, 61, 89, 121, 157
NBC Blue Network, 22, 26, 61
Newton, Ernie, 65
Noblesville, Ind., 24
Norris, Cari, 203
Novelodeons, The, 30, 60, 147. *See also* Otto and the Novelodeons
Nye, David E., 171

Oermann, Robert K., 13, 58
O'Halloran, Hal, *113*, 176
Ohio River Folk Festival, 194
Olaf the Swede, 6
Old Homestead Records, 27
Old Southern Sacred Singers, 51
Old Timers, 174
Opryland, 115
Ossenbrink, Luther, 49. *See also* Arkie the Arkansas Woodchopper
Otto and the Novelodeons, 56. *See also* Morse, Ted "Otto"; Novelodeons, The
Otto and the Tune Twisters, 60. *See also* Morse, Ted "Otto"
Overstake, Eva, 53, 82. *See also* Three Little Maids, The
Overstake, Evelyn, 82. *See also* Three Little Maids, The
Overstake, Lucille, 81. *See also* Carson, Jenny Lou; Three Little Maids, The
Overstake Sisters, 37. *See also* Three Little Maids, The
Owen, Tom, 43
Owen's Barn Dance Trio, 44

Paige, Mabel, 85
Paoli, Bob, 65

Paramount, 84
Parker, Chubby, 29, 41, 42, *46*, 53
Parker, Linda, 1, 10, 11, 13, *34*, 37, 51, 52, 122, 161, 162, *163*, 164, 174, 191
patriarchy, and the Great Depression, 153–67
Peabody, Eddie, 81, 86
Pemwright, C. A., 43
Penny, Lee, 59, 180
Peoria, Ill., 23
Peterson, Richard A., 4, 6, 9, 200
Peterson, Walter, 40, 60. *See also* Kentucky Wonder Bean
Petterson, "Pat," 106
Phantom Stallion, The, 180
Phillips Petroleum, 89, 181
Pickering, M. J., 189, 194
Pie Plant Pete, 29, 41, 42, 60, 64
Pinex Cough Syrup, 157, 176
Pinex Merrymakers, 45, 58
Pinex Merrymakers, 52
Plan of Chicago, 109
polka, popularity of, 92
Popular Culture and the Enduring Myth of Chicago, 108
Porter, Edwin S., 170
Porter, Rocky, 91
Powell County, Ky., 13
Prairie Farmer, 5, 6, 21, 22, 104, 121, 170
Prairie Farmer and WLS: The Burridge D. Butler Years, 183
Prairie Farmer Publishing Company, 136
Prairie Ramblers, The, 14, 27, *28*, 31, 42, 45, 54, 57, 55, 59, 64, 65, 66, 73, 74, 86, 87, 91, 94, 106, 147, 176, 202. *See also* Sweet Violet Boys, The
Prairie Sod Boy, 106
Presley, Elvis, 92, 96
Pridmore, Jay, 103
Priest, James B., 44
Princess Tsianina, 13
Promised Land, The, 182
promoters, as artificers, 195
Pullman Palace Car Company, 108
Purina Mills, 56

race: and denunciation of urban jazz culture, 139–48; and emphasis of rural identity, 139–48
radio: distribution of, 2; and extension of the hearth, 35; as nationalizing phenomenon, 127; as new medium, 33–34
Radio's Intimate Public, 127
Radio Voices: American Broadcasting, 1922–1952, 126
Ramsey, Ill., 63
Randolph, Robert I., 110
Rautenberg, Louise, 52
Red Brand Farm Fence, 137
Redpath Lyceum Bureau, 55, 178
Reneau, George, 51
Renfro Valley, 194, 195
Renfro Valley Barn Dance, 52, 157, 194. *See also* Renfro Valley
Renfro Valley Boys, The, 51
Republic Pictures, 79, 180
Rhododendron Festival, 188
Rice, Al, 86
Rice, Harry, 202
Richard, Ramey, *140*
Richards, Jerry, 87
Ritter, Tex, 179
Roberts, Sue, 173
Robison, Carson, 28
Rockcastle County, Ky., 194
Rock Creek Rangers, The, 30
Rodgers, Jimmie, 56, 58, 59, 64, 65, 170, 172, 191
Rogers, Kenny, 117
Rogers, Roy, 181, 202
Roosevelt, Eleanor, 160
Roosevelt, Franklin D., 124, 160
Roosevelt, Theodore, 169
Rose, Paul, 59, 86, *105*, 177
Rosenwald, Julius, 136
Ross, Betsy, 183
Rough Riders, 170
Rowell, Glenn, 36
Rowley, Cy, 87
Royalton, Minn., 13
Rube Tronson and His Texas Cowboys, 37, 44, 62, 87, 93. *See also* Tronson, Rube
Ruppe, Gene, 51
rural identity: and popular culture, 130–33; and tradition adapting to modernity, 133–38
rural market, 202
Rural Music Age, 7
Rush, Ford, 36
Russell, Tony, 28, 29, 42, 46
Rustic Revelers, The, 44, 45

Sackett Sisters, 88
Safford, Harold, 187
Sage Riders, 77, 87, 89, 90, 96
Satherley, Art, 172, 173
Sears, Roebuck and Company, 6, 21, 41, 114, 120, 136, 137, 170, 173, 200
Second Annual National Folk Festival (Chattanooga), 191
Second Great Migration, 116
Sennett, Mack, 85
sentimental mother, 162, 164
Setters, Jilson. *See* Day, J. W.
Shea, Jeff, 173
Shelton, Robert, 25
Showboat (minstrel company), 142
Show Boat (NBC variety program), 55
shuttle migration, 116

Sinclair, Upton, 102
singing cowboy, 169, 172. *See also* Allen, Rex; Autry, Gene
Sleepy Hollow Gang, 180
Smile-A-While, 77, 138
Smith, Blaine and Cal, 42, 64
Smith, Harry, 195
Smith, Joe, 143
Smith, Jonathan Guyot, 175
Smulyan, Susan, 5, 11, 200
Snyder, Glenn, 32, 58, 62, 83, 86, 183
Social Origins of the Urban South: Race, Gender, and Migration in Nashville and Middle Tennessee, 1890–1930, 114
Soubier, Clifford "Old Pappy," 143
Southern Diaspora: How the Great Migration of Black and White Southerners Transformed America, The, 11, 104
Southern Migrants, Northern Exiles, 116
Southern mother, 156
Spareribs, 11, 143, *144*, 174
Spoor, George K., 170
Sprague, Carl T., 170
Square Dance Festival of Chicago (1949), 91
Stafford, Check, *113*, 192
Stand By! 23, 202
Steele, Harry, 47
Stokes, Dwight "Tiny," 87
Strolling Guitarists, The, 65
Sullivan, Louis, 102
Summum, Ill., 175
Sunbonnet Girls, The, 76. *See also* Linder Sisters, The
Sunny Southland, 142
Suppertime Frolic, 52
Swain, Chuck, 77. *See also* Blue Grass Boys, The
Swanson, Holly, 15. *See also* Cousin Tilford
Sweet Violet Boys, The, 55. See also Prairie Ramblers, The

Tatum Sisters, The, 77
Taylor, Hartford Connecticut "Harty," *34*, *38*, 51, *163*, 191. *See also* Karl and Harty
Taylor, Jack, *28*, 54, 87, *105*, *177*
Texas Valley Folks, 77
"That Silver-Haired Daddy of Mine," 9, 57, 173, 174. *See also* Autry, Gene
Thomas, Jean, 188
Thomson, James C., 96, 97
Three Hired Men, 36
Three Little Maids, The, 37, 63, 64, 82
Three Neighbor Boys, The, 30, 36
Tin Pan Alley, 30, 36
Tint, Al, 141
Tioga, Tex., 172
Tom and Don, 42
Tommy Dandurand and his Barn Dance Gang, 44. *See also* Dandurand, Tommy
Tommy Dandurand and His Gang of WLS, 40. *See also* Dandurand, Tommy
Tom Owen's Barn Dance Trio, 40
Travelers, The, 52
Tribe, Ivan, 26
Trietsch, Ken "Rudy," 60, *95*, 106
Trietsch, Paul "Hezzie," 60, *95*, 106
Tronson, Rube, *35*, 44, 45. *See also* Rube Tronson and His Texas Cowboys
Trout, Max "Sambo," 141
Tumbling Tumbleweeds, 9
Turner, Frederick Jackson, 169
Tyler, Paul L., 4, 10, 200

Uncle Ezra, 60, 61, 140, 202. *See also* Barrett, Pat
United Paramount Theatres, Inc., 93
University of the West, 59
uptown hillbilly, 32
urbanization, 103

Vaillant, Derek, 125, 126
Valentine's Day Massacre, 110
Van Wert, Ohio, 44
Vickland, Bill, 174
Vickland, William, 30
Victory Garden program, 79, 80, 81
Virginian, The, 170
Vogue label, 90

Wake Up and Smile, 59
Walberg, Tony, 87
WAPO (Chattanooga), 77
war bond campaigns, 79–80
Ward, Cecil and Esther, 65
Ward, Charles Otto "Gabe", 60, *95*, 106
WBAP (Fort Worth), 1, 20, 133
WBBM (Chicago), 87, 181
WBOS (Boston), 84
WCAU (Philadelphia), 180
WDAN (Danville, Ill.), 87
WDZ (Tuscola, Ill.), 63, 175
Weaver Brothers and Elviry, 53
Wellington, Larry, 55, 178, *179*
WENR (Chicago), 85
WENR-TV, 89
West, Penny, 77
Westerners, The, 29, 36, 55, 65, 178, *179*. *See also* Louise Massey and the Westerners; Massey Family, The
Westinghouse, 120
WFAA (Dallas), 19
WGN, 27, 96
WGN Barn Dance, 96, 97
WHA (Wisconsin), 125

WHAS (Louisville), 176
WHAS Renfro Valley Barn Dance, 145
"When the Work's All Done This Fall," 170
White, Don, 87
Whiteness, emphasis of, 133, 148
White Top Folk Festival, 188, 192
Whitlock, Ralph, 36
Whitney, Penny, 77
WHO Iowa Barn Dance Frolic, 145
WIBW (Topeka), 178
WIL (St. Louis), 58
Wilbur and Ezra, 174
Wilgus, D. K., 13, 31, 132
Willcox, Ariz., 77
Williams, Ann, 173
Williams, Michael Ann, 6, 201
Williamson, J. W., 171
Wilson, Colleen and Donna, 202
Wilson, Don, 65
Wilson, Donna and Colleen 88
Wilson, Grace, 30, 34, 73, 74, 80, 89, 91, 92, 93, 94, *105*, 122, *123*
Winnie Lou and Sally, 37
Winston County, Ala., 106
Wiseman, Linda Lou, 165
Wiseman, Lulu Belle, 157, 162, 165. *See also* Cooper, Myrtle Eleanor; Lulu Belle; Lulu Belle and Scotty
Wiseman, Scotty, 14, 52, 53, 165, 183, 193, 194. *See also* Lulu Belle and Scotty
Wister, Owen, 170
Wittke, Carl, 142
WJJD (Chicago), 52
WLAV (Grand Rapids), 77
WLS: and airwave community, 10, 138; and marketing program, 10
WLS Artists Bureau, 23, 55, 62, 78, 83, 91
WLS Creed, 131, 165
WLS Family Album, 23, 30, 75, 93, 138, *139*, 164, 165, 202
WLS National Barndance, 62
WLS National Barn Dance Gang, 62
WLS Rangers, 86, 90
WLS Show Boat Junior, 60
WLW (Cincinnati), 41, 52, 58, 87, 157, 194
WMMN (Fairmont), 53
WNBI (NBC International), 84
WNOX (Knoxville), 50
WOC (Davenport), 54
Wolfe, Charles, 32, 46, 50, 52, 200
women: as metaphors, 162; and pay discrepancies, 41
Workman, Sunshine Sue, 30
World's Columbian Exposition of 1893, 109, 110, 169
WOWO (Fort Wayne), 60, 77
WRCA (NBC International), 84
Wright, Frank Lloyd, 102
WSM (Nashville), 32, 114
WSM Barn Dance, 114. *See also* Grand Ole Opry
WSM Grand Ole Opry, 141, 145
WTAM (Cleveland), 60
WTTM (Trenton), 180
WWVA Wheeling Jamboree, 145
Wylie, David, 202

XERA (Mexico), 58, 81

YMCA College, 155
YMCA College Quartet, 47
yodeling, popularity of, 64

Music in American Life

Only a Miner: Studies in Recorded Coal-Mining Songs *Archie Green*
Great Day Coming: Folk Music and the American Left *R. Serge Denisoff*
John Philip Sousa: A Descriptive Catalog of His Works *Paul E. Bierley*
The Hell-Bound Train: A Cowboy Songbook *Glenn Ohrlin*
Oh, Didn't He Ramble: The Life Story of Lee Collins, as Told to Mary Collins *Edited by Frank J. Gillis and John W. Miner*
American Labor Songs of the Nineteenth Century *Philip S. Foner*
Stars of Country Music: Uncle Dave Macon to Johnny Rodriguez *Edited by Bill C. Malone and Judith McCulloh*
Git Along, Little Dogies: Songs and Songmakers of the American West *John I. White*
A Texas-Mexican *Cancionero:* Folksongs of the Lower Border *Américo Paredes*
San Antonio Rose: The Life and Music of Bob Wills *Charles R. Townsend*
Early Downhome Blues: A Musical and Cultural Analysis *Jeff Todd Titon*
An Ives Celebration: Papers and Panels of the Charles Ives Centennial Festival-Conference *Edited by H. Wiley Hitchcock and Vivian Perlis*
Sinful Tunes and Spirituals: Black Folk Music to the Civil War *Dena J. Epstein*
Joe Scott, the Woodsman-Songmaker *Edward D. Ives*
Jimmie Rodgers: The Life and Times of America's Blue Yodeler *Nolan Porterfield*
Early American Music Engraving and Printing: A History of Music Publishing in America from 1787 to 1825, with Commentary on Earlier and Later Practices *Richard J. Wolfe*
Sing a Sad Song: The Life of Hank Williams *Roger M. Williams*
Long Steel Rail: The Railroad in American Folksong *Norm Cohen*
Resources of American Music History: A Directory of Source Materials from Colonial Times to World War II *D. W. Krummel, Jean Geil, Doris J. Dyen, and Deane L. Root*
Tenement Songs: The Popular Music of the Jewish Immigrants *Mark Slobin*
Ozark Folksongs *Vance Randolph; edited and abridged by Norm Cohen*
Oscar Sonneck and American Music *Edited by William Lichtenwanger*
Bluegrass Breakdown: The Making of the Old Southern Sound *Robert Cantwell*
Bluegrass: A History *Neil V. Rosenberg*
Music at the White House: A History of the American Spirit *Elise K. Kirk*
Red River Blues: The Blues Tradition in the Southeast *Bruce Bastin*
Good Friends and Bad Enemies: Robert Winslow Gordon and the Study of American Folksong *Debora Kodish*
Fiddlin' Georgia Crazy: Fiddlin' John Carson, His Real World, and the World of His Songs *Gene Wiggins*
America's Music: From the Pilgrims to the Present (rev. 3d ed.) *Gilbert Chase*
Secular Music in Colonial Annapolis: The Tuesday Club, 1745–56 *John Barry Talley*
Bibliographical Handbook of American Music *D. W. Krummel*
Goin' to Kansas City *Nathan W. Pearson, Jr.*
"Susanna," "Jeanie," and "The Old Folks at Home": The Songs of Stephen C. Foster from His Time to Ours (2d ed.) *William W. Austin*

Songprints: The Musical Experience of Five Shoshone Women *Judith Vander*
"Happy in the Service of the Lord": Afro-American Gospel Quartets in Memphis *Kip Lornell*
Paul Hindemith in the United States *Luther Noss*
"My Song Is My Weapon": People's Songs, American Communism, and the Politics of Culture, 1930–50 *Robbie Lieberman*
Chosen Voices: The Story of the American Cantorate *Mark Slobin*
Theodore Thomas: America's Conductor and Builder of Orchestras, 1835–1905 *Ezra Schabas*
"The Whorehouse Bells Were Ringing" and Other Songs Cowboys Sing *Guy Logsdon*
Crazeology: The Autobiography of a Chicago Jazzman *Bud Freeman, as Told to Robert Wolf*
Discoursing Sweet Music: Brass Bands and Community Life in Turn-of-the-Century Pennsylvania *Kenneth Kreitner*
Mormonism and Music: A History *Michael Hicks*
Voices of the Jazz Age: Profiles of Eight Vintage Jazzmen *Chip Deffaa*
Pickin' on Peachtree: A History of Country Music in Atlanta, Georgia *Wayne W. Daniel*
Bitter Music: Collected Journals, Essays, Introductions, and Librettos *Harry Partch; edited by Thomas McGeary*
Ethnic Music on Records: A Discography of Ethnic Recordings Produced in the United States, 1893 to 1942 *Richard K. Spottswood*
Downhome Blues Lyrics: An Anthology from the Post-World War II Era *Jeff Todd Titon*
Ellington: The Early Years *Mark Tucker*
Chicago Soul *Robert Pruter*
That Half-Barbaric Twang: The Banjo in American Popular Culture *Karen Linn*
Hot Man: The Life of Art Hodes *Art Hodes and Chadwick Hansen*
The Erotic Muse: American Bawdy Songs (2d ed.) *Ed Cray*
Barrio Rhythm: Mexican American Music in Los Angeles *Steven Loza*
The Creation of Jazz: Music, Race, and Culture in Urban America *Burton W. Peretti*
Charles Martin Loeffler: A Life Apart in Music *Ellen Knight*
Club Date Musicians: Playing the New York Party Circuit *Bruce A. MacLeod*
Opera on the Road: Traveling Opera Troupes in the United States, 1825–60 *Katherine K. Preston*
The Stonemans: An Appalachian Family and the Music That Shaped Their Lives *Ivan M. Tribe*
Transforming Tradition: Folk Music Revivals Examined *Edited by Neil V. Rosenberg*
The Crooked Stovepipe: Athapaskan Fiddle Music and Square Dancing in Northeast Alaska and Northwest Canada *Craig Mishler*
Traveling the High Way Home: Ralph Stanley and the World of Traditional Bluegrass Music *John Wright*
Carl Ruggles: Composer, Painter, and Storyteller *Marilyn Ziffrin*
Never without a Song: The Years and Songs of Jennie Devlin, 1865–1952 *Katharine D. Newman*
The Hank Snow Story *Hank Snow, with Jack Ownbey and Bob Burris*
Milton Brown and the Founding of Western Swing *Cary Ginell, with special assistance from Roy Lee Brown*
Santiago de Murcia's "Códice Saldívar No. 4": A Treasury of Secular Guitar Music from Baroque Mexico *Craig H. Russell*
The Sound of the Dove: Singing in Appalachian Primitive Baptist Churches *Beverly Bush Patterson*

Heartland Excursions: Ethnomusicological Reflections on Schools of Music *Bruno Nettl*
Doowop: The Chicago Scene *Robert Pruter*
Blue Rhythms: Six Lives in Rhythm and Blues *Chip Deffaa*
Shoshone Ghost Dance Religion: Poetry Songs and Great Basin Context *Judith Vander*
Go Cat Go! Rockabilly Music and Its Makers *Craig Morrison*
'Twas Only an Irishman's Dream: The Image of Ireland and the Irish in American Popular Song Lyrics, 1800–1920 *William H. A. Williams*
Democracy at the Opera: Music, Theater, and Culture in New York City, 1815–60 *Karen Ahlquist*
Fred Waring and the Pennsylvanians *Virginia Waring*
Woody, Cisco, and Me: Seamen Three in the Merchant Marine *Jim Longhi*
Behind the Burnt Cork Mask: Early Blackface Minstrelsy and Antebellum American Popular Culture *William J. Mahar*
Going to Cincinnati: A History of the Blues in the Queen City *Steven C. Tracy*
Pistol Packin' Mama: Aunt Molly Jackson and the Politics of Folksong *Shelly Romalis*
Sixties Rock: Garage, Psychedelic, and Other Satisfactions *Michael Hicks*
The Late Great Johnny Ace and the Transition from R&B to Rock 'n' Roll *James M. Salem*
Tito Puente and the Making of Latin Music *Steven Loza*
Juilliard: A History *Andrea Olmstead*
Understanding Charles Seeger, Pioneer in American Musicology *Edited by Bell Yung and Helen Rees*
Mountains of Music: West Virginia Traditional Music from *Goldenseal* *Edited by John Lilly*
Alice Tully: An Intimate Portrait *Albert Fuller*
A Blues Life *Henry Townsend, as told to Bill Greensmith*
Long Steel Rail: The Railroad in American Folksong (2d ed.) *Norm Cohen*
The Golden Age of Gospel *Text by Horace Clarence Boyer; photography by Lloyd Yearwood*
Aaron Copland: The Life and Work of an Uncommon Man *Howard Pollack*
Louis Moreau Gottschalk *S. Frederick Starr*
Race, Rock, and Elvis *Michael T. Bertrand*
Theremin: Ether Music and Espionage *Albert Glinsky*
Poetry and Violence: The Ballad Tradition of Mexico's Costa Chica *John H. McDowell*
The Bill Monroe Reader *Edited by Tom Ewing*
Music in Lubavitcher Life *Ellen Koskoff*
Zarzuela: Spanish Operetta, American Stage *Janet L. Sturman*
Bluegrass Odyssey: A Documentary in Pictures and Words, 1966–86 *Carl Fleischhauer and Neil V. Rosenberg*
That Old-Time Rock & Roll: A Chronicle of an Era, 1954–63 *Richard Aquila*
Labor's Troubadour *Joe Glazer*
American Opera *Elise K. Kirk*
Don't Get above Your Raisin': Country Music and the Southern Working Class *Bill C. Malone*
John Alden Carpenter: A Chicago Composer *Howard Pollack*
Heartbeat of the People: Music and Dance of the Northern Pow-wow *Tara Browner*
My Lord, What a Morning: An Autobiography *Marian Anderson*
Marian Anderson: A Singer's Journey *Allan Keiler*

Charles Ives Remembered: An Oral History *Vivian Perlis*
Henry Cowell, Bohemian *Michael Hicks*
Rap Music and Street Consciousness *Cheryl L. Keyes*
Louis Prima *Garry Boulard*
Marian McPartland's Jazz World: All in Good Time *Marian McPartland*
Robert Johnson: Lost and Found *Barry Lee Pearson and Bill McCulloch*
Bound for America: Three British Composers *Nicholas Temperley*
Lost Sounds: Blacks and the Birth of the Recording Industry, 1890–1919 *Tim Brooks*
Burn, Baby! BURN! The Autobiography of Magnificent Montague *Magnificent Montague with Bob Baker*
Way Up North in Dixie: A Black Family's Claim to the Confederate Anthem *Howard L. Sacks and Judith Rose Sacks*
The Bluegrass Reader *Edited by Thomas Goldsmith*
Colin McPhee: Composer in Two Worlds *Carol J. Oja*
Robert Johnson, Mythmaking, and Contemporary American Culture *Patricia R. Schroeder*
Composing a World: Lou Harrison, Musical Wayfarer *Leta E. Miller and Fredric Lieberman*
Fritz Reiner, Maestro and Martinet *Kenneth Morgan*
That Toddlin' Town: Chicago's White Dance Bands and Orchestras, 1900–1950 *Charles A. Sengstock Jr.*
Dewey and Elvis: The Life and Times of a Rock 'n' Roll Deejay *Louis Cantor*
Come Hither to Go Yonder: Playing Bluegrass with Bill Monroe *Bob Black*
Chicago Blues: Portraits and Stories *David Whiteis*
The Incredible Band of John Philip Sousa *Paul E. Bierley*
"Maximum Clarity" and Other Writings on Music *Ben Johnston, edited by Bob Gilmore*
Staging Tradition: John Lair and Sarah Gertrude Knott *Michael Ann Williams*
Homegrown Music: Discovering Bluegrass *Stephanie P. Ledgin*
Tales of a Theatrical Guru *Danny Newman*
The Music of Bill Monroe *Neil V. Rosenberg and Charles K. Wolfe*
Pressing On: The Roni Stoneman Story *Roni Stoneman, as told to Ellen Wright*
Together Let Us Sweetly Live *Jonathan C. David, with photographs by Richard Holloway*
Live Fast, Love Hard: The Faron Young Story *Diane Diekman*
Air Castle of the South: WSM Radio and the Making of Music City *Craig P. Havighurst*
Traveling Home: Sacred Harp Singing and American Pluralism *Kiri Miller*
Where Did Our Love Go?: The Rise and Fall of the Motown Sound *Nelson George*
Lonesome Cowgirls and Honky-Tonk Angels: The Women of Barn Dance Radio *Kristine M. McCusker*
California Polyphony: Ethnic Voices, Musical Crossroads *Mina Yang*
The Never-Ending Revival: Rounder Records and the Folk Alliance *Michael F. Scully*
Sing It Pretty: A Memoir *Bess Lomax Hawes*
Working Girl Blues: The Life and Music of Hazel Dickens *Hazel Dickens and Bill C. Malone*
Charles Ives Reconsidered *Gayle Sherwood Magee*
The Hayloft Gang: The Story of the National Barn Dance *Edited by Chad Berry*

The University of Illinois Press
is a founding member of the
Association of American University Presses.

Composed in 10/14.5 Janson Text LT Std
with ITC Clearface display
by Barbara Evans
at the University of Illinois Press
Designed by Kelly Gray
Manufactured by Sheridan Books, Inc.

University of Illinois Press
1325 South Oak Street
Champaign, IL 61820-6903
www.press.uillinois.edu